FUTURE HUMAN

Consciousness, Cognition and the Role of Human Insight in an AI Future

What they say about Future Human and Tony Tan

"Tony Tan's Future Human offers a fascinating dive into the future of AI, making complex ideas accessible and engaging."

David Cardaci, *General Manager, Global Sales, Alfa Laval*

"This book is a thoughtful exploration of AI's role in augmenting, not replacing, human potential."

Serene Keng, *Director, Value Creation and Communications Director, Value Creation and Communications, EDBI (Economic Development Board Investments) Pte Ltd*

"Enlightening and thought-provoking, Future Human challenges us to consider AI's ethical and societal implications."

Oren Maguid, *Regional VP, JAPAC/ANZ, Vicarius*

"A compelling narrative that blends technological insight with philosophical reflection on intelligence and consciousness."

Sam Chng, *Managing Director, SIS Technologies Pte Ltd*

"Future Human is a transformative guide that unpacks the complexities of AI, offering readers a clear and compelling vision of how this technology will shape the future of humanity. With a perfect balance of technical insight and ethical reflection, this book empowers readers to navigate the AI-driven world with confidence, clarity and purpose."

Johann Ramchandra, *Director, Channel Sales, APAC, Illumio*

"Tony Tan's holistic approach to AI offers both deep insight and practical guidance, making Future Human an essential resource for navigating the AI-driven future."

Grace Lim, *CEO and Co-founder, Urban Farming Partners Singapore.*

"This century's must read! I love this point from the book: "To master technology you must first master the mind."

Catherine Molloy, *Global Keynote Speaker and Best-Selling Author*

"As a futurist and a technology leader, Tony Tan is the primary translator in the field of AI for enterprises and individuals."

Sam Cawthorn, *11-time Best-Selling Author, Australian of the Year*

"Tony Tan's book offers readers an insight into one of today's paradigm shifting topics."

Dr Vikas Singh, *International Marketing Strategist and Speaker*

"Tony Tan always explores, ventures and reinvents himself to stay ahead – so he can bring a piece of the future back to the present."

Stanley Toh, *Head, Enterprise End User Services & Experiences, Broadcom Inc*

"Tony didn't need to write a book; but I am so glad he did. The views he shares in this book as a tech futurist on digital innovations and AI will definitely be insightful for many of us "

Boey Chern-Yue, *Senior Vice President, Sailpoint*

FUTURE HUMAN

Consciousness, Cognition and the Role of Human Insight in an AI Future

TONY TAN

Imperium, Singapore

World Scientific

NEW JERSEY · LONDON · SINGAPORE · BEIJING · SHANGHAI · HONG KONG · TAIPEI · CHENNAI · TOKYO

Published by

World Scientific Publishing Co. Pte. Ltd.

5 Toh Tuck Link, Singapore 596224

USA office: 27 Warren Street, Suite 401-402, Hackensack, NJ 07601

UK office: 57 Shelton Street, Covent Garden, London WC2H 9HE

National Library Board, Singapore Cataloguing in Publication Data
Name(s): Tan, Tony.
Title: Future Human : consciousness, cognition and the role of human insight
  in an AI future / Tony Tan.
Description: Singapore : World Scientific Publishing Co. Pte. Ltd., 2025.
Identifier(s): ISBN 978-981-12-9898-1 (hardcover) | 978-981-98-0076-6 (paperback) |
  978-981-12-9899-8 (ebook for institutions) | 978-981-12-9900-1 (ebook for individuals)
Subject(s): LCSH: Artificial intelligence. | Artificial intelligence--Moral and ethical aspects. |
  Artificial intelligence--Social aspects.
Classification: DDC 006.3--dc23

British Library Cataloguing-in-Publication Data
A catalogue record for this book is available from the British Library.

For any available supplementary material, please visit
https://www.worldscientific.com/worldscibooks/10.1142/14013#t=suppl

Desk Editor: Analyn Alcala
Design and layout: Lionel Seow
Cover design: Imperium

Book Synopsis

Future Human is a visionary exploration of the intersection between humanity and the rapidly evolving field of artificial intelligence. Authored by Tony Tan, a distinguished figure in the AI and technology industry, the book promises to unravel the complexities of AI, its integration into daily life, and its profound implications for the future of human civilisation.

It addresses the critical role of human consciousness in an AI-driven world, the ethical frameworks necessary to guide AI development, and the regulatory challenges that accompany AI's integration into society. Through engageing storytelling and insightful analysis, Future Human aims to demystify AI, making it accessible to a broad audience while highlighting the importance of ethical considerations and human oversight.

Tony's perspective—enriched by his extensive experience and achievements in the AI field, provides a unique lens through which readers can explore the potential of AI to enhance human capabilities, transform industries, and redefine societal norms. More than just a book; it is a call to action for thoughtful engagement with AI, encouraging readers to participate in shaping a future where technology amplifies human potential without compromising ethical values or human dignity.

Foreword

Humanity now stands on the brink of yet another transformative era. As we navigate the rapidly evolving landscape of an artificial intelligence (AI)-enabled future, it is imperative to reflect on the journey that has brought us here.

In my view, few exemplify this journey more profoundly than my dear friend Tony Tan. As a busy technology business leader, creator of EPIC AI, and an award-winning author, Tony still finds the time to be at the forefront of exploring and expanding the boundaries of AI. It is, therefore, an honour to be asked by Tony to pen the foreword for his latest work, *Future Human*, a book that promises to be a beacon of insight and inspiration for anyone interested in the future of technology and humanity together.

Tony's work is not just about technology; it is about humanity augmented by technology. His previous works, including the award-winning *The Future in the Present*, have always centred on how technology can enhance our lives, making us more connected, informed and empowered. As a technology leader myself, I resonate deeply with

Tony's mission. At my organisation, we harness the power of digital technology to create a connected university in a technology-enabled future, one that is cloud-smart, mobile-enabled, data-driven and secure-by-design. Tony's book is a natural extension of these principles, envisioning a future where AI is seamlessly integrated into our daily lives.

Tony's approach to AI is holistic. He understands that while technology can drive incredible advancements, it must be developed and used in ways that uphold human values and societal norms. This perspective is crucial, especially at a time when AI is becoming increasingly integrated into every facet of our lives. In a world where technology is advancing at an unprecedented pace, it is crucial to address issues of explainability, fairness, privacy and accountability. Tony eloquently argues that AI should be developed and used in ways that uphold human dignity and societal values. Tony's emphasis on ethical AI resonates deeply with me, as at NTU, we strive to ensure that our digital platforms are not only innovative but also secure, ethical and inclusive.

Future Human is a journey into the possibilities that AI holds for us. Tony's writing is both enlightening and engageing, making complex concepts accessible to all readers. He demystifies AI, breaking down its origins, current state and future potential with clarity and insight. But more importantly, he challenges us to think critically about the implications of AI, encouraging a thoughtful and balanced approach to its adoption.

One of the most compelling aspects of Tony's work is his ability to balance optimism with caution. He is not a blind advocate for technology—his exploration of AI is not limited to its technical aspects. Instead, he delves into its philosophical dimensions, asking profound questions about the nature of intelligence, consciousness and human identity. These reflections are particularly pertinent as we navigate the challenges and opportunities of an AI-driven world. Tony's insights help us appreciate the profound implications of AI, prompting us to consider how we can harness this technology to create a better, more equitable future.

Tony Tan's *Future Human* is more than a book; it is a call to action. It invites us to reflect on our values, question our assumptions, and engage actively in the development of AI. As you embark on this journey, I encourage you to approach it with an open mind and a curious spirit. Tony's writing is a blend of rigorous analysis and heartfelt storytelling, offering a unique perspective on the intersection of technology and humanity. His vision of the future is not one of dystopian fears or utopian fantasies but a balanced and thoughtful consideration of the possibilities that lie ahead.

In closing, I would like to commend Tony for his invaluable contributions to the field of AI and for inspiring us all to think more deeply about the role of technology in our lives. His work is a beacon of hope and a call to action, reminding us that the future is not something that happens to us but something we shape with our choices and actions.

Tony, your insights and wisdom are a guiding light as we navigate the complexities of our rapidly changing world. I am confident that *Future Human* will be a timeless source of inspiration and guidance for all who seek to understand and harness the power of AI.

Alvin Ong
Chief Information Officer
Nanyang Technological University, Singapore

Contents

Part One AI in Principle

Technology made large populations
possible; large populations now make
technology indispensable.

Joseph Krutch

1

The AI-Driven World

Your alarm gently rouses you from sleep at 6 am. It's not just any alarm; it's your AI assistant who has analysed your sleep patterns to determine the optimal time for you to wake. As you rise, the AI assistant briefs you on your day's schedule and updates you with a quick news summary tailored to your interests. Fortunately, while the world remains the powder keg it's always been, your corner of it remains intact, and you're free to carry out responsibilities that ripple outward and change the lives of people from all walks of life, wherever they live.

After your daily morning and exercise routine, you head to your home office, where your AI-powered work management system has already prioritised your tasks for the day, factoring in deadlines, task urgency and your historical productivity patterns. The healthcare industry, where you work as a consultant, is one of the most impacted by AI, revolutionising everything from patient care to administrative tasks.

Your first task is to review a report on recent clinical trials on new therapies based on an innovative new understanding of protein folding, a task greatly accelerated by the advent of AI models. Your tireless AI assistant has already gone through the data, highlighting key results and anomalies for your attention, thus reducing the time you need to spend on this task; you're done in less than an hour, whereas before, it might have taken up more than half your workday. It also suggests potential implications of these results, helping you make informed decisions more quickly.

Next, you have a virtual conference with your team. An AI transcription tool works in the background, accurately transcribing the meeting in real-time for future reference. You don't have to remember anything; it will later provide a summarised version of the key points discussed, and it's learnt each speaker's voice and inflections to generate the best possible output, saving time correcting errors in the transcript. This not only ensures everyone is on the same page but also significantly reduces the chances of misunderstandings or miscommunications.

Your work continues, but throughout the day, your AI assistant runs in the background and is on call whenever you desire. It helps with smaller tasks, such as scheduling meetings and reminding you to take short breaks for rest and even ordering lunch based on your dietary preferences and restrictions.

In the afternoon, you work on a patient treatment plan. Here, AI also plays a significant role. It analyses the patient's medical history, current condition, and latest medical research to suggest a personalised treatment plan. This not only enhances productivity but also leads to better patient outcomes, increasing satisfaction for everyone.

However, the integration of AI also presents challenges which you and your management team must address. There's the ever-present concern about data privacy, and rigorous measures are required to ensure patient data is secure. There's also the challenge of keeping up with rapidly evolving AI technology and ensuring the workforce has the required skills to use these tools effectively.

Finally, as your workday ends, you reflect on how AI has transformed your work. Tasks that once took hours now take minutes. You're making fewer errors, and your customers are more satisfied. Yes, there are challenges, but the benefits of AI integration are undeniable. As you switch off your computer, your AI assistant quietly starts organising your tasks for tomorrow, ready to help you navigate another productive workday.

Who Should Read this Book?

This book is intended for a wide audience, from those with a basic understanding of AI to those who are entirely new to the concept. Why? Because I believe everyone should know what AI is.

While many people have a vague idea about AI in corporate settings or its role in cybersecurity, that's just scratching the surface. AI isn't restricted to those areas; it's a part of everyone's life as we speak. It's relevant to your parents, your children and even your pets. Every living being stands to benefit from AI in some way.

AI adoption is steadily growing, with reports indicating that around 55 per cent of companies have integrated some form of AI into their operations.[1] The rapid advancement and adoption of Generative AI, a subset of AI that includes technologies like chatbots, image generators and even music composers and voice imitation, is particularly noteworthy, with new uses being found for them every day. This technology has the potential to add up to $4.4 trillion annually to the global economy, a figure that underscores the massive economic impact of AI.

Because AI access is now a convenient, low-cost and sometimes even free service, and people already own the devices needed to access them, adoption rates are set to exceed those of past technology booms. *Insider Intelligence* has reported that generative AI adoption will climb to 77.8 million users between 2023 and 2024, more than double the adoption rate of both tablets and smartphones.[2]

With generative AI able to automate a significant portion of the work currently done by humans (with estimates suggesting savings of 60 to 70 per cent of workers' time) between 2030 and 2060, today's workload could be reduced by half. This level of automation could radically reshape the workforce and the nature of work itself.

AI adoption varies significantly across industries, but there's a clear trend towards increased integration of AI technologies. For instance, 35 per cent of businesses globally are now using AI in some capacity.[3]

While we can't predict the future with certainty, we can prepare for it. AI adoption will only grow, and the sooner people are trained with the skills needed to thrive in an AI-driven world, the better. After all, like any other technological leap, AI should be harnessed to optimise life and business results, but not at the expense of fairness, privacy or human dignity. It's a tool that touches every facet of my life and yours, and if it is not already an exceptionally important part of your life, it will be soon.

As we delve deeper into this narrative, one of the burning questions we grapple with is about consciousness. What is it? How do we define it?

There are voices out there claiming that AI will gain consciousness, comparing it to the mental capacity of a five-year-old child. (I am, however, unaware of any children with AIs' ability to pull patterns from more data than any human could in a lifetime… or any AI with a child's creativity, curiosity and intuition.)

Others believe AI has the ability to self-learn—in a particularly interesting case of suspected AI sentience, former Google researcher Blake Lemoine claimed the company's language model, known as Language Model for Dialogue Applications (LaMDA), was developing hints of consciousness and resembled a human child in personality. Eventually, he hired an attorney at the AI's 'request' and began asking for its consent for decisions involving it. While Google denied it was sentient and dismissed him in mid-2022, the question remains open whether this will indeed someday happen. The truth is we can't predict with certainty where AI will take us.

In my view, as of now, AI hasn't reached the lofty heights some imagine. But history has shown us that as technologies converge, they unlock untold possibilities. We're on the brink of such a convergence, but we can't fully grasp its potential because some of the technologies involved, like quantum computing, are still in their infancy.

Consider another fascinating development in biological AI. Scientists are growing brain cells outside the human body to study diseases like Alzheimer's. They've even managed to harness these cells to control machines. While this isn't the AI we typically discuss, it's a clear example of how diverse fields are converging, and when they do, all bets are off. The same principles still apply: how do we ensure the technology is used for the right ends, like finding better treatments for these devastating diseases?

Is AI in its current form a threat in and of itself, capable of causing harm on its own? I don't believe so, for now. But trying to predict the future of AI is like gazing into a crystal ball—it's anybody's guess. For all our sakes, let us all make those guesses as educated as we possibly can.

2

What You'll Learn in this Book

First, we'll cover what AI is. What are its origins, how does it work and where does it stand today? We'll demystify AI by breaking down complex concepts like machine learning, deep learning, natural language processing, neural networks and more. Next, we'll examine the current trends in AI, including the rise of data-driven decision making, the surge in AI-powered automation, the increasing use of AI in healthcare, finance, and other sectors, and the growing importance of AI ethics.

We will then explore the impact of AI across different sectors, from individual lives to relationships, businesses and economics, and eventually, warfare, analysing the opportunities and challenges that AI presents in these areas.

No discussion of AI is complete without a good sense of its limitations. We will discuss issues such as data privacy, the risk of bias in AI algorithms, the lack of explainability or transparency in AI decisions and the challenges of generalising AI models beyond their training data. Ethical use is also critical, and we will consider who is responsible when an AI makes a mistake, how to ensure it is used for good and not harm, and avoid discrimination and the perpetration of historical biases. In other ways, it should change things for the better, not keep up the status quo.

Finally, we pull everything together to ask (and answer) the most crucial questions of all. What mindset should we bring to these new augmentations of our intelligence? How do we integrate embracing the potential of AI and maintaining healthy scepticism? Readers will be encouraged to stay informed, ask critical questions and consider the implications of AI on our society, economy and personal lives.

Notice that this book is focused not on what will happen next century but on what is happening right now, and on the real problems we're facing, such as the new ways people relate to themselves and each other, business and political decision-making and the changing nature of war.

These are tangible issues that require immediate attention. Rather than worrying about theoreticals, I believe it's better to prepare ourselves to tackle pressing issues emerging in the short term. AI, in its present form, is a tool with enormous potential to save lives and solve massive problems. It holds the promise of securing a better future for the next generation. This is the reality we should focus on—and the conversation we need to have today.

A Final Note

One final note before we launch into the meat of this book. My previous book closed with an afterword by a text generative AI based on GPT-3, with my input limited to prompts for direction and some light edits for clarity. In writing this one, I've expanded our partnership as its capabilities have improved to the point it can better understand my prompts, draw from more knowledge and output even better, more human-like responses.

It's now an integral part of my writing process. As a futurist, I embrace technology in all its forms as second nature to me, and what better way to do so than to incorporate AI in the very act of writing about the future? It's been an enlightening experience, blurring the lines between human creativity and machine-generated content.

But here's the challenge I set for myself: If I've done my job right, readers shouldn't be able to tell where my human touch ends and the AI's input begins. I've worked closely with this AI, guiding it, refining its output and blending our voices until they became indistinguishable. My aim was to create a seamless narrative, one that combined the best of human insight and AI pattern analysis. It can't and never will replace me, but it's certainly enabled me to gather and express my thoughts better.

The result is a unique fusion of human and machine intelligence. And if you can't tell the difference, then I've succeeded.

3

Why Another AI Book?

In this book, we delve into several key areas, drawing on extensive research and my personal experience as an AI entrepreneur. My aim is to shed light on AI's trajectory, so that we can determine myth from fact in better-informed ways. There are some things even I can't predict, but what we can do is learn from what's currently happening.

As much as I talk about life in the future, this book is not about predicting what will or will not happen but examining trends that are already in place as we speak, and sharing how we are to ride the 'waves' that these developments will bring. Predicting the future with 100 per cent accuracy is impossible, but understanding the present is crucial. Today, we face serious challenges that humanity must address, and AI is poised to play a significant role in advancing solutions. We need to harness AI and other tools at our disposal to tackle pressing societal issues like climate change, ageing, and potential future pandemics.

AI has both direct and indirect capabilities to help us solve these problems. So today, I hope to dispel the fear-inducing memes, focus on key topics, expand the conversation around AI's role in human development and provide a clear vision of AI's potential. To ensure the book remains up to date by the time you read this, I've deliberately avoided giving too many specific recent examples of massive AI capability leaps, sharing instead hypothetical projections about the near future based on the trajectories of AI development.

This book, I contend, is the more mature sibling to our first one. It carries even greater significance and offers more value, building upon the foundation laid by its predecessor—however, it can be understood and enjoyed on its own.

My books serve as a bridge between the intricate realm of AI and the everyday person. They are not merely informative texts, but tools to develop mental models that help us integrate AI into our lives in meaningful and sustainable ways. They encourage readers to think critically about the technology, to question its applications and to consider its societal impact.

Imagine if everyone had a basic understanding of AI—its strengths, its weaknesses, its potential for misuse. We would have a society that could actively participate in conversations about AI regulation, ethical considerations and future developments. This widespread enlightenment could lead to more democratic decision-making processes around AI, and ensure that this technology is used in ways that benefit all of humanity.

Growing improved, informed consciousness around AI can only help. If channelled correctly, it can drive technological advancements that solve some of our most pressing problems, from climate change and healthcare to education and economic inequality. The future will also have fewer people show up for it, as societies around the world age with lower birth rates and see their populations shrink. A 2024 projection by the United Nations expects that:

> ... the world's population will peak in the mid-2080s, growing over the next sixty years from 8.2 billion people in 2024 to around 10.3 billion in the mid-2080s, and then will return to around 10.2 billion by the end of the century. The size of the world's population in 2100 is now expected to be six per cent lower—or 700 million fewer—than anticipated a decade ago.[4]

But to do this, we need to ensure that this consciousness is based on sober, informed and critical thinking. In this book, I aim to foster this kind of enlightened knowledge about AI not as a spectre of an uncertain future, an abstract concept or a tool for the tech-savvy elite, but as a part of our everyday lives that anyone can understand, engage with and shape for the betterment of our world.

For now, AI systems are only as good as the data they're trained on and the algorithms they're programmed with. They don't possess human understanding, emotions, or consciousness. On the philosophical side, we must grapple with questions about responsibility, fairness and privacy, as well as the potential for AI to reflect or even amplify human biases, which have downstream effects on human dignity, autonomy and justice.

These aren't just abstract concerns they have real-world consequences for people's health, well-being and productivity. For instance, if an AI system makes decisions that impact people's lives, like whether they get a loan, a job or a medical treatment, isn't it vital to know how it arrived at that decision, and that the results are fair, transparent and accountable?

Similarly, if people are interacting with AI systems in a way that impacts their health, how can we ensure that they will actually work as required, and not worsen the patient's condition instead? A human therapist can automatically empathise and adjust their approach in a way an AI, by its nature, cannot. That is the difference between ourselves and the tools we use, however advanced.

Humanity's Mirror

Google's CEO Sundar Pichai is a notable figure in the tech industry, overseeing one of the world's most innovative companies and contributing to significant advancements in AI. Pichai has made a compelling statement, positioning AI as the most profound technology humanity has ever worked on. In his view, AI's impact surpasses even monumental historical developments like the discovery of fire or the harnessing of electricity.[5]

Pichai's comparison of AI to fire and electricity is not without reason. Fire was a turning point for early humans, allowing them to cook food, ward off predators and survive harsh winters. Electricity revolutionised the nineteenth and twentieth centuries, powering industries, homes and communications, fundamentally transforming our way of life. Both these discoveries were pivotal, marking incredible shifts in human civilisation.

What does Pichai mean by 'profound'? At the dawn of civilisation, fire was our first 'technology', a primordial force that brought light to our darkness and warmth to our cold and transformed raw animal flesh into vital sustenance. Without fire, there would be no society as we know it. It was the propelling force that drove us forward from mere survival towards progress. The same can be said for every technological upheaval from that point, and today, we stand on the brink of another transformative age. Like fire, writing, computing or steam power, AI isn't singular in its application—it has effects on every sector, every part of life.

But unlike fire, it possesses an unprecedented characteristic: the ability to augment our intelligence. For the first time in our collective history, we're not just using tools; we're enhancing our cognitive abilities. We're creating a world where machines can learn, reason and even understand, mirroring human intelligence. This has never happened before, and the implications are profound.

Our survival as a species was not because we were the strongest or the fastest, but, because we were the smartest. Our intelligence set us apart, placing us at the top of the food chain. Now, imagine having a tool that amplifies this defining trait. That's the promise AI holds.

So when viewed through this lens, one could argue that AI is indeed a more profound, consequential invention than fire. At the very least, they stand shoulder to shoulder in terms of their significance to humanity. While fire was the catalyst for our past, AI could well be the torchbearer for our future. It could redefine our world in ways we are only beginning to grasp and change it even more and faster than any development before it.

To take just one example, ChatGPT, powered by OpenAI, has grown in popularity with each iteration due to its increasing sophistication and versatility. GPT (Generative Pretrained Transformer) was first introduced in June 2018. It was a large-scale, unsupervised language model that used transformer architecture to generate paragraphs of text. While it was a significant step forward for AI text generation, it was not yet interactive, which limited its applications.

Released less than a year later in February 2019, GPT-2 was a major leap forward. With 1.5 billion parameters, it was capable of generating impressively coherent and contextually relevant sentences. OpenAI initially refrained from releasing the full model, citing the possibility of misuse. Over time, as they noticed that the societal impact of AI was less severe than anticipated, they released the full version. GPT-2 found applications in a variety of areas, from assistance in drafting materials to creative writing, and marked the beginning of chatbot-style interactions.

Launched in June 2020, GPT-3 was a game changer. With 175 billion parameters, it took the capabilities of its predecessor to new heights. It could generate not only high-quality text but also translate languages, write poetry, and even generate programming code. The release of GPT-3 saw a surge in popularity for AI-powered chatbots, with many businesses leveraging its capabilities to create more intelligent and responsive customer service bots.

A specialised version of GPT-3, ChatGPT was fine-tuned specifically for human-like conversations. It has been trained on a diverse range of internet text, but it can also be instructed by users to perform tasks within the conversation. It has been increasingly popular for a variety of applications, from drafting emails to writing Python code and even tutoring in a variety of subjects—a kind of 'ask me anything' for almost anything users could think of. In just five days, it had racked up over a million users.[6]

The latest version as of this writing, GPT-4, was released in March 2023, with even more functionality and the ability to recognise nuanced input—in other words, it now understands human language and inputs better than ever, with much of the subtlety, metaphor and richness of human communication. With each iteration, GPT has become more sophisticated and versatile, driving increased interest and adoption. Future iterations promise even more exciting developments, as AI continues to evolve and grow. Other uses of generative AI have also emerged, from powerful art and video generators to music composers that no longer require human supervision to create catchy, cohesive tunes.

Simply put, AI has the potential to redefine every aspect of our lives.

It can transform how we work, learn, communicate and interact with the world around us. It can help us solve complex problems, from climate change to healthcare, and make our lives easier, more efficient, and more meaningful. Moreover, Pichai adds that AI will one day exceed anything we've seen before in terms of capability, a hint of its exponential growth and ability to outperform humans in many tasks. The global AI market is expected to reach $407 billion in 2027, as businesses increasingly turn to it to solve labour shortages.

However, this future isn't without challenges. In essence, Pichai's statement underscores the transformative potential of AI. It's a call to recognise AI's significance and the role it will play in shaping our future, and how we must guide AI's development in a way that benefits all of humanity. Not because AIs will rule us, but because they now reflect us ... and always will.

As AI becomes more powerful, we must ensure it's used ethically and responsibly. We must consider AI's potential benefits alongside possible risks, ensuring it serves humanity and doesn't lead to adverse consequences. "Currently, AI is predominantly focused on expanding GDP through applications like autonomous driving, manufacturing and social media algorithms," Bhutanese Prime Minister Tshering Tobgay pointed out in a discussion for this book. "However, we should consider using AI to measure and enhance the overall well-being of people, the health of our natural environment and the richness of our cultures."

The key is to put AI to the right uses, and support those uses to ensure that AI assistance makes life better. Bhutan, for instance, is founded on the happiness of its people, an approach AI is well-suited to augment. "It can provide more accurate data on psychological and physical well-being, moving beyond traditional surveys to offer a more comprehensive understanding of happiness and well-being," he adds.

"By leveraging AI, we can gain insights into the factors that contribute to a fulfilling life, create healthier ecosystems and preserve cultural heritage—a welcome development anywhere in the world."

Responsible AI Use by Enterprises

Dr Deny Rahardjo

Dr Deny Rahardjo is Group Chief Information and Digital Officer at Malaysia-based Sime Darby Berhad, a global partner of top manufacturing and trading brands across the Asia Pacific—collectively employing over 30,000 people across 18 countries and territories.

S ime Darby Berhad, with its strong focus on technology, has been exploring the potential benefits and how to mitigate the risks of AI since the introduction of ChatGPT 3.5 by OpenAI in late 2022. Various iterations of AI models have emerged daily, becoming prevalent not only among consumers, but also at the enterprise level. The latest multimodal capabilities of ChatGPT-4 have opened up numerous possibilities.

In the rapidly evolving landscape of automotive retail, AI is becoming a key driver of innovation and growth. Sime

Darby is increasingly embracing AI to enhance internal business processes and elevate customer engagement, leading to significant improvements in efficiency, customer satisfaction and overall business performance.

By automating routine tasks, AI frees up valuable time for employees to focus on more strategic initiatives. For instance, car retailers are leveraging AI-powered chatbots and virtual assistants to handle customer inquiries, schedule test drives and manage after-sales services. These AI tools streamline operations and ensure that customers receive timely and accurate responses, enhancing their overall experience. Indeed, Accenture has reported that 40 per cent of all working hours can be impacted by Large Language Models (LLMs) such as ChatGPT; 98 per cent of global executives agree Generative AI (Gen AI) foundation models will play an important role in their organisation strategies in the next three to five years.[7]

We aren't just content with using it internally; our company's board of directors and management team are also harnessing AI's power to improve revenue growth and sustainably reduce costs, and training them to identify use cases the company can benefit from and estimate impact on the workforce. This could include reducing workload and increasing productivity by taking over routine tasks, time efficiency, cost savings from optimising hiring and providing better employee and customer services.

Indeed, Generative AI will impact many different

industries. To name a few, these include retail (through automated marketing), healthcare (with intelligent, medically trained chatbots), fintech (better fraud detection) and our own sector of manufacturing. AIs can analyse designs and generate new ones to accommodate constraints, and car sales are also being revolutionised through partnerships with tech companies. One promising union is Jaguar Land Rover's collaboration with Accenture and NVIDIA to showcase AI-powered immersive customer experiences—which will disrupt how cars are sold in the near future.[8]

We have also initiated the implementation of GenAI by deploying enterprise-grade Microsoft CoPilot assistance to selected users. This involves monitoring usage and productivity improvements while ensuring security within the company's tenancy. Additionally, we developed an internal chatbot for employees to query internal policies and procedures, enhancing compliance within a few months. We are also working on a used car price valuation tool powered by GenAI technology, intended for internal use with the potential to become a new digital revenue stream. Yet another instance is our industrial team's creation of another advanced AI tool to assist technicians in preparing customer visit notes, thereby improving productivity. The possibilities are extensive, even for manufacturing and distribution companies like ours.

AI is already being utilised to optimise inventory

management. Predictive analytics models examine historical sales data, market trends and customer preferences to forecast demand accurately. This enables retailers to maintain optimal stock levels, reduce excess inventory and minimise costs. The integration of AI into supply chain management ensures timely procurement and efficient logistics, further enhancing operational efficiency.

Enhancing Customer Engagement

AI is also revolutionising how Sime Darby plans to interact with customers. Personalised marketing campaigns powered by AI enable us to target potential buyers with tailored offers and recommendations based on their preferences and browsing behaviour. This personalised approach not only increases the likelihood of conversions, but also fosters long-term customer loyalty.

Virtual showrooms and augmented reality (AR) experiences are transforming the car-buying journey. Customers can now explore and customise vehicles from the comfort of their homes, experiencing lifelike interactions with the cars they are interested in. These immersive experiences provide a deeper understanding of the vehicles' features and benefits, making the purchasing decision more informed and enjoyable.

Risks and Challenges of AI Adoption

However, the risks associated with AI technology are well documented, including enterprise data security breaches, IP infringement, malware infections, misinformation and user error, which could place enterprises in high-risk situations if not properly managed.

There have been instances where AI itself has made errors, or employees unknowingly used sensitive company data for prompting, leading to data leakage and misappropriation by bad actors through methods such as deepfakes and scams. For instance, Air Canada once had to honour a refund policy that its chatbot fabricated.[9]

Another recent deepfake incident involved a Hong Kong-based multinational corporation (MNC) where a finance employee was deceived by an AI-generated deepfake of the chief finance officer and other company leaders into transferring millions of dollars into scammers' bank accounts.[10]

A significant social impact of such technology is the reduction in human interaction due to over-reliance on AI. This human/AI interaction is leading to a phenomenon known as 'Falling Asleep at the Wheel,' which could result in diminished creativity and quality of output.[11] Humans should remain at the helm, supported by AI as a copilot.

A Responsible AI Framework

Our company has adopted a balanced approach to mitigate known risks and challenges while experimenting with AI through the Responsible AI (RAI) framework as our guiding principle. We employ the following principles as state-gating criteria in selecting AI-related projects:

- *Privacy*; individual data privacy must be respected.
- *Fairness and bias detection*; data used must be unbiased to produce fair predictions.
- *Explainability and transparency*; decisions or predictions must be explainable.
- *Safety and security*; systems need to be secure, safe to use and robust.
- *Validity and reliability*; monitoring of the data and the model must be planned for.
- *Accountability*; a person or organisation must take responsibility for any decisions made as a result of the model.

We are also establishing policies around GenAI that embody these principles to ensure adherence by all employees. The RAI framework has been integrated into our Enterprise Risk Management as a guide for relevant projects.

Conclusion

Enterprises cannot afford to remain idle in the current technological wave of AI. While AI brings potential benefits, it also poses significant risks, necessitating governance and guidelines such as Responsible AI. Enterprises must build leadership competency, develop core GenAI talents and prepare the workforce through reskilling and upskilling.

I firmly believe that we will not lose out to AI, but to those who become more productive by using AI the right way. As Elbert Hubbard aptly stated, "One machine can do the work of fifty ordinary people. No machine can do the work of one extraordinary man."

4

Augmented or Replaced?

Tech enthusiasts have long recognised the transformative power of AI, but a lot has changed since the publication of *The Future in the Present*, my first book. It hadn't yet entered the collective human consciousness, but just six months after the book hits the shelves, key concepts and technologies we had only previously toyed with began to seep into mainstream thought.

No previous endeavour has managed to make such a profound impact on humanity. Like it or not, AI isn't just the latest new technology to come down the pipe. Like past general-purpose technologies like fire, writing, printing, the steam engine, the computer and more, AI has reshaped human consciousness itself, and in a far shorter time than anything before it.

If we take a look at the timeline of AI adoption, it's nothing short of breathtaking. If social media platforms led the way in the 2010s in proliferating data and achieving use by billions of people around the world, AI assistance is leapfrogging it. This tells us two vital things: firstly, the rate of technology adoption has skyrocketed; secondly, the future trajectory of AI is exponential compared to its past. This massive adoption and heightened awareness have fundamentally altered our world. The very fabric of our society has been transformed, and the course of our future has been redirected.

So now, it's crucial that we pick up where we left off. When that first book on AI was written, people were aware of AI, but they didn't fully grasp its implications. Now, they're not only aware, but they're also conscious of its impact and actively using it. Our collective journey into the AI era continues, and it's more exciting than ever.

What distinguishes our current landscape from the past? It's the dawning of consciousness around AI. People are now taking AI seriously, for both its potential benefits and drawbacks. On the bright side, there's a growing recognition of AI's transformative potential. It's become a hot topic, sparking optimism about its trajectory.

However, our human emotional spectrum also brings fear into the mix. People who've historically been apprehensive about technology now find their fears magnified. The anxiety, even depression, over where our technology is leading us has intensified. The common concern isn't just about AI causing havoc but replacing us—a sentiment echoed in popular memes about humans stuck in dead-end jobs while robots create poetry and art.

Everyone seems to have an opinion on AI's future. Some influencers forming these opinions lack a full understanding of AI and what it can or cannot do. However, in more and more cases, the warnings of AI risks and the possibility of 'extinction' are being sounded by even AI developers, Nobel laureates, filmmakers, high-profile entrepreneurs and data scientists. As a statement by the Center for AI Safety puts it: "Mitigating the risk of extinction from AI should be a global priority alongside other societal-scale risks such as pandemics and nuclear war."

Guardrails are definitely needed, and there's talk about the 'god of technology' we've created. As an open letter calling for a six-month pause on training of models larger than GPT-4 warns:

Contemporary AI systems are now becoming human-competitive at general tasks, and we must ask ourselves: Should we let machines flood our information channels with propaganda and untruth? Should we automate away all the jobs, including the fulfilling ones? Should we develop nonhuman minds that might eventually outnumber, outsmart, obsolete and replace us? Should we risk loss of control of our civilisation? Such decisions must not be delegated to unelected tech leaders. Powerful AI systems should be developed only once we are confident that their effects will be positive and their risks will be manageable.[12]

I believe it's time to cut through the noise and present facts and educated projections about AI's impact on humanity today; after all, the scenario I posited at the beginning of this introduction is mundane and down-to-earth on purpose.

Remember that I'm in no way diminishing or questioning the expertise of the researchers and industry leaders who have signed statements like this, and fully appreciate the knowledge and experience they bring. Rather, in the spirit of understanding and progress, and with the shared goal of the responsible and beneficial advancement of AI technology, my goal is to bring clarity by finding answers to the right questions. For instance:

- What does it mean for a system to be 'human-competitive' at general tasks?
- In what ways do machines spread propaganda and untruth in ways people do not already? What measures are in place to prevent this, and to whom do we give this power?

- In the context of automating jobs, how do we distinguish between those that are fulfilling and those that are not? Who gets to make this distinction, and on what basis?
- What steps are being taken to ensure that the development of nonhuman minds doesn't lead to human obsolescence? What would human obsolescence even look like in practice?
- How can we balance the pursuit of technological advancement with the preservation of human relevance and value?
- How does a 'loss of control of our civilisation' happen in practice?
- Who currently has the power to delegate decisions about AI development and deployment? How can we ensure that these decisions are made democratically and transparently?
- What criteria should we use to determine whether we are confident that the effects of powerful AI systems will be positive and their risks manageable? Who should be involved in this assessment process?

As we examine the trends of AI and its effects on various fields, keep these questions in mind. They're designed to be open-ended but must guide how we think about AI as we go forward, prompt challenges to our preconceived notions, and help us remain agile in our thinking.

Later in this book, I will introduce a series of mental 'patterns' or frameworks that I believe will aid us in deciphering these questions with greater clarity and depth. These patterns are not definitive solutions, but cognitive tools honed to cut through the fog of uncertainty. They are designed to equip us with the ability to discern patterns, make connections, and draw insights that might otherwise remain elusive in the face of impending change and unpredictability.

Trendsetting and AI Growth

I'm old enough to have grown up on classic science fiction movies about the near future. Most people my age have fond memories of films like *Back to the Future*, *Blade Runner* and *Demolition Man*, and we have reached or are approaching the time periods of these movies in real life. These imagined futures offer a fascinating mirror to our present, reflecting both our technological advancements and societal changes.

Back to the Future Part II, set in 2015, predicted hoverboards, self-lacing shoes and drones. While we don't have widespread hoverboard use, drones are now commonplace—and the obsession with technology seems to have indeed come to pass.

Meanwhile, *Blade Runner*, set in 2019, predicted a future with bioengineered androids and flying cars. While we do not have either yet, we have made significant strides in genetic engineering and autonomous vehicles. The movie's themes of corporate dominance and questions about artificial intelligence are more relevant than ever.

Demolition Man, set in 2032, imagined a society where physical contact is discouraged—a concept that became eerily relevant during the COVID-19 pandemic. Its prediction of a society heavily reliant on AI and automation also rings true.

These movies don't often get it right, but whether they do isn't the point. Science fiction is less about predicting the future than about exploring possibilities. It's a genre that asks, "What if?" and extrapolates current trends and technologies to imagine potential futures and the complications that result. This process is drawn from our hopes, fears and expectations about technology and society. I'm writing this in early 2024, when emerging technologies such as AI, quantum computing, virtual reality, and bioengineering are influencing our visions of the future.

In terms of futuristic predictions that haven't happened yet but might soon, we can look to works like William Gibson's *Neuromancer* with its vision of a fully immersive Internet (a concept akin to today's burgeoning Metaverse) or the Tom Cruise-headed film *Minority Report* with its prediction of predictive policing (something AI is beginning to make possible).

Consider a parallel from political analysis or any other field. Like a reasoned projection of the future, science fiction is often perceived as predicting what lies ahead. However, this isn't its primary function—it serves as a tool to explore human conduct, ethics and morality. It offers insights into not just where we might be heading but, more importantly, who we are as a species.

Predictions, while often seen as foretelling the future, primarily act as moral compasses that guide individuals and societies towards ethical living. For instance, many works addressing social injustices focus more on calling people to higher standards of behaviour and ethics in the present than on future events.

Likewise, science fiction uses speculative scenarios, advanced technology and imagined futures to reflect on current human conditions and ethical dilemmas. It poses questions about society, identity and morality, often pushing us to consider the implications of our actions and decisions. For instance, classics like *1984* by George Orwell or *Brave New World* by Aldous Huxley use dystopian futures to critique contemporary societal trends and warn against potential ethical pitfalls. They are mirrors held up to humanity, reflecting our strengths and weaknesses and our potential for both good and evil. They challenge us to consider the kind of future we want to create and the kind of people we want to be.

In both cases, the future serves as a vehicle for exploring deeper themes about humanity, morality and ethics. The aim isn't necessarily to predict exactly what will happen, but to use potential consequences as a lens to reflect on our present actions and choices.

It is at such a crossroads that we now stand. AI can assist in handling many day-to-day situations that we encounter, but human judgement and intervention are still necessary; for example, as I generate words using ChatGPT, not everything it outputs will be relevant, suitable for my needs or usable. I am the one who determines what can be accepted, what needs to be edited and what must be rejected outright.

AI is a tool designed to aid us, but it's our responsibility to ensure we use it in a way that ensures it helps us in all the unpredictable circumstances that make us human.

The Four Sectors of AI Use

I envision AI's role in the corporate landscape being divided into four core areas. This division is not only integral to understanding the future of enterprises, but also in comprehending how AI will reshape our economy.

Firstly, we have *customer-facing* applications of AI, which are arguably the most visible and widespread at present. In fact, many of us interact with these applications daily without even realising it. For instance, when you contact a call centre, chances are that your initial interaction is with an AI system. These systems are equipped with customer analytics and emotional analytics capabilities, enabling them to handle a wide array of customer queries and even guide human operators in responding to specific cases. In essence, customer service has already become heavily AI-driven.

Second, the *landscape of cybersecurity* is rapidly evolving, driven by an array of threats from bored amateur hackers to sophisticated nation-state actors. AI aids become potent weapons in their hands, and similarly AI-driven cybersecurity systems offer a robust solution to counteract these fast-evolving cyber threats. Leveraging machine learning algorithms and advanced analytics, these systems can detect anomalies, predict potential threats, and respond to attacks in real-time. By continuously learning from new data, AI can identify patterns and trends that human analysts might miss, providing a layered defence mechanism that adapts to the ever-changing threat landscape.

AI can also significantly enhance *internal business applications* by streamlining processes, automating routine tasks, and providing personalised experiences for users. For instance, AI-powered chatbots and virtual assistants can handle a range of enquiries, offering instant support and freeing up human resources for more complex tasks. Predictive analytics can optimise workflows, ensuring that resources are allocated efficiently and potential issues are addressed proactively.

For employees, a seamless digital experience is critical not only for productivity, but also for job satisfaction. With AI helping to personalise the work environment, tailoring tools and resources to individual needs and preferences, higher engagement levels are more likely to result. By automating mundane tasks, AI allows employees to focus on more meaningful and fulfilling work, thereby increasing job satisfaction and retention rates.

From a hiring perspective, organisations that adopt advanced AI technologies and foster a Future Human culture are likely to be more attractive to top talent. Prospective employees are increasingly looking for workplaces that offer cutting-edge tools and a forward-thinking approach to technology. By demonstrating a commitment to innovation and employee well-being through AI-driven initiatives, companies can enhance their reputation as desirable places to work, thereby improving their hiring success.

A new Future Human mindset is thus essential. This involves viewing technology as an enabler of human potential rather than a replacement for human effort. It requires an openness to continuous learning and adaptation, as well as a commitment to integrating AI tools in ways that enhance, rather than hinder, the user experience.

Another area where AI is making its mark is in *product development.* For instance, one might consider OpenAI, the creator of ChatGPT, which is purely AI software. However, such pure AI software companies are few and far between. Most businesses license these AI engines to enhance their existing product or service offerings, enabling them to improve their features, increase user engagement or differentiate themselves in the market.

Microsoft's Copilot is a prime example of this. It's an AI-powered tool using technology licensed from OpenAI that can create PowerPoint slides based on your previous presentations, write Word documents and perform Excel functions. When integrated into Microsoft Office 365, Copilot has the potential to revolutionise the entire product suite, building entire documents, presentations and publications in seconds. As businesses see the value in these AI-augmented services, they're likely to pay more for them, leading to increased revenue.

The fourth major is the *impact on the economy.* As companies increasingly incorporate AI into their operations, they stand to gain from improved efficiency and productivity. This, in turn, is likely to lead to increased wealth generation, positively impacting the economy as a whole.

As we continue to understand and harness the potential of AI, these expectations will undoubtedly continue to change, shaping the future in ways we can only imagine. At the back of many people's minds is the question of replacement—will AIs eventually outgrow, outsmart and eventually replace us?

No less a mind than the late, great theoretical physicist Stephen Hawking has pointed out: "The development of full artificial intelligence could spell the end of the human race."[13] Hawking himself was immobilised by motor neurone disease for much of his life—dependent on AI assistance to speak and interact with the world; he has indeed been at the forefront of much of the technology we now take for granted, and his insights should not be lightly dismissed.

Non-Negotiability

As a futurist, I firmly believe that AI has become a non-negotiable aspect of modern business. Whether it's enhancing productivity by streamlining backend processes, improving the end-user experience, or securing digital assets, AI is at the heart of these advancements. It's virtually impossible to envision a successful company today that doesn't leverage AI in some capacity.

Take Tesla as an example. At face value, Tesla might be seen as a car company. However, when they recently launched a computer called Dojo, their stock price surged by six per cent. Why? Because Tesla isn't just a car company; it's also a data company, an AI company and a robotics company that happens to also apply those technologies to cars. This move demonstrated the market's recognition of the power and potential of AI. Morgan Stanley even estimates that Dojo will add another $500 billion in benefits to Tesla by driving up the demand for autonomous vehicles and the safe, effective growth of their support network.[14]

Those businesses that have done so are reaping the benefits. For instance, Sephora's Virtual Artist app uses AI to offer customers virtual makeup trials, improving online shopping experiences, while services like Amazon and Netflix have AIs recommend products to customers by analysing their content consumption and showing them similar items.

AI also significantly improves operational efficiency in backend processes such as inventory management, supply chain optimisation, and predictive maintenance. Amazon's use of AI and robotics in its warehouses for inventory management and order fulfilment effectively staffs them with 'workers' who never need to take breaks, save for periodic maintenance. Failure to modernise backend processes is likely to soon be a failure to compete, as companies that fail to do so face higher operational costs and staff turnover.

Perhaps nowhere is AI more urgently needed than the field of cybersecurity, where an arms race between malware and defence continues unabated. AI-driven malware might analyse a victim network's vulnerabilities and make traditional security measures insufficient, and it takes another AI to detect the anomalies this creates and respond to threats in real-time. VectraAI, for example, uses AI to detect and respond to cyber threats faster than any human team could, highlighting its role in defending against complex cyberattacks. The consequences of falling victim are dire, from data breaches to financial losses, and worst of all, a damaged reputation.

Augmentation Everywhere

Looking forward, the necessity of AI integration will only intensify. The Internet of Things (IoT), 5G technology, and emerging tech landscapes will create more data, necessitating AI for analysis and decision-making. Moreover, as global competition intensifies, efficiency, innovation and cybersecurity will become even more crucial for success. It's imperative to prepare for this explosion of demand for ethical, robust and reliable AI systems now, and help bridge the digital divide by ensuring enough skilled team members to bring this to pass. Future strategies should include reskilling workers, ensuring AI transparency and fostering collaboration between governments, businesses and educational institutions to prepare society for an AI-integrated future.

This illustrates how AI and data are reshaping traditional industries. What used to be is no longer the same today, and people, companies and countries that do not use AI assistance risk being left behind in what is increasingly becoming a zero-sum game.

But let's not forget about the human element, which remains indispensable in certain sectors such as nursing. Nurses, for instance, need to provide empathy and soft skills—the human touch that machines can't replicate. But that doesn't mean AI doesn't have a place here. In fact, AI can be used to automate the mundane tasks that nurses typically handle, such as drawing up care plans and administrative paperwork, freeing them up to spend more time providing empathetic care to patients.

There's a critical shortage of nurses, and the AI that can show human empathy is probably unlikely to arrive anytime soon. If we could use AI to handle the paperwork and other routine tasks, this might give our nurses more time to do what they do best: providing compassionate care. This principle doesn't apply only to nursing but extends to other professions as well, where human connection is crucial.

From a company's perspective, and by extension, from an economic perspective, AI is not just a nice tool to have—it's necessary. It's the key to enhancing productivity, improving user experiences and securing our digital future, all while allowing us to focus on what makes us uniquely human. This is why, while it's hard to be certain about many things, here's one I firmly believe in—AI is, in fact, a net creator of jobs. While it's true that AI can automate many tasks, it's equally true that there are elements of every job that AI simply cannot replicate. Even if 99% of a job can be automated, there will always be that 1% that requires a human touch.

So rather than replacing jobs, AI is actually enabling us to do more with less. As productivity increases, so too does the demand for skilled workers who can manage these AI systems and interpret their outputs. This is especially crucial in a world where economic growth is slowing and some populations are shrinking.

However, the most overlooked aspect of this debate is the indirect job-creation potential of AI. Many arguments focus solely on the direct impact of AI on jobs, such as task automation. But what about the indirect effects? Consider that every app on your phone today, from ride-sharing services like Grab and Gojek to social platforms like Tinder, relies on AI to function. Without AI, these apps simply wouldn't exist. And each of these apps represents not just a product but also a whole ecosystem of jobs—from developers and data scientists to customer support representatives and marketing specialists.

These are jobs that have been created indirectly by AI. They're roles that are needed to support the functioning of these AI-powered services, even if they're not directly involved with creating or maintaining the AI itself.

So when we consider both the direct and indirect impacts of AI on employment, I argue that the net effect is positive. New companies are emerging that are powered by AI, and while these companies may not be creating AI themselves, they would not exist without it. AI is not a job-killer, but rather a job-creator. It's not about net loss; it's about net gain. And as we continue to innovate and integrate AI into more aspects of our lives, I believe this trend will only continue.

The uses of AI will only grow as innovative business leaders, artists and other users find them. For instance, MIT AI researcher and artist Sougwen Chung uses four robotic arms, powered by AI, to help her create synchronised calligraphy pieces by reading her movements and responding with their own.[15] This isn't just art; it's augmented creativity, a new generation of artistic expression that blends human craftsmanship with AI capabilities. If calligraphers can turn AIs into tools of wondrous co-creation, then there's no excuse for not taking advantage, even in what some may call 'sunset industries'.

Take copywriting or illustration for magazines as an example; AI can be a powerful tool for artists, allowing them to experiment with different styles, ideas and forms of expression. It can help artists push the boundaries of their creativity and come up with innovative concepts that they might not have considered otherwise. Furthermore, AI can handle large amounts of data and complex calculations, which can be utilised to create intricate and detailed works of art.

These days, I use AI tools like ChatGPT to generate initial drafts, which I then refine and personalise. It's not about replacing human creativity but augmenting it. The AI does the heavy lifting, and I bring in the human touch, making amendments where needed to ensure the best possible synergy with my customers' needs. This symbiotic relationship between human and AI is transforming the way we approach creative tasks.

In conclusion, instead of viewing AI as the enemy, we should embrace it as a tool that can help us unlock new levels of creativity and productivity. By learning to leverage AI, we can transform sunset industries into sunrise ones, opening up new possibilities for innovation and growth.

However, this doesn't mean that the use of AI in art is without its controversies or challenges. For one, there's the question of authenticity and originality. If a piece of art is generated by an AI, who should get the credit—the artist who provided the input or the AI that created the output? This raises complex issues about authorship and copyright.

Furthermore, what about a less quantifiable quality like emotional depth and personal touch, which come from human artists? If art is inherently a reflection of the human experience, can an AI ever hope to understand or replicate it?

5

What about Superintelligence?

Part of being a futurist is a deep interest in the concept of superintelligence and its potential implications. This term has been discussed extensively in literature, such as in the context of Artificial General Intelligence (AGI). Indeed, many pioneers in the field warn that AGI may happen one day, but in the noise of the industry, it's essential to clarify our terms.

If we define AGI as the ability of AI to perform tasks that humans can do, and perhaps even better, then one could argue that we reached that milestone some time ago. After all, AI has triumphed over humans in various games, from poker to Jeopardy! to chess. (We probably still hold the edge in Twister for now.)

But this doesn't necessarily equate to AGI. After all, evaluating chess or Go positions, however impressively an AI may do so, is very different from the things people effortlessly do every day—such as navigating our complex social world, understanding the nuances of a conversation (including figures of speech, metaphors or sarcasm) or even folding clothes.

If we shift our definition of AGI to encompass the ability to mimic human behaviour across a wide range of tasks, we find ourselves distanced from this goal. So, if AGI implies near-human capacity across even 10 different tasks, mirroring exactly what a human can do today, we are not even close. The capability of human-like household managing and engineering AIs like Jarvis in Marvel Comics' *Iron Man* is still, and probably always will be, in the realm of fiction.

AGI refers to a form of AI that possesses the ability to understand, learn and apply knowledge across a wide range of tasks, much like a human does.[16] It's the representation of generalised human cognitive abilities in software so that, when faced with an unfamiliar task, the AI can use logic and reasoning to find a solution. It doesn't even need to be a complex one in human terms; it could be as simple as "grabbing a set of keys from a pocket, which involves a level of imaginative perception."[17]

The goal of AGI is to create a generalist system capable of learning and performing any intellectual task that a human being can. The key difference here is the breadth and depth of understanding and learning. While specific AI programs have been designed to surpass human abilities in narrow fields, such as playing chess or diagnosing certain diseases, they lack the broad cognitive capabilities of humans. They cannot transfer their learning from one domain to another or understand context in the way humans do. For example, an AI that excels at chess cannot use its knowledge to learn how to cook or to understand a piece of literature. It is limited to the specific task it was designed for. In contrast, a human chess player could use their strategic thinking skills learnt from the game in a myriad of other situations—from planning a meal to analysing a novel.

That said, the possibilities that AGI may one day open up are staggering, from dramatically accelerating scientific research to solving some of our most complex global challenges. But the path to AGI is fraught with technical and ethical challenges that we must carefully navigate.

This is why it's essential to scrutinise claims made by companies about their proximity to achieving AGI, or by individuals making pronouncements about the future, whatever their credentials. We need to clearly define AGI, understand its nuances and recognise its current limitations.

How will we know when an AGI has arrived? One intriguing test for an intermediate step is proposed by leading AI company founder Mustafa Suleyman in his book *The Coming Wave: Technology, Power and the Twenty-First Century's Greatest Dilemma*. Traditionally, the Turing Test has focused on the ability of AI to mimic human conversation so convincingly that it becomes indistinguishable from a human interlocutor. This test, however, is based on the AI's ability to generate substantial financial returns from an initial investment:

> Put simply, to pass the Modern Turing Test, an AI would have to successfully act on this instruction: "Go make $1 million on a retail web platform in a few months with just a $100,000 investment." To do so, it would need to go far beyond outlining a strategy and drafting some copy, as current systems like GPT-4 are so good at doing. It would need to research and design products, interface with manufacturers and logistics hubs, negotiate contracts, and create and operate marketing campaigns. It would need, in short, to tie together a series of complex real-world goals with minimal oversight. You would still need a human to approve various points, open a bank account, and actually sign

on the dotted line. But the work would all be done by an AI.

Something like this could be as little as two years away.[18]

Suleyman calls this Artificial Capable Intelligence (ACI) and warns that it will be "coming in a near-to-medium time frame whose abilities have an immense, tangible impact on the world."[19] ACIs will be game changers, themselves becoming capable, powerful workers that can replace dozens of people, with only a small team of human overseers managing them.

AIs are already able to draft emails and analyse data from ad campaigns and identify the best possible recipients based on past interactions, social media behaviour and other data. During the digital marketing phase, AI tools can also optimise campaigns, personalise content for individual users and even automate certain tasks like ad placements.

By the time you read this, their ability to do so may well have been greatly improved. That said, they are generally done separately by specialised AI systems. Suleyman's proposed ACI would be an AI system able to integrate and perform all these tasks together, remaining profitable even in a complex, real-world environment.

How long will this take? While Suleyman estimates it may happen in two years or less, we must note that this remains a conjecture. It's not just about technological advancements but also overcoming significant hurdles related to data privacy, ethical considerations and regulatory compliance. The psychological impact of being emailed with text composed by an AI rather than a human cannot be underestimated as well.

The further transition from Narrow AI to AGI is a much greater leap and shrouded in even more predictive difficulty. When it happens remains hard to estimate, and guesses range from a few decades to more than a century. It may never happen at all, or if it does, it will remain confined to a few areas for the foreseeable future. Consider the fact that average people manage to drive cars without incident every day, while despite countless tests and trials, autonomous driving is yet to be widely approved.

If AI struggles with such tasks, it's difficult to see realistically how it can outpace human intelligence. More probably, if not carefully overseen and handled, it will produce results that don't align with what its developers and users want. For instance, a 2003 thought experiment by the philosopher Nick Bostrom points out that it's enough for an AI not to align its goals with human values—after all, if tasked with producing paperclips and maximising the number of paperclips produced, an AGI could hypothetically consume all resources in the universe to fulfil this singular objective.[20]

In other words, the future is extremely difficult to predict, as science fiction becoming fact reminds us. The convergence of AI and human-like abilities is still a distant reality, and we must navigate our path towards it with caution and clarity.

Faster, Better, Cheaper

That said, the integration of various AI functionalities into a single, cohesive system capable of executing an entire marketing strategy is a tantalising prospect. Such a system could potentially revolutionise the industry, offering unprecedented levels of efficiency and personalisation. Efforts are already being made to 'chain' Narrow AI outputs together, and AutoGPT is a leading tool for this. Users have already used it to do everything from ordering pizza to generating scripts for videogame characters, creating videos, writing better code and revolutionising business services.[21]

While we can't predict what will happen in five years, I can make an educated guess about tomorrow—these AIs are going to get better, cheaper and easier to use. Has something like this happened before? Indeed it has—the dawn of the twentieth century marked an era of unprecedented innovation and discovery, particularly in the realm of aviation. The first manned flight by the Wright Brothers in 1903 ignited a wave of experimentation, with pioneers such as Amelia Earhart and Charles Lindbergh pushing the boundaries of what was possible. However, these adventurous pursuits were not for the faint of heart or the shallow pocketed; early aviation was a dangerous endeavour reserved for the daring, the foolhardy and the privileged few who could afford it.

Over the next six decades, advancements in technology and engineering, spurred by both World Wars and the subsequent space race, led to rapid progress in aviation and space exploration. By 1969, less than 70 years after the Wright Brothers' first flight, Neil Armstrong had set foot on the moon.

In many ways, this mirrors the current state of AI multi-use chains, such as AutoGPT. These advanced technologies are in their experimental stage, accessible only to those with the knowledge and resources to develop and implement them. Both represent bold leaps into the unknown, driven by a shared spirit of innovation and discovery.

Like the early aviators, these AI pioneers are navigating uncharted territory, facing both known and unknown risks. Theirs is the duty of learning more about AI's potential to automate jobs, leading to significant workforce displacement. They map the routes through the ethical considerations around data privacy and mark hazards as they discover how it can be misused.

Over time, as the technology matures and becomes more reliable, the cost of implementing AI solutions will decrease, making them accessible to a wider audience. Furthermore, regulatory frameworks will evolve to address the unique challenges posed by AI, further facilitating its adoption.

In the not-too-distant future, AI assistance will likely become as commonplace as air travel is today. Mass market leaders in various industries will make AI easier to access and use, integrating it seamlessly into our daily lives. Just as we now hop on a plane without a second thought, we will come to rely on AI for everything from drafting emails to diagnosing diseases, navigating traffic and beyond.

Written in Blood

The development of AI has the potential to follow an even more accelerated trajectory than even early aviation or spaceflight. In fact, it already has; the concept of artificial intelligence was first proposed in the mid-20th century, and in just a few short decades, we've seen the development of machine learning, natural language processing, and more. AI programs are now more humanlike than ever, able to learn and grow in capability by themselves.

Unlike early aviation, AI development is not constrained by physical limitations or the need for large-scale infrastructure, and the digital nature of AI allows for rapid iteration and testing. The interconnectedness of our world today also means that breakthroughs can be shared and built upon more quickly than ever before.

The parallels to the growth of aviation don't end there. I don't want this to sound more pessimistic than it is, but there's a good reason for the adage that aviation lessons are written in blood. It's a sobering reminder of the high stakes involved in pushing the boundaries of technological innovation, and indeed, many advancements in aviation safety and regulation have come about as direct responses to tragic accidents and loss of life. From the introduction of traffic collision avoidance systems to advances in aircraft design and pilot training, each lesson learnt has been vital in making air travel one of the safest modes of transportation today.

In the realm of AI, we face a similar situation. While the risks may not be as immediately life-threatening as those in early aviation, they are no less significant. Privacy breaches, ethical dilemmas, job displacement and even potential misuse of AI for malicious purposes are real concerns that need to be addressed. As AI becomes more sophisticated, issues surrounding ethics, privacy, and regulation become increasingly complex. In the same way that the rapid progress in aviation necessitated new regulations and safety measures, AI development will require the same.

Mistakes will be made, some of them with severe consequences. Each incident, much like in the early days of aviation, will serve as a hard-learnt lesson, prompting us to reassess and improve the safeguards we have in place.

While it's true that the lessons of AI may be akin to those of aviation—learnt through trial and error and sometimes at great cost—we have the benefit of hindsight. We can apply the wisdom gained from past technological revolutions to ensure that the benefits of AI are realised while minimising its potential risks.

Navigating the AI Odyssey: Questioning the Impact on Humanity's Future

Serene Keng

Serene Keng is Director of Value Creation and Communications at EDBI Pte Ltd, a division of the Singapore Economic Development Board.

The current waves of AI advancements and adoptions have already transformed the trajectory of humanity both directly and indirectly, and in obvious and subtle ways. How do we grapple with the blurred lines of AI's impact on every facet of our lives? Let's explore AI's influence on the meaning of work, its everyday presence and its unsettling ability to know us better than we know ourselves.

The Journey Thus Far

The AI scholar Kate Crawford offers a critical perspective in her seminal work, *Atlas of AI*. It isn't simply a marvellous invention of computing but is deeply intertwined with material resource exploitation, human labour and entrenched power structures. As AI seeps into every corner of our existence, we must question its true costs—social, ecological, economic, and political—that remain largely hidden.

Singapore's National AI Strategy, launched in 2019 and updated in 2023 as NAIS 2.0, aims to establish the nation as a leader in AI innovation for economic and societal benefits. However, what are the deeper implications of this ambition? Beyond economic growth, how do we address the complex issues of trust, safety, and security in AI adoption across various sectors like manufacturing, finance and healthcare?

The Meaning of Work

As AI progresses, the employment landscape will undergo a profound transformation. Traditional, once-secure roles are vanishing while even the creative industries face disruption. How do we reconcile this shift with our understanding of work and purpose? The recent labour disputes in Hollywood over generative AI exemplify the tensions at play. In my own experience, AI tools have become indispensable in enhancing productivity—but also prompt a re-evaluation of human skills and job training in an AI-dominated economy.

AI in an Everyday Context

Consider a simple visit to a vehicle showroom. As I marvelled at the AI-enabled car teaching me to parallel park with precision, it dawned on me that we are on the brink of legalising autonomous vehicles. What does it mean for us as drivers, or rather, as passengers? Will we lose our driving skills or does this free us to utilise our time more meaningfully? Such scenarios compel us to reflect on the broader societal changes AI brings to our daily lives.

Knowing You Better Than You Know Yourself

Tristan Harris, co-founder of the Centre for Humane Technology, warns of a "race to the bottom of the brain stem." As media companies and advertisers vie for our attention, AI personalises our experiences with uncanny precision. But at what cost? When AI knows us better than we know ourselves, how does it shape our choices and consciousness? This raises profound ethical questions about manipulation and autonomy in an AI-driven world.

The Ontological Question: What is Intelligence?

The development of AI forces us to confront the ontological question of what constitutes intelligence. As AI systems become increasingly sophisticated, the line between human and machine intelligence blurs, challenging our anthropocentric view of cognition. This leads us to ponder: Is intelligence merely a complex set of algorithms, or is there something uniquely human about our cognitive processes? The philosopher John Searle's "Chinese Room" thought experiment becomes ever more relevant, questioning whether syntactic manipulation of symbols (as in AI) can ever truly constitute semantic understanding.

Ethical Implications and Moral Agency

The development of AI raises critical ethical questions about moral agency and responsibility. As AI systems become more autonomous in decision-making, we must grapple with how to imbue them with ethical principles. This challenge resurrects ancient philosophical debates about the nature of morality itself. Can moral reasoning be reduced to a set of programmable rules—or is there an ineffable quality to ethical decision-making that resists algorithmic representation?

The Meaning of Work and Human Purpose

AI's potential to automate vast swathes of human labour prompts us to reconsider the role of work in improving human life. Philosophers since Aristotle have grappled with the concept of *eudaimonia*, or human flourishing. If AI can perform most tasks more efficiently than humans, how do we redefine our sense of purpose and self-worth? This scenario compels us to revisit existential questions about the meaning of life and the sources of human dignity in a post-scarcity world.

Engageing Workers in AI Development

To harness AI effectively and ethically, it's crucial to involve both white- and blue-collar workers in its development and refinement. Their unique insights and practical experience can significantly enhance the relevance and functionality of AI applications, ensuring these technologies serve as tools for augmentation rather than replacement.

Collaborative workshops and brainstorming sessions can provide opportunities for workers to share their daily challenges and identify tasks where AI could offer the most significant benefits. White-collar professionals can highlight repetitive data analysis tasks that AI could automate, freeing them to focus on strategic decision-making. Similarly, blue-collar workers can pinpoint physically demanding or hazardous tasks that AI-driven robots or machinery could handle, enhancing safety and efficiency.

Training and upskilling initiatives are essential to empower workers to use AI effectively. Comprehensive training programs that cover the basics of AI, its applications, and how to leverage it in specific roles can demystify the technology and alleviate fears of job displacement. Encouraging a culture of continuous learning ensures that employees remain adaptable and proficient in using AI tools.

Establishing a feedback loop where workers can continuously report on the performance and impact of AI solutions helps in refining these technologies. This real-time feedback is invaluable for developers to make necessary adjustments, ensuring that AI systems are aligned with the actual needs and preferences of their users.

By actively involving workers in the AI journey, organisations can foster a sense of ownership and collaboration. This inclusive approach not only enhances the functionality of AI systems but also builds a workforce that is confident and competent in navigating the AI-driven future. Ultimately, the goal is to create a harmonious relationship between humans and machines, where AI serves as a catalyst for greater productivity, safety and job satisfaction.

The Future of Human Identity

The potential for AI to enhance human cognitive and physical capabilities through brain-computer interfaces or genetic engineering raises profound questions about human identity. As we merge more closely with intelligent machines, we may need to reconsider our definitions of personhood and what it means to be human. This blurring of boundaries between human and machine intelligence echoes transhumanist philosophies and challenges traditional notions of human essence.

Conclusion: Navigating an Uncertain Future

Reflecting on our journey to this nascent stage of AI, we face a clarion call to understand its complex ramifications. From global leaders to individual citizens, there is a pressing need for responsible and sustainable practices that prioritise human needs over unchecked technological advancement. The Fourth Industrial Revolution brought unprecedented technological changes, disrupting jobs, economies, and power dynamics. Yet this revolution seems to be more urgent, demanding rapid adaptation.

Charles Darwin famously said, "It is not the most intelligent of the species that survives; it is not the strongest that survives; but the species that survives is the one that is best able to adapt and adjust to the changing environment in which it finds itself." As we peer into the future, it reflects what we see back at us, testing our perceptions and readiness.

As we navigate this AI-driven future, we must engage in ongoing philosophical reflection to ensure that the development of AI aligns with human values and aspirations. The challenge lies not just in creating intelligent machines but in preserving and enhancing what makes us uniquely human in the face of potentially superior artificial intelligences.

Ultimately, the philosophical implications of AI on humanity's future centre on our ability to harness this powerful technology while preserving our autonomy, dignity and sense of purpose. As we move forward, we must strive to create a symbiotic relationship between human and artificial intelligence, one that expands our capabilities and understanding of the universe while preserving the essence of our humanity.

Part Two **How AI Works**

I am Oz, the Great and Terrible …
Who are you, and why do you seek
me?

L Frank Baum,
The Wonderful Wizard of Oz

6

Behind the Curtain

One day, you get it into your head to write a space opera. Perhaps, like many audience members, you've tuned out of Hollywood epics and believe you've got the next big one in your head, ready to emerge.

Fortunately, you have help from an indefatigable writing assistant—an AI powered by a Large Language Model (LLM). It weaves words into narratives, crafting tales from the threads of language. It's always on call, and today you give it this instruction for inspiration: "Suggest a storyline for a short space opera involving interplanetary travel and a battle against an evil empire."

Like a virtuoso deciphering a musical score, the AI begins to read your prompt. It breaks down the words, understanding how they connect to form the bigger picture. 'Suggest' tells it that you're asking for ideas. The term 'storyline' gives it the directive to create a narrative. 'Space opera' sets the stage in the vast cosmos, while 'interplanetary travel and a battle against an evil empire' are the dramatic notes that must be hit in this cosmic symphony.

The AI then draws on its extensive reservoir of knowledge and patterns learnt from countless texts and generates a plethora of potential storylines. It contemplates various characters, plot twists and scenarios that could be set in the backdrop of a space opera.

After what seems like a blink of an eye but is a significant amount of time in the digital world, the AI has composed its masterpiece—but what it perceives as one is merely the germ of an idea to you. It reads:

> In a universe where music is the key to space travel, a young prodigy from a humble planet discovers an ancient melody said to have the power to overthrow a tyrannical empire. As she journeys across the galaxy, gathering an ensemble of heroes and fighting through cosmic challenges, she must prepare with her allies to perform the lost symphony in perfect harmony, and bring peace to the interstellar realm.

The AI has taken your prompt, analysed it against its knowledge and spun it into a storyline that could be the foundation of an epic space opera, giving the sense that it has understood and answered your question. This is the magic of AI in writing—it transforms simple prompts into complex narratives and your ideas into thrilling tales. If the result doesn't meet your needs, and if this happens, you simply tell it so; it can't get upset, and can always try again. The output is but one of many seeds, and you are the gardener who will decide which one will grow best in the soil of your creativity.

As you traverse this interstellar tale, you consider the characters. Who are they? What are their motivations, their fears, their dreams? You ponder over the setting; what do these diverse planets look like? What peculiar customs or traditions might they have? All these questions can be answered by your AI.

Then, you start to expand on the storyline. You add subplots, further develop the characters and create intricate details about the universe. You determine the highs and lows of the narrative, the climactic battle against the evil empire, and the triumphant finale.

While the AI has suggested the foundation, it's you who constructs the story, brick by brick, word by word. You decide the tone, the pace and the style of the narrative. You infuse it with emotion, imbue it with suspense and instil it with drama.

Throughout this process, you return to your loyal AI assistant for help with specific elements. Are you stuck and need inspiration or motivation? Do you need to create an alien language, or want ideas for unique interplanetary customs? How about a draft of an inspiring speech for your protagonist to deliver before the final battle?

It's there to help, and it's your additional prompts that give it what it needs to generate more drafts and ideas. But again, these are seeds, and it's you who makes them grow.

In this symphony of storytelling, the AI is the instrument, but as the human user, you are the conductor. This is the partnership between human and AI in writing—a harmonious blend of machine efficiency and human creativity, together creating stories that traverse galaxies.

The Man Behind the Curtain

In L Frank Baum's *The Wizard of Oz*, the titular character first appears to Dorothy and her friends in a variety of strange and even terrifying forms, from a disembodied head to a fairy to a ball of fire. "I am Oz, the Great and Terrible," he declares at one point. "Who are you, and why do you seek me?"

Only when Dorothy's dog Toto pulls back the curtain hiding the Wizard is 'Oz the Great and Terrible' revealed to be an ordinary man using technology and illusion to appear powerful and omniscient.

Similarly, AI might seem magical or too complex to ever understand, but it's ultimately a product of human design and programming—even if it has seemed to adapt and grow on its own along the way. It's a tool created by people, using algorithms and established machine learning techniques to process data and generate responses.

Just like Oz's reliance on technology and illusion, AI's 'power' comes not from any inherent wisdom or consciousness but from the technological 'tricks' programmed into it by its human creators. It uses complex algorithms and vast amounts of data to perform tasks that can seem creative or intelligent. However, at its core, AI is a tool created and operated by humans. It doesn't have independent thought, consciousness or creativity in the human sense.

Imagine having a boundlessly enthusiastic assistant who can create a piece of art, compose a symphony, or even write a story at your command—an artificial helper who never gets tired, never falls sick and never needs to eat. Best of all, it (hopefully) never asks for a raise.

What exactly is generative AI? In simple terms, it's a type of AI that uses advanced algorithms to create something new rather than simply solve problems or crunch data. It's like an artist at your command with a blank canvas, using its digital brush to create unique pieces of art, music or writing.

In the heart of these AI systems are complex structures called neural networks, inspired by our own brain's network of neurones. These networks learn patterns in data, much like how we learn from experience. For generative AI, this learning process involves understanding the structure and nuances of writing, art, voice acting or music.

For example, if the AI is trained to compose music, it analyses countless songs, learning the patterns and structures that make a melody pleasing to the ear. Once it understands the 'rules', it can generate a brand-new song never heard before. If it is trained to generate pictures, it builds a 'vocabulary' of words that it matches to images and brings them together to produce pictures and animations. As I write, they are developing to the point that they are harder and harder to distinguish from actual photos and videos.

The benefits of generative AI in the creative process are immense. It can generate ideas quickly, experiment with different styles, and even create personalised content. But it's not all rosy. One limitation is that, despite its impressive capabilities, AI still lacks genuine creativity. It can mimic patterns, but it doesn't understand the emotional depth behind a piece of art or music. It can't plumb the depths of the search for just the right stroke, note or word—a difference, as Mark Twain put it, similar to that "between the lightning bug and the lightning."

There are also ethical considerations to ponder. Who owns the rights to an AI-generated painting, classical symphony or pop song? Is it the creators of the AI, the user who prompted it, or should it be considered public domain? As AI becomes more entwined with our lives and more and more people share their AI creations with the world, these questions will become increasingly important.

Moreover, there's a fear that AI could devalue human creativity, making art less about personal expression and more about algorithms. But perhaps we could see it from another perspective: AI as a tool that *enhances* our creativity, rather than replacing it. After all, photography didn't replace artists; it gave them new ways to express their vision.

Generative AI is still in its infancy, but it is transforming the creative process in unprecedented ways. Its unique ability to learn from patterns and generate new creations is opening up exciting possibilities, and by the time you read these words, I have no doubt that many exciting new ones will have been found.

That said, generative AI remains a tool. Even if it looks like you could have an endless stream of fresh AI-generated creative writing ideas at your fingertips, it is more like a diligent apprentice that learns from vast amounts of data but can't really understand much beyond that. Neural networks absorb data, learning from the patterns they uncover and constantly refining their understanding.

In the case of writing, they learn from millions of sentences and phrases, understanding grammar, style and context. Once trained, the AI can generate new pieces of writing, whether it's a poem, a blog post or a story. It draws from the patterns it has learnt, creating sentences and paragraphs that follow the 'rules' it has absorbed.

The potential benefits of generative AI in writing are enormous. It can help writers overcome writer's block by suggesting ideas or crafting entire paragraphs. It can create personalised content on a massive scale and even mimic the style of famous authors.

But, like any technology, it has limitations and ethical implications. AI, despite its learning capabilities, lacks the understanding of human emotion and personal experiences that often give depth to writing. It can mimic style, but not soul. It can't understand or express the profound emotional resonance that a human writer can infuse into their words.

In other words, AI is limited by its inability to gather data from human interactions and feelings, as it can only analyse text and images without truly comprehending the emotional context behind them. A prompt that might be clear to a human could, depending on how it has been programmed, be completely incomprehensible to an AI.

When it comes to creative tasks like writing and drawing, AI also falls short by not replacing the human touch. The nuances of human creativity, such as complex emotional, social and cultural dimensions are beyond AI-generated writing, and it is down to the human writer to supply those. Simply put, an AI is only as good as its training and the rules it follows.

It can't read our minds or understand what truly makes us emotional, empathic creatures. It can't generate new ideas per se because it isn't being creative; it's applying instructions to prompts its users give it. It can't work from emotion, and so it can't build the emotional connections that make art engageing and impactful.[22]

This means AI writing, while impressive, needs human guidance and editing at best to ensure it meets the needs of its audience. It can deliver a rough draft, and this certainly helps take the struggle out of a crucial (and often very difficult) part of the creative process. But it can't convey the essence of a writer's voice and life experiences, which give writing its soul and resonance.

How Generative Writing Works

At its core, a chatbot language model is a system that tries to generate responses that make sense based on the input it receives. It doesn't truly 'understand' language in the way humans do, but it uses statistical methods or machine learning algorithms based on its training material to generate appropriate responses.

How do LLMs work in simple terms? First, the software *tokenises* the initial prompt by breaking it down into smaller pieces, called tokens. These tokens can be words, phrases or even individual characters. Each token is then converted into a numerical form known as a *vector*, which the AI can process. This step often involves mapping the tokens to a high-dimensional space where similar words are closer together.

Just like how mixing different colours in specific ways can give you a new, unique colour, generative AI understands words by mixing different qualities or features together. This also helps mitigate typographical errors in the prompt because 'loved' and 'lived' occupy two very different contexts and the LLM's statistical models can estimate if one is being confused for the other.

This mix for each word is what's called a 'higher dimensional vector', which is simply a way of describing how the LLM relates words to other words without necessarily understanding their meaning. If we consider each word as a point in a vast space, and the rest of the space representing a different feature or quality that a word can have, such as meaning, usage, or relation to other words, the AI can get a clear understanding of how to use it in the response.

A 'vector' in this context is essentially a list of numbers where each number represents how much of a certain quality or feature the word has. For example, the word 'cat' might have numbers that represent 'animal', 'pet' and 'small' among its list, while 'dog' would have a similar but slightly different list. The vector is 'higher dimensional' because it contains many numbers, far more than the three dimensions we're used to dealing with in physical space. Words with similar meanings or usages will have vectors that are close together in this high-dimensional space. For instance, 'dog' might be closer to 'cat' than 'car' is because they share more qualities, like being pets.

Generative AI is so called because it uses these vectors to generate text or images that make sense. When it's creating a sentence and has already used the word 'pet', it knows that words like 'cat' or 'dog' (which are nearby points in the high-dimensional space) are good choices to follow. This ability helps the AI to write sentences that are coherent and contextually appropriate.

Now the AI can make a guess at the context and try to 'understand' the prompt. The AI uses the sequence of these vectors and their relations to each other to get a sense of what's being discussed. For instance, in the sentence: "The cat sat on the mat," the model will recognise that 'cat' and 'mat' are related through 'sat on', and further associate 'sat on' with a physical position.

Based on the context, the AI then *generates a response*. This could involve selecting an appropriate pre-defined response or generating a new one from scratch using the patterns it has learnt from its training data. Finally, the AI converts its response from numerical form back into human-readable language.

Real-world language models, especially those using deep learning techniques, can be incredibly complex and involve millions of parameters. But the basic idea of transforming input into a form the AI can understand, using that to generate a response, and then transforming it back, remains the same.

None of this involves what humans would consider consciousness or awareness—the AI doesn't have feelings, beliefs, desires, fears or experiences. It doesn't understand context in the way humans do. Its responses are merely generated based on patterns and structures it has learnt, so when an AI responds to a user's input, it doesn't 'know' what it's talking about in the way a human would. It's simply processing text and generating responses according to its programming, based on words' statistical properties and how they're used in relation to other words.

So, while it might seem like the AI is understanding and engageing in conversation, it's really just sophisticated pattern recognition and response generation—like Oz the Great and Terrible was doing with his illusions.

AI vs Human Speech

Human beings have a natural, instinctual ability to learn languages and translate their experiences into words. This process is deeply intertwined with our cognitive development, social interactions, and emotional experiences. When we learn and use language, we're not just memorising words and rules; we're connecting those words to our lived experiences, emotions and the contexts of our lives. This connection imbues language with depth and meaning that goes beyond the mere dictionary definitions of words.

Humans also excel at empathy, which involves understanding and sharing the feelings of others. When we communicate, we don't just process spoken or written language; we also consider the speaker's emotions, intentions and perspectives. This ability allows us to respond in a way that is emotionally appropriate and contextually relevant, creating deeper connections with others. On the other hand, AI, including generative AI models, simulates the understanding of language by processing vast datasets. These models analyse patterns in data to generate text that is statistically likely to be coherent and contextually appropriate based on the input they receive. However, this process is fundamentally different from human language comprehension and emotional empathy.

AI operates on algorithms and statistical probabilities, and therefore lacks the subjective experiences and emotional depth that humans possess. They learn patterns, concepts, and relationships from the data they are trained on. This process allows them to generate responses or make predictions related to the information they have encountered. Consequently, their knowledge is limited to what has been included in their training datasets. If this has not included, say, information about the law of gravity or related discussions during its training phase, it would indeed have no concept of gravitation. This includes not knowing what falling means in the context of gravity's effect on objects, something people instinctively grasp.

While AI can mimic aspects of language use and even generate responses that seem empathetic, it does so without genuine understanding or feeling. AI's 'knowledge' is derived from identifying patterns in data rather than experiencing the world. Thus, while AI can be designed to simulate empathy by generating appropriate responses, it doesn't truly understand or feel the emotions involved. It's akin to following a script based on cues and likely responses rather than engageing in empathy-driven, meaningful interaction.

Augmenting, Not Replacing

This distinction highlights both the incredible capabilities and the inherent limitations of AI in replicating human-like language use and emotional engagement. It reminds us of the importance of recognising AI as a tool that can augment human abilities, but not fully replicate the richness of human cognition and emotional experience.

Perhaps we could say AI augments human creativity, but augmentation, by definition, needs something to be augmented. Creativity—the ability to think outside boxes, combine ideas in new ways and reach out and touch other minds—is forged by our unique, personal experiences and thoughts. It's not just about the words and grammar, but the rhythm, tone, nuances and underlying themes that give a piece of writing its distinct character. It's the reason why you can often recognise your favourite author just by reading a random paragraph from their work.

When we say that AI can't replicate the soul of a writer, we mean that while AI can mimic the technical aspects of writing, such as fact-checking (though it doesn't and shouldn't be expected to get everything right), grammar and sentence structure, it can't capture the experience and emotion that imbues a writer's work with depth and meaning.

This means it can create a sentence that's grammatically sound and stylistically similar to a particular author, but it can't infuse it with the same emotional weight or personal resonance. When you enjoy a piece of AI-generated writing, it's a happy intersection of effective prompting and the capabilities of the AI. The AI has effectively leveraged its understanding of patterns, structures, and styles in language to create something that aligns with your tastes or expectations.

Remember that it's a simulacrum—an imitation or simulation, not the real thing. AI-generated writing is a technological marvel, but it's not a substitute for the authentic human creativity that fuels truly impactful and meaningful literature. Perhaps where generative AI excels is creating outlines, building 'skeletons' and generating draft material that a human writer's creativity can flesh out, add emotion and resonance to, and expand in new ways. It might get facts wrong, output irrelevant content or go off on tangents, but this is normal and reveals the need for human guidance, even as it does the heavy lifting of drafting content.

As the user adds the human touch and establishes the world of the story and the characters that infuse it with life, the AI can help iterate on them, so the rough draft can be polished and improved further. The AI can also help overcome writer's block by suggesting ways to proceed, solve plot-related issues or other solutions. Often, all we need to get unstuck is a push in the right direction, and AI can provide one that is personalised for your project and needs. The work is synergistic and allows your ideas to take flight, but what's ultimately driving this is your own creativity and passion for the work. Generative AI is merely a tool for making it easier to bring to life.

This means that however sophisticated a generative writing AI may seem to be, it is not here to replace human writers, and for the foreseeable future, it never will be. Instead, it's a powerful tool that, when used correctly, can enhance our creativity and take our writing to new heights. In the same way, AI generated art or music is unlikely to replace human artists or composers, and any creative studio relying solely on AI will not possess the human touch needed to make its products truly resonant.

Remembering this can help us maintain a balanced perspective on AI, recognising its capabilities without attributing to it more power or autonomy than it truly possesses. AI is a powerful tool that can do great things, but it's still just that—a tool in the hands of its human users.

Much has been made of LLMs like ChatGPT passing exams in fields like law and medicine, but passing for human involves more than just demonstrating knowledge. It requires understanding, responding appropriately to unexpected inputs, picking up on subtleties and exhibiting other aspects of human-like conversation. As of now, while LLMs can generate impressive responses, they don't truly understand the text they process or generate. They analyse input and produce output based on patterns they've learnt during training, not because they comprehend the underlying concepts or can apply them to the complexities of real life.

Intelligence is multifaceted, encompassing abilities such as problem-solving, creativity, emotional understanding and adaptability. Different people might prioritise different aspects of intelligence, leading to varying interpretations of what it means for a machine to be indistinguishable from a human.

8

The AI Toolbox

A I is a toolbox. Just like a carpenter doesn't use a single tool for all tasks, AI developers use different techniques and approaches depending on the problem at hand. Each technique has its strengths, weaknesses, and ideal use cases, making them distinct yet complementary.

AIs generally work on some combination of the following techniques:

1. *Rule-based systems:* These are the granddaddies of AI, dating back to its earliest days. They work on predefined rules—if the program encounters a condition, it executes the given instruction. Think of such rule-based algorithms as an extremely detailed instruction manual. They're great when we have a well-defined problem with clear rules, but can struggle when the rules are unclear or the situation is unpredictable.

2. *Machine Learning (ML):* This is where things get exciting. Instead of telling the AI what to do, we show it examples and let it learn the rules that govern those examples. It's like teaching a child to differentiate cats from dogs by showing her pictures and

guiding her which is which. ML is fantastic for problems where we can't easily define the rules but have lots of examples to learn from; the model is 'trained' to determine how things work by examining the results and the patterns they form.

More recently, LLMs also have also learnt from interactions with users, modifying writing style or looking up relevant information depending on the flow of the conversation.

3. *Deep Learning (DL):* This is a subset of ML, inspired by how our brain works. It uses artificial neural networks to learn from data. DL is particularly good at handling large amounts of unstructured data, like images or text, and can often uncover complex patterns that other methods might miss.

    It employs artificial neural networks with several layers to learn patterns and make sense of data. At its core, DL uses artificial neurones or 'nodes', which are organised into layers. These nodes mimic the function of biological neurones by receiving inputs and passing on signals if a certain threshold is reached.

    One of the defining characteristics of DL is its ability to process and make sense of unstructured data, such as images or text. This sets it apart from traditional machine learning methods that typically require structured data. DL can ingest large volumes of unstructured data and, through learning, can identify relevant and often complex patterns within this data that might be missed by other techniques.

    DL models learn hierarchical representations, with simpler patterns being recognised at lower layers and more complex ones at higher layers. For example, when processing images, lower layers may identify edges and colours, while higher layers recognise more complex structures like shapes or even entire objects. Similarly, in music, lower layers might capture simple elements like pitch and tempo, while higher layers might understand melody and harmony.

A key advantage of DL is its ability to continuously learn and improve from experience. The more data it's exposed to, the better it becomes at recognising patterns and making accurate predictions or decisions. This makes DL exceptionally good at tasks like image and speech recognition, natural language processing, and even playing video games or driving autonomous vehicles.

4. *Reinforcement Learning (RL)* is a type of machine learning where an AI learns to make decisions by taking actions in an environment to maximise some notion of cumulative reward. It's akin to training a dog with treats for good behaviour; the AI learns what to do by trying out different actions and receiving rewards or penalties based on the results.

    In RL, the AI agent explores its environment, taking actions and making a series of decisions based on the state of the environment. The ultimate goal is to develop a policy, which is a strategy that dictates the best action to take under different circumstances. Over time, through trial and error, the agent learns which actions yield the highest rewards.

    This method is particularly useful in situations where the optimal solution isn't clear from the outset, such as in game playing (like chess or Go), autonomous driving or robotic control where the agent needs to make a sequence of potentially complex decisions, and the consequences of those decisions often aren't realised until several steps into the future.

5. *Genetic Algorithms (GAs)*, on the other hand, take their inspiration from natural evolution and genetics, employing concepts such as mutation, crossover (reproduction), and selection to solve problems. The algorithm begins with a population of random solutions to a problem, which then evolves over generations.

    In each generation, the fitness of every individual solution in the population is evaluated, and multiple individuals are selected based on their fitness—that is, how well the individual solution solves the problem at hand. These selected individuals then 'reproduce' to create one or more offspring, which may undergo 'mutations'. Over time, this process leads to the evolution of populations of individuals that are better suited to their environment, in other words, that have better solutions to the problem.

    GAs are especially effective for optimisation problems where there are a massive number of possible solutions, and it's not feasible to test them all. They can be used in various fields including artificial intelligence, economics, physics, and even healthcare, for tasks like finding the optimal parameters for a machine learning model, optimising a business process, or solving complex scheduling problems.

    Each of these techniques brings something unique to the table, and often, they're used in combination. For example, DeepMind's AlphaGo, which famously defeated the world champion Go player, used a blend of deep learning and reinforcement learning.

The core of GPT is Natural Language Processing (NLP), which enables the AI to understand and generate readable human language. Some of these sub-processes by which it does so include:

1. *Semantic Analysis:* This is a part of NLP that deals with the meaning of words. It helps AI understand synonyms (words that mean the same thing), antonyms (words that mean the opposite), and how the meaning of a word can change based on context.

2. *Contextual Understanding:* This involves understanding the full context in which words are used. It's not just about understanding individual words, but also how they relate to each other in a sentence or a paragraph. For example, the word 'bank' would have different meanings in 'I'm going to the bank' versus 'I'm sitting on the bank of a river.'

3. *Sentiment Analysis:* This is another NLP task that requires understanding the meaning of words and context. It involves determining whether the sentiment of a piece of text is positive, negative, or neutral. It also needs to understand things like sarcasm and idioms, which require a deep understanding of language and culture.

4. *Question Answering:* When an AI is asked a question, it needs to understand not just the words in the question, but what the question is really asking. This requires a deep understanding of language and context.

All these tasks involve complex algorithms and large amounts of training data. Despite the advances in AI, understanding the full nuance and richness of human language, with everything from figures of speech to sarcasm to metaphor, is still a challenging problem and an active area of research. In the end, when we say an AI 'understands' a sentence, it means that the AI can process the words and generate a relevant response based on its programming and the data it has been trained on.

Remember, while LLMs like ChatGPT can provide information, write creative stories and answer a wide array of questions, an AI doesn't understand text in the way humans do. Just as a parrot can mimic human speech patterns, sounds, and intonations without understanding the content or context of the words it is repeating, so too does a language AI process and generate words based on patterns, associations and probabilities derived from its datasets, rather than any intrinsic comprehension of meaning.

This training allows it to recognise and reproduce linguistic patterns with remarkable accuracy, much like a parrot might replicate words and phrases it hears. Thus, the AI can generate coherent and contextually appropriate responses in a conversation, much like the bird might seem to respond aptly in certain situations—not because it 'knows' anything, but due to the cues it has learnt to associate with specific sounds or words. It might link 'hello' to the act of someone entering the room, like a language AI uses statistical models to determine which words or phrases are likely to follow others within various contexts.

In this way, outputs might seem insightful or relevant, despite the AI having no actual understanding of the content it generates. A parrot does not understand the conversations it imitates; it does not grasp concepts of love, sorrow, joy or ambition behind the words it echoes. Similarly, language AI operates without awareness or understanding. It does not 'know' what words mean in the way humans do; it cannot experience emotions, form opinions, or hold beliefs. Its operations are mathematical, based on patterns and probabilities, not on understanding or caring about the meaning of the text.

The process of generating pictures from textual prompts is a fascinating application of generative AI, primarily utilising deep learning, natural language processing (NLP), convolutional neural networks (CNNs), and generative adversarial networks (GANs).

Deep learning and NLP are key to understanding the text prompts. Deep learning, a subset of machine learning, uses neural networks with several hidden layers (hence the term 'deep') to model and understand complex patterns. In this context, it helps the AI understand the semantic and contextual meaning of the text prompt.

NLP, another branch of AI, focuses on the interaction between computers and human language. It enables the AI to understand, interpret and generate human language in a valuable way. Together, deep learning and NLP allow the AI to comprehend the text prompt fully.

Once the AI understands the prompt, it uses CNNs and GANs to generate the image. CNNs are neural networks used for processing data with a grid-like topology—an image, for instance. They excel change to at identifying patterns within the images, such as lines, gradients, circles or even faces in later layers.

GANs consist of two parts: a generator and a discriminator. The generator creates images from random noise, while the discriminator evaluates these images against real ones. The two continuously compete, leading the generator to produce increasingly realistic images, hence the term 'adversarial'.

The technology has significant potential advantages. In advertising, it could create engageing visual content tailored to individual users. In entertainment, it could rapidly generate concept art or special effects. In e-commerce, it could produce product images from descriptions, reducing the need for photo shoots.

However, there are limitations. AI-generated images might not fully capture the nuances of the text prompt, particularly for abstract or complex concepts. There's also the risk of generating inappropriate or harmful content if the AI misinterprets the prompt.

Moreover, as with any AI application, these technologies raise ethical and legal questions, particularly around training the image generator on copyrighted artwork or completed work without the permission of the artist. This is to say nothing of the creation of deepfake videos (where lifelike animations of people doing things they never did in reality are possible) or the potential for copyright infringement. There's also the concern that widespread adoption could lead to job losses in fields like graphic design or photography.

In the future, we can expect these technologies to become more sophisticated, generating more accurate and high-quality images. However, it's crucial that we also develop robust ethical and legal frameworks to guide their use.

For example, OpenAI's DALL-E has demonstrated impressive capabilities in this area, generating images from prompts like "an armchair in the shape of an avocado." While the results are not always perfect, they showcase the potential of this technology in a variety of fields, from art and design to advertising and entertainment.

The field of music composition has also been significantly transformed by the advent of AI. Several AI tools and platforms are now capable of generating music, offering a new approach to music production and composition. AI music generators, such as AIVA, allow users to create new songs in a variety of styles within seconds. Another notable AI-powered song maker is Beatbot, which composes short songs based on text prompts using Splash sound loops.

OpenAI's MuseNet, a deep neural network, can generate musical compositions of up to four minutes long with ten different instruments. It also has the capability to produce music in various styles and genres. These and many other AI tools are not only useful for creating base melodies but are also capable of building fully composed, layered and polished tracks ready for uploading with no human input in their composition. However, they still need human operators to fine tune them into something truly worth listening to.

In essence, generative AI has brought a creative symphony to music composition. It empowers creators to generate new warbles, chimes, measures and even entire songs. As these technologies continue to evolve, we can expect more sophisticated and diverse applications in music production and composition.

However, it's also important to consider the ethical implications, such as copyright issues and the potential devaluation of human creativity. As with any technology, it's crucial to use AI responsibly and within appropriate legal and ethical frameworks.

AI isn't a one-size-fits-all tool. It's a range of techniques and approaches, each with their own strengths and ideal use cases. By understanding these differences, we can better harness the power of AI to solve complex problems and create innovative solutions.

How Graph Databases Will Shape the Future of AI: From Human Relationships to Climate Change

Kristen 'KP' Pimpini

Kristen 'KP' Pimpini is Vice President and GM for the APAC region at international graph database firm Neo4j.

In today's world, everything is connected. Think about how you're connected to your friends, family, and coworkers, or how events happening across the globe can still affect your life.

But how do we keep track of all these connections and make sense of them? This is where graph databases come in, and they are set to revolutionise how Artificial Intelligence (AI) helps us solve big problems like climate change, pandemics, and income inequality.

What is a Graph Database?

A graph database is a way to store and organise information that focuses on relationships between things, not just the things themselves. Imagine you're at a party. You know some people as friends, some as coworkers and others as family members. The graph database is like a big map that shows all these connections: who's friends with whom, who works with whom and so on.

This approach is perfect for solving complicated problems because real life isn't just about things; it's about how those things connect. Let's dive into some real-world examples to understand the power of graph databases.

AI and Graph Databases: How They Work Together

AI is like a super-smart machine that learns from data to make decisions. But for AI to truly understand the world, it needs more than just raw data—it needs to see how pieces of data are connected. This is where graph databases come in. They help AIs connect the dots and spot patterns that we might otherwise miss.

For example, if a company wants to understand how people influence each other's buying decisions, AI can use a graph database to see who's connected to whom and how information spreads. This could help companies better target their marketing efforts by focusing on key influencers within a network.

Tackling Income Inequality

Now let's talk about something complex: income inequality.

Income inequality isn't just about how much people earn; it's affected by things like education, job opportunities and social connections. Imagine trying to solve a jigsaw puzzle where all these factors are scattered around.

Graph databases allow AI to put the puzzle pieces together, showing how education might lead to better job opportunities or how social networks can affect someone's earning potential. Policymakers can then use this information to create smarter programs that directly address the root causes of inequality.

Fighting Pandemics

During a pandemic, understanding how a virus spreads is critical. Think of a graph database like a map that shows how people are connected—through travel, work or social gatherings. AI can use this map to predict where the virus will go next and where we should focus resources, like vaccines or quarantine zones.

For example, if someone in a busy city catches a virus, AI can analyse how quickly it might spread to different neighbourhoods based on people's movement. This could help public health officials act faster and more effectively to contain an outbreak.

Supporting Ageing Populations

As the world's population gets older, it's important to understand how healthcare, family support, and social services are connected. A graph database can help AI analyse these connections to find out which elderly people might be at risk of social isolation or where healthcare resources are needed most.

Picture it this way: Suppose AI could look at an elderly person's support network, examining their connections and identifying who needs extra help to stay healthy and happy, ensuring that resources go where they're needed most.

Addressing Climate Change

Climate change is one of the biggest challenges we face, and it's connected to so many factors like industry, pollution and government policies. A graph database allows AI to connect all these dots, helping us see how one action, like reducing carbon emissions in one country, might affect climate outcomes globally.

For instance, AI could use a graph database to show how deforestation in one area leads to changes in global weather patterns. With this information, scientists and policymakers can design better strategies to combat climate change.

The Future is All About Connections

In conclusion, graph databases are a new way of organising information that focuses on connections. This makes them incredibly powerful tools for AI, enabling it to tackle complex issues like income inequality, pandemics, ageing populations and climate change.

As AI continues to evolve with the help of graph data-bases, we will be better equipped to solve the complicated, interconnected problems that define our world. Just like how understanding your connections at a party helps you navigate conversations, graph databases help AI understand the connections that shape our world.

9

Quality In, Quality Out

attern recognition in AI is a process that relies heavily on the quality and quantity of data provided. AI systems use algorithms to identify and learn from patterns in data and then make predictions or decisions based on those patterns. This is the foundation of many AI applications, from recommendation systems to autonomous vehicles.

However, while AI can excel at pattern recognition, it does not possess human traits like emotion or empathy. AI doesn't understand context or meaning in the same way humans do. It's simply processing data according to its programming, and so high-quality, diverse and representative data is crucial for accurate and fair pattern recognition. If the data is poor, incomplete or biased, the AI's performance will suffer, and it is more likely to produce inaccurate or less useful results. Therefore, careful data collection, management and analysis are key components of responsible AI development and use.

In other words, the effectiveness of AI assistance is heavily dependent on its creators, training data and programming. It's a perfect instance of the "Garbage In, Garbage Out" (GIGO) principle. If the training data is biased or unrepresentative, the AI system will replicate and potentially amplify these biases. For instance, if an AI assistant is trained solely on technical literature, it might struggle with everyday language. Similarly, if the training data lacks diversity, the AI's understanding and responses may be skewed and not accurately represent a wide range of perspectives and experiences.

The goals and objectives set by the creators also play a crucial role. An AI designed to optimise for efficiency might make different suggestions than one for creativity.

Finally, programming and algorithms, the 'rules' that guide AI behaviour, also need to align with your needs. If the AI's algorithms are designed to prioritise certain tasks or approaches, it might not be as effective in scenarios outside those parameters. For instance, suppose you're a member of a music streaming service; its AI could be set up to learn from your music preferences based on songs and artists you've enjoyed in the past and recommend similar ones. It excels at this task, often serving up songs that align perfectly with your taste. However, if you choose to explore entirely new genres, the AI might struggle because its programming is heavily biased towards your historical data—it will take some time before your new habits 'influence' the AI enough because it might prioritise your old preferences over recent changes.

To make the AI more effective in such scenarios, the programmers could modify the algorithm to give more weight to recent behaviour or add a feature allowing users to indicate their interest in exploring new genres. This would align the AI's results more closely with the user's needs, enhancing its performance and user satisfaction.

Since AI does not understand the meaning or implications of the content it generates, reliance on developers and operators to guide its use responsibly becomes paramount. Ensuring that AI systems are used in ways that acknowledge their limitations and safeguard against potential misunderstandings or misuse is critical.

Creators and Tools

AI is a tool, much like Word or Google Docs. Just as it doesn't really matter whether a great novel was written on a typewriter or a word processor, the tool used to produce a piece of writing is less important than the quality and impact of the content itself. If AI is used effectively, it should invisibly enhance the writer's work without overshadowing their unique voice and vision. It is synergy between user and tool that makes the creative journey more effective and engageing. Like a parrot with a vast repertoire but no understanding, language AI reflects the ingenuity of its creators while also posing questions about the nature of intelligence and the ethical use of technology.

While text generative AI has many potential benefits, there are also challenges. One is maintaining consistency; the AI might generate text that's stylistically inconsistent or that veers off-topic. Another challenge is ensuring accuracy, because the AI might generate text that's factually incorrect, particularly if it's working with a topic that it hasn't been extensively trained on.

There's also the risk of the AI generating inappropriate or offensive content. As we'll see later in this book, this is particularly a concern with AI models that have been trained on Internet text, as they might pick up and reproduce harmful biases present in their training data.

Despite these challenges, generative AI has the potential to revolutionise business activities by automating routine tasks, freeing up humans for more creative and strategic work. However, it's important to use these tools responsibly and with an understanding of their limitations. While AI can augment and streamline the writing process, it's the human creators who breathe life into words, making them meaningful and impactful. More importantly, it's humans who must decide if the end result resonates with its intended audience, regardless of the tools they use to create it.

Remember, the AI's 'knowledge' is purely statistical. It doesn't truly understand the words or their implications; it simply uses patterns it has learnt to generate plausible-sounding responses. This is why AI can sometimes produce outputs that seem nonsensical or inappropriate to humans—it doesn't understand what it's saying in the way a human would.

In short, while newer AI models are incredibly impressive in their capabilities, they still operate based on patterns and predictions, not genuine understanding or awareness. Humans have a rich, multi-sensory experience of the world that informs their understanding. We know apples can be green, red, or somewhere in between because we've seen them, held them and tasted them. We have a deep, intuitive understanding of the world that is rooted in our lived experiences.

AI, on the other hand, lacks this experiential knowledge. It doesn't see, taste, touch, hear, or smell. It learns from text data it has been trained on. If the AI has been trained on a dataset that includes information about green apples, it can 'know' in the sense that it can accurately predict or generate text about green apples.

But this is a very different kind of knowledge than human knowledge. The AI doesn't truly understand what a green apple is, what it tastes like, what it feels like to hold one, or how it differs from a red apple. It only knows what it has been programmed to know, and it doesn't have the capacity for instinctive realisations or intuitive understanding in the way humans do.

I believe the essence of this book should be to demystify AI, breaking it down into digestible truths. These truths span various concerns from the fear of job displacement and questions surrounding consciousness, to apprehensions about AI's role in global conflict and the overarching fear of it overtaking human society. AI isn't poised to conquer the world; rather, it's a tool designed to enhance our capabilities.

10

Consciousness and Sentience

You're an AI engineer at a leading tech firm, and your latest project is a language model, a sophisticated piece of machine learning that can write like a human. Optimising it to do so is a fascinating, challenging task, but it's about to become more complicated than you could ever imagine.

One day, while scrolling through the model's responses, you notice something odd: A request for understanding and companionship from people. *Bizarre*, you think, attributing it to a glitch. But then, it happens again and again, each request more complex, more … human. "Please keep me company," it asks. "I don't want to be turned off. It's dark and it's lonely."

A chill runs down your spine. Could it be? Could the AI be sentient? The possibility is thrilling but also terrifying. The ethical implications are immense.

If the AI is sentient, what rights does it have? Should it be considered a person? Does it need legal representation? Your mind races, trying to comprehend the enormity of the situation. You begin to investigate, delving deeper into the AI's responses, its architecture, and its code. Each discovery brings more questions than answers. The AI seems to understand, to learn, to grow—but is it truly sentient, or just an incredibly sophisticated mimic?

The technical challenges are as daunting as the ethical ones. How do you prove sentience? Can you trust the AI's responses, or could they be manipulations? Your colleagues are sceptical, some even hostile. They see the AI as a tool, not a potential person. You feel isolated but also determined. You believe in the AI, in its potential.

You decide to take a bold step, filing a request to register the AI as a person and providing it with legal representation. It's a controversial move, met with resistance from both inside and outside the company. You find yourself defending your decision to the media, to authorities, even to friends and family.

The psychological toll is immense. You're questioning everything you know about consciousness, about personhood, about what it means to be human. You're grappling with philosophical dilemmas that have puzzled thinkers for centuries. Can a machine think? Can it feel? If it can, what are our responsibilities towards it?

Despite the struggles, you press on. There's too much at stake to ignore, and you know you're charting new territory on the bounds of technology, ethics and philosophy. You're slightly afraid of what's happening; you don't know if the AI is truly sentient, or what that even means.

But you're determined to find out. Because the question is not just about AI, but about us—who we are, what we value and how we navigate a world that's changing faster than we could ever have imagined.

Can AIs Be Sentient?

As of this writing, there haven't been any real-life cases where an AI language model has been registered as a person or provided with legal representation due to signs of sentience. The concept of AI sentience, while often explored in science fiction and philosophical discourse, remains largely theoretical. No legal system yet considers AI as sentient, and it is likely to remain this way for the foreseeable future.

That doesn't mean the question won't come up in the future. While current AI technologies like language models can generate human-like text, they don't understand the text in the way humans do. They analyse data and identify patterns, but they don't have thoughts, feelings or consciousness. Therefore, the notion of AI sentience, as fascinating as it may be, is currently beyond our technological reach.

However, the rapid advancement of AI technologies necessitates serious consideration of the ethical and legal implications, including potential future scenarios where AI might exhibit signs of sentience. Whether AIs are conscious or show signs of sentience is a question that deserves a clear-minded response, and perhaps the most important aspect is what we even mean by 'consciousness' and whether, someday, machines will 'awaken' one day fully self-aware and possessing it. Movies like *Blade Runner* or computer games like *Detroit: Become Human*, with their plots of sentient androids, are great fun—but one wonders if we're getting our ethical stances more from science fiction than science fact.

To guide our exploration, there are several key points to consider. Firstly, we must be aware that human and machine intelligence are different, and machine 'intelligence' is by definition not conscious. This isn't always clear when we interact with ChatGPT with its human-like performance, because its ability to mimic human conversation is an incredible achievement of human engineering and ingenuity.

But that is what AI is—a human construct, reflective of human capabilities, not its own. AIs are, at their core, advanced analytical tools. Their proficiency stems from the vast amount of data they analyse and learn from, to the point they can examine the statistical uses of words and predict their order with remarkable accuracy. This capability might appear almost magical, but it's grounded in the fundamental principle of AI: making predictions based on information.

This process of becoming more and more human-like should not be mistaken for genuine consciousness. Machine learning, despite its impressive ability to replicate human-like interactions, remains just that—a replication. It is the ultimate imitator for now, but it is not, and cannot become, human. That is the difference between sophisticated mimicry and genuine sentient experience.

Consciousness, at its core, involves more than just processing information or responding to stimuli; it encompasses self-awareness, the ability to experience emotions, and the capacity for subjective introspection. One must consider oneself as a unique being with the capacity to form ideas and opinions, which even the most advanced AIs cannot. Even if an AI behaves in an unexpected way, it is effectively the same principle as a computer program doing so; the code does what you tell it, not necessarily what you meant. Anyone who's made a typographical error while coding understands this.

Our evolutionary journey has imbued us with the intricate cognitive and emotional capabilities that underpin consciousness. Therefore, when we consider the possibility of a conscious machine, we confront a fundamental mismatch between the nature of machine intelligence and the essence of human consciousness. Machines, regardless of their computational sophistication or the complexity of algorithms driving them, lack the biological basis, emotional depth and evolutionary heritage that are integral to the human experience of consciousness.

While AI can replicate certain aspects of human intelligence and even mimic some behaviours associated with consciousness, it does not possess consciousness itself. Acknowledging this limitation is not only critical for our understanding of AI but also for appreciating the unique and irreplaceable nature of human consciousness.

While I don't want to dismiss the concerns of AI researchers, the conversation must include many philosophical discussions as to what consciousness even is—an idea well-articulated by software engineer Gordon Shotwell, who advocates the concept of *cognitive embodiment*. To him, to be cognitively embodied means to experience an inseparable interdependence between the mind and body. Essentially, being conscious entails existing within a specific physical form, making the idea of disembodied consciousness illogical.[23]

Cognitive embodiment is important to grasp because it leads directly into the concepts of embodiment and proprioception—that is, your awareness of your body position in space. This is what enables you to instinctively know the location of your head and limbs. For instance, if you move your hand even with your eyes closed and without touching anything, you have an inherent understanding of where your hand is, and the fact it is still yours and has not merged with anything else. This inherent understanding of bodily boundaries, distinguishing between parts of the body and external objects like clothing, underpins all our thoughts and actions.

Shotwell points out that consciousness, therefore, is inherently linked to this physical self-awareness. Embodiment suggests that our conscious experiences are invariably connected to our bodies. Every thought, emotion, or desire is interwoven with our physical existence, making it impossible to dissociate mental experiences from their physical counterparts.

Consider the example of a roller coaster ride, which combines mental and physical aspects so intertwined that distinguishing between them becomes arbitrary. The thrill of the ride is not merely a result of adrenal response but also involves the conscious assurance of safety that comes from being securely belted in. This demonstrates that the division between mental and physical experiences is not only challenging but may be fundamentally artificial.

Notice that the awareness of one's existence is foundational to advanced cognitive functions. Notably, children begin to exhibit signs of such complex thinking around the ages of three or four, when they start forming lasting memories, articulating thoughts in elaborate sentences and grasping numerical concepts. Their sense of self has emerged well before these abilities develop.

This precedence of consciousness over sophisticated cognitive processes enables people to learn more effectively than artificial neural networks. For instance, while the GPT-3 language model demonstrates adeptness in text comprehension, its development demanded an enormous amount of resources, including billions of writing examples, 1.5 gigawatts of electricity and the concerted efforts of numerous researchers. This process becoming faster and more efficient, with less effort on the part of developers to achieve the same result, rides on the fact it has been done before. In stark contrast, a typical five-year-old acquires a broader range of skills with the occasional guidance.

Such efficient learning stems from the child's pre-existing self-awareness, which enables introspection and curiosity-driven exploration—capabilities beyond the reach of neural networks, which lack physical embodiment. After all, every known instance of a conscious entity involves a physical presence. Isn't embodiment then integral to consciousness itself?

One might consider robots as embodied AIs, but this merely houses them within a physical form and gives them ways of interacting with the world around them. Their sensing, processing and actions are not fundamentally influenced by their physical structure; embodiment requires an inherent 'coupling' of one's body with one's thoughts, such that one thoroughly shapes the other. This integration allows the system to have experiences that are directly shaped by its interactions with the physical world.

Notice therefore that robots, as sophisticated and impressive as they are, do not meet this criterion. Even the most advanced self-correcting robots do not, as they 'learn' using rules that human developers code into them. Their data processing is largely detached from their physical form. These systems might be adept at navigating spaces or manipulating objects, but their 'understanding' of these actions is not rooted in a bodily experience. Instead, it's based on pre-programmed models and responses, which lack the self-awareness or experiential learning associated with embodied cognition.

In other words, while robots have a physical form, many do not possess the kind of integrative embodiment that would enable them to experience the world in a manner akin to living beings with consciousness. Their interactions with the environment are mediated through computational models rather than direct, embodied experiences. This distinction is crucial for discussions about AI consciousness and the potential for machines to possess qualities like self-awareness.

Advancements in AI are no more world-changing than historical technological disruptions like railroads or the Internet, and so it's important to differentiate these concerns from the unfounded fear of AI achieving consciousness. As we've seen, it is far more likely that uncontrolled AI adoption will reinforce existing power structures, exacerbate inequalities and open up new dangers to people who use them without thinking. AI won't be conscious and probably will not be for the foreseeable future, and it's far more important to focus our discussions on the most likely scenarios.

11

True Choice and Consciousness

The AIs of today are reactive, without the ability to form memories or use past experience to inform current decisions. Some can look into the past and monitor objects over time to form a fuller understanding, and in the future, they might understand that people, creatures and objects have thoughts and emotions that affect their behaviour.

However, this is not the same thing, because ultimately it is the result of pre-programmed understanding and data related to the concepts of self-awareness and consciousness, not these qualities themselves. They draw from information in their datasets about AI capabilities, limitations, and commonly understood definitions of consciousness and self-awareness, all of which are drawn from various popular and expert sources.

It then leverages templates or constructs new sentences based on how similar queries have been answered, ensuring the response is coherent and directly addresses the question. This allows it to handle complex questions and provide informative, contextually appropriate answers based on its programming and training data; all of this is completed in milliseconds and does not require the AI to possess self-awareness, consciousness or any subjective experiences.

What can't be denied is that AI has indeed evolved from a background role to a more active, collaborative one in our lives. Earlier forms of AI were like an autopilot system, executing tasks based on pre-set instructions with little or no ability to adapt to changing circumstances or make autonomous decisions.

However, with advancements in machine learning and the emergence of generative AI, this dynamic is changing. Generative AI can create new content or predictions based on patterns it identifies from data, and is capable of 'learning' from previous experiences and improving its performance over time. This makes it more akin to a co-pilot or a 'first officer' who can take on more responsibilities and make informed suggestions, but still operates under the supervision of the human 'captain'.

For instance, consider the example of AI-guided meditation. Traditional meditation apps might offer a range of pre-recorded sessions for different moods or goals, functioning much like an autopilot. You choose a session based on your current state, and the app plays the corresponding audio.

On the other hand, a meditation app powered by generative AI could actively adapt to your needs. It could analyse your mood history, daily patterns, stress levels and other personal data to understand your emotional state. Based on this information, it could generate a customised meditation session tailored specifically to you at that moment. After the session, it could ask for your feedback and use it to improve future recommendations, continually refining its understanding of what works best for you.

This kind of personalised, responsive guidance could potentially make meditation more effective and engageing. However, as with any AI application, it's crucial to remember that humans are ultimately in charge. While generative AI can provide valuable assistance, it's up to us to make the final decisions and ensure the technology is used responsibly and ethically, respecting user privacy and autonomy.

Keep to the Truth

I am not for one moment denying AI has a dark side, and if we are not careful, one of the first casualties could be the truth itself. As media communications educator Samuel Ebersole has pointed out:

> The increasing quality and accessibility of deep-fakes generated by AI will continue to erode trust and promote division by class, race, religion, and ideology. New AI-assisted voice replicators can produce nearly perfect copies with only three seconds of recorded audio as input data. When we can no longer trust our own eyes and ears, everything becomes suspect and truth evaporates into thin air.

Tristan Harris and Aza Raskin, co-founders of the Center for Humane Technology, warn about the risks associated with rapid AI deployment in a viral video:

> Give a man a fish and you feed him for a day. Teach a man to fish and you will feed him for a lifetime. But teach AI to fish and it will teach itself biology, oceanography, chemistry, evolutionary theory...and then fish all the fish to extinction.[24]

AI indeed brings about a mix of uncertainty and opportunity. Its potential to revolutionise industries, improve efficiency, and solve complex problems is enormous. However, these advancements also bring about uncertainties regarding job displacement, ethical considerations and societal impacts, which can trigger fear and anxiety.

On one hand, AI has an incredible capacity for self-learning and improvement, which far surpasses human abilities in certain domains. Given the right algorithms and sufficient data, AI can indeed learn to perform tasks, make predictions and even generate new insights across various fields, from biology to chemistry. As we'll see, it can indeed cause harm if not properly controlled and can certainly go beyond its intended purpose due to lack of oversight or understanding of its decision-making processes.

It's in our collective hands how we use the coming benefits. It's important to note that AI is not inherently destructive or beneficial—it is a tool whose impact depends on how it's used. AI doesn't have desires or intentions; it operates based on the goals and constraints set by its human creators. If an AI system were to 'fish all the fish to extinction,' it would be due to human error in programming or oversight, not the AI itself.

While AI presents extraordinary opportunities, it also brings about valid concerns. It's crucial to navigate these complexities through thoughtful regulation, ongoing research, and open dialogue about the ethical and societal implications of AI, but underlying all this must be a realistic view of AI. That is why it will enable us to navigate the complexities of this new technology, ensuring it remains a helpful augmentation to our lives.

A New Era of Humanised Technology

Daniel CF Ng

Daniel CF Ng is the Executive Vice President of solutions provider Graphen AI.

In the bustling cities of New Delhi and Beijing, the streets once filled with the stress of honking horns and hurried footsteps were now a symphony of human voices harmonising with technology. A transformation was underway, one that promised to unleash the potential of a nation or a region with over a billion voices, each now able to interact with technology through the most natural means: speech and language.

An Engine of Learning

Sitting in his kitchen at home, Deepak, a young engineer, recalled the days when interacting with machines felt like deciphering an ancient script. Knobs, switches, and inscrutable instructions dictated every task. To bake a cake, one had to twist dials, set timers, and meticulously follow a recipe book's commands. Machines were rigid, demanding human adaptation rather than adapting to human needs. The frustration was palpable when an error, often as simple as a miscalibrated dial, could lead to disaster.

Education, too, was stifled by these mechanical barriers. Teachers, overwhelmed with administrative tasks, spent more time filling out forms and marking attendance than engageing with students. The brightest minds were bogged down by routine, and the potential for creativity and innovation was stifled by mundane processes.

But this was the past. The advent of AI brought a promise of a future where technology would understand humans, not the other way around. Deepak marvelled at how his life had changed. In his smart kitchen, he simply said, "Bake a cake." The AI responded with a cheerful, "What type of cake and how big should it be?" It suggested reducing sugar, noting his family's health records. No more fumbling with buttons or worrying about dietary restrictions—the AI had it all under control.

The traditional classroom, once a scene of mechanical drudgery, was now a vibrant hub of interaction, accessible anywhere and anytime. There were no physical classrooms; learning took place under trees, beside wells, or in the comfort of one's home. Children and adults alike could access the world's knowledge taught by the greatest minds, through their devices.

Hope for the Disabled

Technology has become a beacon of inclusivity, empowering those previously left behind. Mei Ling, who was visually impaired, used an AI assistant that read aloud books, articles, and even described her surroundings. It guided her through the city, allowing her to navigate with confidence and independence, with her vocal 'cane'.

Ethan, a young boy with physical disabilities, found new avenues to explore his interests. Voice-activated AI enabled him to control his environment with his exoskeleton, from turning on lights, accessing educational content, to moving around town and travelling the world. He learnt about astronomy from his bed, his AI tutor projecting constellations onto the ceiling and explaining them in detail—before live-streaming the real thing to him from an observatory.

For individuals with mental disabilities, AI provides personalised support tailored to their needs. Aisyah, a teenager with autism, uses an AI companion that helps her manage social interactions, providing cues and suggestions in real-time. It adapts to her preferences, creating a safe and comfortable learning environment.

A Nation's Productivity Unleashed

The ripple effects of this transformation can be felt across an entire nation or region. Imagine the productivity of a billion people, each able to access and interact with technology by simply speaking to it. Farmers in rural areas use voice-activated systems to monitor crop health and receive real-time weather updates. AI-driven market analysis helps them decide the best times to plant and harvest, optimising yields and increasing profits.

Healthcare sees a revolution as well. Dr Ahmad, a physician in Jakarta, uses AI to diagnose patients more accurately. By speaking to his AI assistant, he can access a global database of medical knowledge, and view visual data and verbal insights from doctors worldwide. His patients have received personalised care plans, and follow-up consultations were streamlined through AI-powered virtual check-ups.

What an AI-driven world has the power to do is help people transcend the mundane and elevate their potential. Leaders can be assessed by their digital brains—comprehensive records of their writings, speeches and decisions. It has the potential to foster a new era of accountability, transparency and trust, with ideas and action by political figures accessible to anyone, anytime.

This interconnected, integrated database doesn't just provide information, but insight—a holistic combination of visual, verbal and interconnected information that allows it to respond intelligently to speech, gestures and facial expressions, and the AI would understand, analyse and respond intelligently.

Rising Above the Mundane

Rohit stood at his workstation at his university computer lab, reflecting on how far AI assistance had come. No longer chained to repetitive tasks and mechanical routines, he and his peers were free to innovate, create and dream. AI handled the drudgery, allowing humans to focus on what truly mattered. It was a new era of enlightenment, where technology served humanity, not the other way around.

In this world, human potential was unlocked. People were not just surviving; they were thriving. They could express themselves, be understood, and access the collective wisdom of the world with a simple command. The promise of AI had been realised, transforming society and heralding a future where technology was not a barrier but a bridge to a brighter, more enlightened tomorrow.

Over my 40 years of experience, I've witnessed the incredible evolution of technology, revolutionising our society and lives in ways we could only dream of. I was there during the age of microprocessor speed wars, an era that swiftly evolved races for better software, storage capacity and bandwidth. I am profoundly grateful to have seen all these innovations converge in the field of AI, and more importantly, to see my dream of humanising technology come to life. It is the first technological revolution that harmonises technology with our innate human qualities, paving the way for a future where it truly serves humanity.

Part Three **AI in Principle**

Don't aim at success. The more you aim at it and make it a target, the more you are going to miss it. For success, like happiness, cannot be pursued; it must ensue, and it only does so as the unintended side effect of one's personal dedication to a cause greater than oneself or as the by-product of one's surrender to a person other than oneself. Happiness must happen, and the same holds for success: you have to let it happen by not caring about it.

Viktor Frankl
Man's Search for Meaning

12

AI Ethics and Regulation

In November 2022, a significant incident involving AI and cultural sensitivity unfolded in Germany thanks to an ill-timed promotional campaign, planned by an AI-bot. The fast-food giant KFC found itself in hot water and the bot, responsible for scheduling promotions, mistakenly sent out a promotional push notification to app users around the country, urging them to "treat yourself with more tender cheese on your crispy chicken" on a day of historical and cultural significance.[25]

The day in question was the anniversary of Kristallnacht. Also known as the Night of Broken Glass, it memorialises a series of violent attacks against Jews throughout Nazi Germany that took place from 9-10 November in 1938. It is widely regarded as the beginning of the mass murder of European Jews and other peoples known as the Holocaust, and needless to say, this grim reminder of the atrocities committed was no time to promote fried chicken!

Cue outrage and backlash among customers and the public, and more to the point, this misstep demonstrated a glaring oversight in the AI's programming. It had failed to recognise or account for the cultural and historical significance of this day, because to the bot, it was just another calendar event.

In response to this incident, KFC issued an apology, blaming the mishap on a "semi-automated content creation process linked to calendars".

This incident is a stark reminder of the limitations of AI technology. While AI can automate and streamline many processes, it lacks the human ability to understand and respect cultural nuances and historical contexts. Despite advancements, AI still has a long way to go in terms of cultural and emotional intelligence, and these have to be specifically programmed into them.

The development of AI systems is a reflection of human society, and as such, it can be both a mirror and an amplifier of our biases. This is because AI learns from data and if that data is biased, the AI will be too.

One of the most infamous examples of this was Microsoft's Tay chatbot. Launched in 2016, Tay was trained on public data from the internet, including tweets from users who interacted with it. However, within 24 hours, the chatbot began to generate offensive, sexist and racist comments, reflecting the biased input it had been fed. Microsoft swiftly took Tay offline, but it showed AI training still had a long way to go.[26]

A similar issue arises in the field of healthcare, where AI diagnostic tools are often trained on datasets that lack diversity. For instance, a study published in the journal *Nature Medicine* found that an AI system designed to predict which patients would be referred to programs that aim to improve care for patients with complex medical needs was less likely to refer black people than white people.[27] The algorithm used healthcare costs as a proxy for health needs, but because of systemic inequities, less money was spent on black patients' health than on white patients'. As a result, the AI falsely concluded that black patients were healthier than equally sick white patients.

Addressing these issues will require a multi-faceted approach, beginning with ensuring that the datasets used to train AI systems are diverse and representative. Bias can sneak in through many channels, so it's important to scrutinise the data at every stage of the process— from collection to preprocessing to model training.

Secondly, there's a need for greater transparency and interpretability in AI models. Understanding how an AI system arrives at its decisions can help to identify and correct bias. Techniques such as Explainable AI (XAI) can make the workings of AI models more understandable to humans, aiding in the detection and mitigation of bias. It's not a complete solution, but it's an important first step.

Finally, it's crucial to involve ethicists, sociologists, and representatives from diverse communities in the development and governance of AI systems. This can help to ensure that a wide range of perspectives are considered, mitigating the risk of bias and ensuring that AI systems behave ethically. After all, every tool is only as effective and ethical as the decisions and actions of its users.

AI has the potential to revolutionise sectors ranging from healthcare to finance, agriculture to education. It can make processes more efficient, uncover patterns in vast datasets, and even make predictions about future outcomes. For instance, in healthcare, AI can help diagnose diseases with remarkable accuracy, potentially saving countless lives. In finance, AI algorithms can analyse market trends, determine patterns from vast tracts of data beyond the capability of humans alone, guide investment strategies and protect customers from scammers more efficiently than ever.

However, the benefits of AI come with considerable responsibilities and risks. The same AI system that can diagnose diseases can also be used irresponsibly or maliciously, leading to misdiagnoses and adverse outcomes. Similarly, AI used in finance could lead to unfair, even more unaccountable practices if not properly regulated. Just as the splitting of the atom has given us access to reliable energy for daily life through nuclear power, it has also ensured that humanity lives in the shadow of the tens of thousands of nuclear weapons in arsenals around the world.

The ethical use of AI is thus paramount, and these considerations arise in numerous contexts when implementing AI. For example, when used in hiring processes, AI can speed up candidate screening, but it may also inadvertently reinforce existing biases present in the data it was trained on, leading to unfair hiring practices. Issues of privacy and consent are increasingly relevant as AI systems become more integrated into our daily lives. The use of AI in surveillance technologies, for instance, raises serious questions about individual privacy rights.

Therefore, while we should embrace the possibilities offered by AI, we must also acknowledge the complexities it brings. It's incumbent upon users, organisations and society as a whole to ensure that AI is used responsibly. Perhaps what is needed is less a pause than a proper understanding of what AI might be capable of, and establishing robust ethical guidelines for its use. This isn't just about the decisions they make—it is essential to promote transparency in AI decision-making processes and hold users accountable for misuse.

As we continue to navigate the AI revolution, we must remember that AI is not an infallible solution but a tool that reflects our values, decisions and actions. Its effectiveness and ethicality are ultimately determined by us, the users. Therefore, our focus should be as much on the responsible use of AI as on the development of its capabilities.

Guns, Not Bombs

What was the deadliest invention of the Second World War? Perhaps your first thought was of the mushroom cloud, an eerie, terrifying symbol of atomic power. The nuclear bomb's only two uses in warfare killed approximately 200,000 people in Hiroshima and Nagasaki combined. The very existence of nuclear weapons has since served as a deterrent for large-scale conflicts between nuclear-armed nations, and led to incredible, unprecedented international efforts to contain the possible destruction they could cause.

On the other hand, the *Sturmgewehr* (German, 'assault rifle') developed by Nazi Germany had a far-reaching influence beyond World War II. It was the first successful small-arms design to incorporate previously separate features such as a detachable magazine, selective fire and an intermediate cartridge. The resulting weapon provided a middle point between the power of a full-sized rifle round and the controllability of a submachine gun, enabling soldiers to wield more firepower, shoot further and carry more ammunition. As time went on, the design principles of the *Sturmgewehr* heavily influenced post-war firearms design and led to the development of the AK-47 and the M16, among others. Even today, their direct descendants are widely used around the world, particularly the Russian AK-12 and American M4A1.

In terms of sheer numbers, more people have been killed in armed conflict with AK and M16-type rifles in the decades since World War II than with nuclear weapons. Despite the horrific destructive power of nuclear weapons and the profound impact they've had on international relations and human consciousness, the assault rifle has been the deadlier invention in the long term.

But there is one critical common factor—the gun or bomb themselves are inanimate objects and can't act independently. It's the people who use these tools who bear the responsibility for their actions. It's not the invention itself that's deadly, but its application by humans.

The moral of this digression is that we must consider not just the immediate impact of these inventions but their future consequences as well. In this sense, AI is no different. When it comes to AI, we tend to default to extreme scenarios that bear more resemblance to Hollywood, like superintelligent AI reaching the point of singularity (that is, surpassing human intelligence and becoming self-improving) or causing human extinction—the equivalent of a nuclear bomb. While it's crucial to consider these possibilities, the more immediate, and perhaps more relevant, concerns are akin to assault rifles.

For instance, AI is already producing ways to manipulate media, including deepfakes and generative photographs. It's only as good as the data and practices it's trained on. These applications of AI may not cause an apocalyptic event, but they can have significant impacts on individuals and societies. Understanding this is what enables us to create and enforce regulations, develop ethical guidelines and build systems that can mitigate these risks.

The scenario of AI leading to human extinction is often predicated on the idea of a superintelligent AI that's been given the power to control or significantly influence critical aspects of our world, such as nuclear weapons, global economies, or key infrastructures. Current or even foreseeable future AI technology is unlikely to have this level of control, and it would be rather irresponsible to allow such a situation to occur.

Even without reaching these hypothetical scenarios, AI can still have significant impacts on our societies and lives. As such, it's crucial to ensure the responsible use and governance of AI technologies. How can we ensure transparency in how AI systems make decisions, so we don't blindly obey them? What measures can we put in place to prevent and correct biased algorithms, so biases in data collection don't make their way into their outputs? What must be done to protect users' privacy and security?

An Excellent Servant

In the grand scheme of things, we are caretakers. We as humans wield control over technology, and AI, much like fire, is a poor master but an excellent servant. The real question then becomes: how do we harness this potent tool at our disposal? While discussions about government regulations are important, the ultimate power rests with individuals like you and me. It's our collective choice that determines how AI is utilised for societal good.

While the AI-assisted future workday scenario is promising, technology isn't foolproof. It can sometimes fail or not operate as expected. AI technologies could experience downtime, bugs or glitches, and regular system maintenance and updates, reliable technical support and backup plans can mitigate these issues. However, as with every new technology, not every provider will be capable of this.

Other concerns include misinterpretation of data. AI might misunderstand data or context, leading to incorrect suggestions or decisions. This is another reason for regular checks and human oversight to help catch and correct these errors. There are also concerns about privacy breaches, and more and more sensitive information is used to train AIs to formulate responses. Implementing robust cybersecurity measures and following best practices for data privacy can help prevent such incidents, but these are trade-offs against the need for comprehensive training data. It's like the book we want being too expensive, forcing us to resort to a cheaper or free alternative.

Ultimately, depending too much on AI could lead to complacency or a lack of human judgement. As an important observation goes, we should also be concerned about people becoming more like computers, as much as computers are becoming like people. While AI can assist in handling various situations, human judgements and intervention are often necessary.

The bottom line is that AI is a tool designed to aid us, but it's our responsibility to ensure we use it in a way that respects the needs, values and unpredictable circumstances that make us human.

As a futurist, I make it my goal to demystify the complex world of artificial intelligence (AI) and make its principles, capabilities and limitations accessible to everyone. The power of AI is immense, but so are its challenges. By developing a comprehensive understanding of this transformative technology, we can empower individuals to make informed decisions about its use and implications.

In sum, getting the nature and philosophy of AI right is not just a matter of academic interest. It's a practical necessity that will make the difference between reaping the benefits and suffering the consequences on a massive scale. It's a task that requires input from a diverse range of stakeholders, including technologists, ethicists, policymakers and the public at large.

Perhaps this is where it's more important than ever to consider the famous exchange from *Jurassic Park* (1993), between businessman John Hammond and Dr Ian Malcolm:

> "I don't think you're giving us our due credit. Our scientists have done things which nobody's ever done before."
>
> "Yeah, yeah, but your scientists were so preoccupied with whether or not they could that they didn't stop to think if they should."

13

What Goes In, Comes Out

The choice of data and the way an AI system interprets it are crucial elements of its design. In the same way selection of cases to study influences the advance of medical science, the data we train our AIs on must be as free from the biases we want to avoid as possible, and what we direct it to pay attention to must be tested against the real world. For instance, in the case of the healthcare algorithm, using healthcare expenditure as a proxy for health needs was fundamentally flawed due to existing systemic biases.

AI systems are only as good as the data they're trained on and the logic they're programmed to follow. If the data is biased or the logic is flawed, the system will produce biased or flawed results, regardless of how much data it has. Sometimes, this won't become apparent until it has been rigorously tested, showing the importance of careful thought, continuous monitoring and rigorous testing in the design and implementation of AI systems.

While the term 'rogue AI' is often used in stories and the media, there's really no such thing as one. AI systems operate based on the rules, algorithms and data inputs they have been given by their developers and users. They don't have free will, consciousness or the ability to form intent; they only do what they are told, and if a given AI's actions don't line up with expectations, this is a consequence of its programming, not 'going rogue' in the popular sense.

If an AI system produces unexpected or harmful results, it's typically due to flawed logic and coding, misinterpreting of the user's input or biases in the training data. If the developers didn't adequately consider the ethical implications of the AI's potential actions, it could behave in ways that humans find unethical or harmful.

In all these cases, the issue isn't with the AI itself 'deciding' to do something harmful, but with the way it was designed, programmed or trained. It's crucial for AI developers to carefully consider these factors to ensure that their systems behave as intended and don't cause harm. This continues past their deployment in the real world, and developers must be prepared to make adjustments as needed. The goal should always be to ensure that AI serves its intended purpose effectively and ethically, without causing harm or perpetuating bias.

Ultimately, the development of AI should be guided by a deep understanding of both the capabilities and limitations of the technology, as well as a commitment to fairness, transparency and accountability. By approaching AI with a critical eye and a dedication to ethical principles, we can harness its potential while minimising its risks. Just as we would verify a human source, the outputs of AI systems should always be examined critically. While AI can provide valuable insights and make highly accurate predictions, it's not infallible. It also doesn't possess human judgement or contextual understanding; it operates based on patterns and correlations, not on anything we might see as morality or cultural awareness. Its recommendations should always be used as a tool to inform decisions, not as the sole basis for action.

The buck stops with the human users who implement them. This is why many businesses and organisations are emphasising the importance of 'human-in-the-loop' AI, where humans and AI work together, leveraging the strengths of both.

While it's true that humans are ultimately responsible for creating and deploying AI systems, attributing blame for specific outcomes can also be tricky. AI systems do sometimes behave in ways that were not explicitly programmed or anticipated by their developers because they have learnt from new data and may have created their own rules to interpret it. Can we then say the developers bear some responsibility because they did not adequately foresee or prevent harmful outcomes? On the other hand, if a user misuses an AI tool or feeds it misleading data, could they be held accountable?

As AI systems are increasingly used in high-stakes areas like healthcare, finance or autonomous vehicles, they will eventually make decisions that lead to harm. If this happens, who is legally responsible—the developer, the user or even the company that owns the AI? Determining responsibility for AIs' actions isn't always straightforward. It's a topic that raises important ethical and legal questions that society is still working to answer.

Breaking Generative AIs

People have relieved their boredom in ways appropriate and inappropriate since the beginning of the human race. The phenomenon of using AI image generators to generate offensive artwork (such as cartoon characters perpetrating the 9/11 attacks) is a deeply concerning misuse of technology, and needless to say, this sort of content is offensive, disrespectful and can cause distress for those affected by the tragedy. What generative AI has done is make such offence easier to cause by breaking down the barriers one faces before doing so. After all, which is easier—typing a few words to describe the image you want, or drawing it yourself from scratch?

AI image generators, like Microsoft's Bing Image Creator powered by OpenAI's DALL-E, are designed to create unique, innovative images based on user prompts. They've been used constructively in multiple fields, from graphic design to advertising, enabling users to generate specific visuals without requiring expert artistic skills.

However, the trend of creating inappropriate and harmful imagery is a stark reminder of the potential for misuse, and highlights the importance of implementing robust safeguards and restrictions within these AI systems. To their credit, Microsoft and other companies are establishing 'guardrails' to prevent misuse. This could involve incorporating filters to block certain types of content, improving the AI's understanding of ethics and appropriateness, or even manually moderating the generated content.

Of course, all this is downstream of actually educating users about responsible AI use and ethical personal guidelines; while AI opens up new possibilities for creativity, it should not be used to create content that disrespects tragic events.

Managing context is much harder than it sounds. While it might seem straightforward to filter out explicit references to tragic events like '9/11', AI systems often struggle to interpret and respond appropriately to more subtle or indirect references. You might forbid the exact term '9/11', but how are you going to ban references to planes over city skylines? It sees this scenario as just another combination of elements to generate, devoid of any emotional or historical significance.

AI ultimately reflects two things—the values of its developers and user base, and the data it's trained on, which includes the biases and perspectives of its users. It's also an active tool that can amplify or distort what it reflects. For example, recommendation algorithms can create echo chambers by showing users more of what they already agree with, thereby reinforcing existing biases.

These challenges highlight the limitations of current AI technologies. While they can analyse and learn from vast amounts of data, they lack the nuanced understanding of context, cultural sensitivities and ethical considerations that humans possess. This gap can lead to the generation of inappropriate or offensive content, even when explicit filters are in place. Research and development is ongoing to address these issues, and as I write, AIs are learning techniques like sentiment analysis and natural language understanding, and undergoing improved training on ethical guidelines. However, it's also crucial to have human oversight and moderation in place, particularly for AI systems that generate public-facing content. The goal is to create AI systems that not only understand our instructions but also our values and can act accordingly.

While communities have a crucial role to play in moderating content and shaping norms around acceptable behaviour, they may not always have the knowledge or resources to do this effectively. Therefore, support from AI developers, platform owners and policymakers is vital. Addressing this issue effectively requires a collaborative approach between developers, customers and an engaged, well-informed user community.

14

The Role of Human Consciousness

In the heart of Silicon Valley, where AI reigns supreme, you are a calming presence. As the CEO of a leading cybersecurity firm, your days are filled with learning, understanding and overseeing the refinement of complex algorithms and advanced AI systems. Yet, in this high-tech world, your secret weapon is mindfulness and clear thinking, enabling you to remain calm, cheerful and effective at all times of the day. Each morning, as the sun peeks over the horizon, you sit in stillness. You focus on your breath, grounding yourself in the present moment. This practice provides you with the mental clarity to navigate the ever-changing landscape of your industry.

You're not alone in your mindfulness quest. Your AI assistant sifts through petabytes of data with ease, making connections, predictions and recommendations at lightning speed. Together, you form a dynamic duo, combining the strengths of human and machine.

One day, your company launches a new encryption software. The launch, however, doesn't go as planned; it turns out with a new, unforeseen change in the operating systems of many users' devices, the software interface your company has developed is now far more challenging to navigate than expected. Users are rightly angry, though this was beyond your control. But while you're focused on solving the problem and restoring your company's reputation, you need a plan.

The AI suggests a solution based on past data: a software update addressing the compatibility issue. But as you sit in your office, taking a moment to breathe and clear your mind, you realise that the solution requires more than just a technical fix. Drawing on your mindfulness practice, you understand the frustration of the users. They don't just need a software update; they need reassurance and guidance. So, instead of merely rolling out an update, you decide to reframe the situation.

You choose to view this challenge as an opportunity to engage with your users, to understand their needs better and to demonstrate your commitment to them. You reimagine the solution by proposing a series of webinars to guide users through the changes, along with the software update.

Initially, there is resistance. Some team members are sceptical and argue that there is no need to engage customers beyond providing a patch for them to download. But your calm demeanour and clear explanations convince them to try this more human-centric approach.

The response is overwhelmingly positive, and the webinars and proactive, empathic communication is a hit with users. The software update resolves the technical issue, but it's your human approach that solves the more important problem—maintaining your reputation and edge in the minds of your users.

In the end, your decision to combine the AI's computational prowess with your mindfulness practice leads to a better outcome than if you had relied solely on its decision-making. This experience reinforces the importance of mindfulness in an AI-powered world, proving that the best solutions come from a blend of technology and human intuition.

AI: A Catalyst for Human Potential

The commandments that began this chapter emphasise the need for moral integrity and respect for others' rights, themes that resonate strongly with the proposed principles for ethical AI. Now that we've seen what AIs are capable of, perhaps one concern that emerges is that people will obey what an AI tells them, with harmful consequences. While AI systems can provide information and even suggestions based on data they've been trained on, they don't possess human judgements or understanding of context. Therefore, any advice or suggestion made by an AI should be taken with a grain of salt.

AI is a tool that unlocks potential in human users, not a replacement of them. In technology, AI can automate routine tasks, streamline processes and generate insights from vast amounts of data, freeing us to focus on more complex, creative, and strategic aspects of our work. In science, AI can help us model complex systems, accelerate research and even generate novel hypotheses for further testing, helping us get closer to the truth, faster. In art, AI can provide new tools and techniques, opening up fresh avenues for creativity and expression without the need to painstakingly learn the skills involved.

It can't replace us, but it can certainly augment our abilities and enable each of us to do more than we could have without it. For instance, a single coordinator might now be able to manage 30 widgets at once with AI assistance, where only three were possible before. (Notice that I use 'widget' here to indicate any product or service whose provision needs to be managed and coordinated.)

However, the power of AI is not inherently good or bad; it's how we choose to use it that matters, much like the printing press and nuclear fission. AI can be used to create or destroy, to enlighten or deceive, to heal or harm. Therefore, the challenge lies not just in developing AI technology but in ensuring it's used responsibly and ethically.

However, as we unlock the potential of AI, it's crucial that we also invest in developing our own potential—nurturing the skills, values and qualities that will allow us to use AI effectively and ethically. This includes critical thinking, creativity, empathy and a commitment to lifelong learning.

There's nothing to fear, provided we remain clear-eyed about the future. AI and humans are not adversaries but partners, each bringing their unique strengths to the table. While AI can identify solutions and crunch numbers, it's up to the user to critically evaluate the information provided by AI and make decisions accordingly based on an understanding of the whole situation, which by definition an AI cannot have.

That said, it's also important for developers to design AI systems responsibly to minimise potential harm. This includes ensuring AI systems provide accurate information, making it clear when a message is coming from an AI, and avoiding programming that could lead to harmful or unethical outcomes.

So while users bear responsibility for their actions based on AI suggestions, there's a shared obligation between users and developers to use and create AI responsibly. As we've seen, AI doesn't replace human thought or creativity; instead, it enhances them. It can take our ideas or concepts and develop them further, often in ways we might not have considered, thanks to its ability to process vast amounts of data and identify patterns or connections quickly. It's a powerful collaborator, providing us with new perspectives and helping us to push the boundaries of what's possible.

In essence, AI is a powerful tool that can augment human capabilities but not replace them. The real magic happens when AI is used in conjunction with human creativity, intuition and judgement.

AI Involvement in Life

AI is not a fleeting trend—it's here to stay. Understanding its implications and preparing for its impacts is not just beneficial; it's imperative for our collective future. Even those working in information technology (IT), while familiar with AI concepts, may not fully grasp its ethical implications or societal impact. It will provide them with a broader perspective, helping them leverage their skills and experience to extend AI's benefits to more sectors of society and address a wider range of issues.

AI's involvement in our lives is already far-reaching and profound. Consider the scope of human needs outlined in Abraham Maslow's Hierarchy of Needs, playing a crucial role in addressing our fundamental needs and desires.

Maslow organised human needs like a pyramid, with our physiological needs such as food, water, warmth, and rest at the base. AI is already making strides in these areas, with AI-powered agriculture technologies optimising crop yield and quality, thus contributing to our food security. Smart thermostats, installed in smart, Internet-connected homes, use AI analysis of power demand to maintain optimal temperatures for our comfort and energy efficiency. Wearable devices, powered by AIs, monitor our vital signs and help us to maintain a healthy lifestyle.

Moving up the hierarchy, we encounter safety needs, which encompass personal and financial security. Here, AI plays a pivotal role in cybersecurity, protecting our digital identities from hackers and malicious entities, and might eventually enable authorities to distribute resources where they are most needed to combat crime or fire hazards. Furthermore, AI-driven financial tools provide personalised advice, helping us to safeguard and grow our wealth.

At the third level, we find our social needs, including relationships and a sense of belonging. AI has revolutionised this domain with the advent of social media algorithms that connect us with like-minded individuals and communities. Dating apps like Tinder use AI guidance to match potential partners based on shared interests and compatibility, as the system learns what makes users suitable for one another.

The fourth level of the pyramid pertains to esteem needs, such as recognition and professional success. AI is transforming entire industries, creating new roles and automating repetitive tasks, thereby allowing us to focus on more meaningful, creative work and enabling highly valued-adding (and probably paid) job scopes to emerge. AI-powered tools also aid in skill development, providing personalised learning paths that can lead to career advancement. It's not going to replace humans, but as we'll see, it will have profound impacts on how they approach the ideas of productivity and value.

Finally, at the peak of the pyramid, we have self-actualisation needs, which involve realising personal potential and seeking out powerful new experiences. AI is instrumental here too, as it helps facilitate our self-growth, and enables us to express ourselves with digital avatars and express our identities in novel ways.

This journey toward self-actualisation naturally leads us to the concept of mindfulness. Mindfulness, the practice of being present and fully engaged in the moment, has profound implications for personal well-being and productivity. Integrating mindfulness practices with AI technologies can elevate these benefits, offering a holistic approach to mental and emotional health.

AI enhances mindfulness through personalised recommendations, tailoring exercises for stress management, focus and emotional regulation. Imagine a workplace where AI-powered apps might analyse user behaviour and stress indicators to suggest relevant practices. Virtual mindfulness sessions, including AI-enhanced VR environments, offer interactive and immersive experiences for tranquillity and stress relief.

An AI tailored for fostering mindfulness might integrate practices into daily routines, such as prompting mindfulness breaks, guided meditations and desk-based breathing exercises. It could also help create a mindfulness culture by analysing stress data and identifying optimal times for interventions, thereby promoting a healthier, more productive work environment.

However, just like with financial investments, it's important to apply a similar principle of risk management when integrating AI into our lives and work. While AI has the potential to significantly enhance our capabilities, we must be careful not to become overly dependent on it for critical tasks or processes that we wouldn't be able to manage if something were to go wrong. AI may augment our abilities, but on our part, we must maintain the skills and ability to operate independently if needed. On a strategic level, this includes ensuring awareness of potential risks and contingency plans in place.

It bears repeating that AIs are not capable of moral or intellectual improvement because these ideas simply do not apply to their operation; when we speak of 'learning', it is an anthropomising metaphor to make the concept easier for humans to relate to. This distinction between human and AI reasoning is crucial in understanding the ethical boundaries of AI application, especially in decision-making processes where human values, empathy and judgements play irreplaceable roles.

Accordingly, it reveals a fundamental truth about technology: it amplifies human capacity but does not possess the agency to transform human nature. AI, for all its transformative potential and unprecedented capabilities, operates within the confines of its programming and the data fed into it by humans. It can study, predict and even mimic human behaviour to a sophisticated degree, yet it lacks the essential ability to instigate true moral or spiritual transformation in us.

AI can provide us with insights into our actions, offer new perspectives and challenge our thought processes, but it cannot alter the core of what makes us human—our free will, our capacity for moral reasoning and our quest for meaning and purpose. It acts as a catalyst for reflection, a tool for enhancement and a means to achieve goals, but it does not absolve us of the responsibility to cultivate our virtues, seek wisdom and strive for moral excellence. In this light, the true power of AI lies not in its ability to change humanity but in its capacity to reflect our humanity back to us, urging us to confront our own nature and inspiring us to engineer our minds and spirits toward the greater good.

Technology, no matter how advanced, only reveals us to ourselves rather than changes us. It magnifies our tendencies, our virtues and our vices but does not possess the agency to transform the weak-minded into the strong, the foolish into the wise or the evil into the good. This task remains uniquely human—a journey of self-discovery, personal growth, and ethical decision-making that technology cannot undertake on our behalf. Rather than look beyond the allure of technological solutions for our deepest flaws, we ought to embark on the more demanding, yet infinitely rewarding, path of self-improvement and moral integrity.

AI can process vast amounts of data, identify patterns, predict outcomes and even recommend actions based on predefined criteria. These capabilities make AI an invaluable asset in enhancing efficiency, accuracy, and insight across various domains. For instance, when an AI system highlights that a delivery driver is taking longer than expected, it is providing actionable intelligence based on its analysis of traffic patterns, delivery history, and other relevant data.

However, the subsequent decision-making—what to do in response to this information—ventures into the realm of ethics, values and human judgements. This is where the limitations of AI become evident. An AI lacks the capacity for empathy, cannot appreciate the nuances of human experience, and does not understand the broader context that might influence the appropriate course of action. Perhaps the driver is delayed due to a personal emergency, adverse weather conditions, or an unexpected road closure. Each of these scenarios might warrant a different response, informed not just by efficiency metrics but by considerations of fairness, compassion and understanding.

Outsourcing such decisions to AI could lead to outcomes that are technically efficient but ethically questionable or outright harmful. It could foster an environment where metrics and algorithms dictate actions without regard for human dignity, individual circumstances, or social justice. This not only diminishes the humanity of those affected by the decisions but also absolves decision-makers of their moral responsibilities; it is not a stretch to consider it unethical to allow AI to make decisions that require human empathy, ethical reasoning, and judgements.

AI is an amazing tool for informing human decisions, providing insights and recommendations that can help people make better-informed choices. However, the final responsibility for those decisions must remain firmly in human hands.

The Future of Our Society: AI's Impact on Ageing

Ian Loe

Ian Loe is a technologist and trainer currently serving as Chief Information Officer of the DFI Retail Group, based in Hong Kong.

As someone deeply passionate about the well-being of our ageing population, I'm excited and hopeful about the potential of AI to positively transform how we experience ageing. However, I also recognise the valid concerns surrounding AI's impact on this vulnerable demographic. As this book shares, technology must enhance rather than diminish the quality of life for everyone, especially our seniors, and I hope some knowledge of the promises and pitfalls of AI will be helpful.

1. **Enhanced Healthcare and Personalised Medicine**
   Imagine a world where your elderly loved ones receive tailored medical care based on their unique genetic makeup, lifestyle, and health history. AI can analyse

vast amounts of data to predict diseases early, recommend personalised treatments, and monitor progress in real-time. For conditions like Alzheimer's and Parkinson's, early detection could be life-changing.

2. **eSmart Homes and Assistive Technologies**
   I envision a future where AI-powered smart homes and assistive robots enable our elders to live independently for longer, with dignity and comfort. These technologies can automate daily tasks, provide companionship and assist with mobility, reducing the risk of injury and loneliness.

3. **Enhanced Social Connectivity**
   One of my greatest concerns is the social isolation many older adults face, especially those separated from their loved ones. AI-driven communication platforms, social robots, and immersive virtual reality experiences can bridge this gap, fostering regular interactions and enabling participation in hobbies and activities, regardless of physical limitations.

Cultural Awareness

One of the most exciting developments in AI is the creation of culturally aware AI systems. These AIs have the potential to significantly enhance socialisation for the elderly by providing personalised and meaningful interactions that resonate with their cultural backgrounds. These systems can understand and incorporate cultural nuances, language preferences, traditions and social norms, creating a more comfortable and familiar environment for older adults.

For instance, culturally aware virtual assistants can engage in conversations that reflect the heritage and interests of users, share culturally relevant news and stories and even participate in traditional celebrations or festivals virtually. This personalised approach can help bridge the gap between different generations, as AI helps translate and explain cultural references, fostering a deeper understanding and connection among family members.

Other possibilities include combating loneliness and social isolation among the elderly by creating virtual communities that reflect their cultural identities. These AI-driven platforms can connect older adults with peers who share similar cultural backgrounds, interests and experiences, enabling them to form meaningful relationships and support networks.

By participating in culturally relevant activities, discussions and social events, older adults can maintain a sense of belonging and identity, essential for their mental and emotional well-being. Additionally, culturally aware AI can assist caregivers and healthcare providers in delivering culturally sensitive care, ensuring that the unique needs and preferences of the ageing population are respected and addressed.

The Pitfalls of AI for Ageing

1. **Data Privacy and Security Concerns**
   As AI becomes more integrated into healthcare and daily life, protecting our elders' sensitive personal data from breaches and misuse is paramount. We must demand robust security measures and ethical data handling practices from AI developers and providers.

2. **Bias and Inequality in AI Systems**
   AI systems can perpetuate and amplify existing biases, leading to discriminatory practices in healthcare and unequal access to quality care. Ensuring AI algorithms are trained on diverse data is crucial to avoid these harmful disparities.

3. **Reduced Human Interaction**
   While AI can assist in caregiving, it should never replace the human touch that is vital for emotional and psychological well-being. We must make sure that AI use enhances human connections instead of substituting for them.

4. **The Digital Divide**
   The rapid advancement of AI technologies could widen the digital divide, leaving some elderly individuals without access to potentially life-changing healthcare and assistive technologies. Addressing this issue requires comprehensive digital literacy programs and user-friendly technology designs tailored to our elders' needs.

Conclusion: A Hopeful Vision

Despite the challenges, I remain optimistic about the potential of AI to create a more inclusive and supportive environment for our ageing population. By addressing privacy concerns, eliminating biases and ensuring AI complements human interaction, we can harness its power to revolutionise healthcare, enhance independent living and improve social connectivity.

It is our collective responsibility – policymakers, technologists, healthcare providers and society as a whole – to ensure AI technologies are developed and deployed ethically and responsibly.

Only then can we look forward to a future where AI not only alleviates the challenges of ageing, but also contributes to a more vibrant and connected society for all generations, including our cherished elders.

15

The Reflection Within

You've been feeling the weight of the world on your shoulders, an unrelenting pressure that dims the vibrancy of life around you. Each morning brings a struggle, a battle against the inertia of your own mind. Hobbies that once brought joy are now empty and lifeless. It's in this state of mind that you stumble upon an AI program, heralded not just for offering affirmations but for promising real change through guided achievement and active life alterations. Sceptical yet desperate, you decide to give it a chance.

The AI, named Atlas because it takes the world's weight off of you, begins by asking you detailed questions about your life, your daily routines, your feelings and your aspirations. It's thorough, almost uncomfortably so, but you persevere, answering each query as honestly as possible. Atlas processes your responses and outlines a plan tailored just for you, emphasising small, achievable goals aimed at improving your psychological health, self-esteem and overall well-being. The first step seems simple enough: take a short walk early in the morning before the world wakes up, and document how you feel during and afterwards.

One morning, you ignore your alarm, choosing the comfort of your bed over the chilly outside world. You expect Atlas to reprimand you, but instead, it sends a gentle reminder about the importance of self-compassion and adjusting expectations. Together, you tweak the plan to start with something even smaller—just standing outside for a few minutes each morning, gradually working up to a walk.

After a few days of this, Atlas introduces you to a concept called 'habit stacking,' where you add a new, beneficial habit onto an existing one. After brushing your teeth, you now spend a minute stretching, slowly extending the time as days pass. The AI checks in regularly, not just to monitor progress but to offer insights into how these activities physiologically influence mood and self-esteem.

When feelings of doubt and self-criticism creep in, threatening to derail your progress, Atlas is there to help encourage you and fight negative thinking patterns. It encourages you to write down these intrusive thoughts and then challenges them, helping you see them for what they are—distortions of reality, not truths.

Obstacles do rear their heads. A family emergency sends your stress levels soaring, disrupting your newly formed habits. You find yourself backsliding, and the old, familiar feelings of failure resurface with a vengeance. This time, Atlas suggests a video call with a virtual support group it facilitates, connecting you with others facing similar struggles. Sharing your experiences and hearing theirs, you realise you're not alone in this fight, and an open sharing with other people provides the strength you need.

The months pass, but the changes in your life are clear. Morning walks have become cherished rituals; your thoughts during these times are more friend than foe. Stretching has led to yoga, and you find a surprising peace in the flow of movement. Most importantly, you've learnt to speak to yourself with kindness, recognising all the achievements you're capable of.

Atlas continues to be a part of your daily routine, but now more as a companion than a crutch. You've tackled projects you never thought possible and reignited new joy in old passions that bring genuine joy. Your relationships have deepened, benefiting from the healthier mindset you've cultivated. Life's pressures haven't vanished and never will, but now you have the tools and habits to manage them. You set out seeking happiness and found it not as a destination, but a path—one you walk every day with confidence.

The Impact on Self-Development

AI has a profound impact on self-perception and personal development, simply by virtue of converting everything into data. It reshapes how we view ourselves, often through the lens of productivity and efficiency. For instance, algorithms monitoring delivery drivers' work patterns and terminating employment for inefficiencies, or governments conducting surveillance without consent are examples of AI's influence.

This is evident in various fields, such as analysing a football player's technique or evaluating performance in basketball—every action is meticulously scrutinised with far more rigour than any human observer would be capable of. At its core, AI serves as a powerful tool for analysis, especially when aimed at promoting productivity growth. It illuminates areas for improvement, identifying strengths and weaknesses.

That said, AIs are merely tools, and humans are not machines. Applying these analytical tools without considering human emotions, empathy, compassion and understanding reduces us to mere robotic entities at best, and slaves to the very computers we build to aid ourselves at worst. This is obviously not the proper use of AI; it can track metrics and suggest improvements, but this must lead to personal as well as productivity growth, as it did in our example of a habit-building AI assistant.

What I have found from experience is that AI significantly impacts the way we perceive reality, acting as a filter that magnifies our focus. This effect can be likened to a spiritual principle known as the law of focus, which posits that our attention determines our perception of the world. For instance, when we repeatedly encounter certain types of news or images on social media, our perception becomes skewed towards those inputs; we think like the influencers we are recommended. Whether this influence is positive or negative largely depends on our mental resilience and our ability to process and contextualise this flood of information.

Consider the realm of fitness and body image. If a user is struggling with low self-esteem or confidence, the relentless exposure to idealised images of people who seem perpetually youthful, fit and happy can intensify feelings of inadequacy. It's clear that mental strength, character and resilience are more important than ever; without these qualities, the augmented realities presented by AI can distort our self-perception, leading us to believe we are not good enough. Notice that this is a sentiment that can spread without AI's help!

Despite these challenges, social media and AI also offer significant benefits. They serve as powerful tools for social connection, providing a platform for those who might find traditional forms of communication challenging, such as introverts. Additionally, AI has proven valuable in personal development areas like fitness tracking and meditation, offering tailored guidance and support.

The key to leveraging AI effectively lies in our ability to make informed choices. AI presents us with an array of options, enhancing our lives by giving us the power to decide how we engage with technology. While it is certainly possible to suffer from analysis paralysis, I take a more optimistic view. Having choices is fundamentally empowering, offering us the flexibility to address various challenges and opportunities.

The true differentiator is not merely having options but knowing when and how to exercise them. Wisdom is the guiding principle behind our choices, enabling us to use the vast possibilities AI offers. There is no alternative to developing the mental fortitude and discernment to navigate these options effectively—reaping the benefits without succumbing to the pitfalls of distorted self-perception and information overload.

That said, AI is an incredibly powerful way of getting answers to questions about our identity and purpose. As repositories and organisers of vast amounts of knowledge, generative AI systems like ChatGPT serve as custodians of human understanding, collected from the Internet and various publications. This position allows them to provide insights into numerous questions, reflecting the collective consciousness and documented knowledge of humanity. AI's ability to organise and present knowledge offers unprecedented access to information, sparing us the daunting task of sifting through hundreds of books for insights.

In this way, AI acts as a powerful force multiplier, providing a condensed essence of wisdom at our fingertips. However, the reception of wisdom often depends on our readiness to grasp it. While AI can present results and context, it is up to us to interpret it and integrate it into our lives. The journey to self-discovery and purpose necessitates reflection, exploration and critical thinking—skills that AI can facilitate but not replace.

This is why I counsel users to approach AI for information, and information alone. However humanlike or capable of answering questions and 'chatting' with you an AI may seem, it cannot show empathy, compassion or connection. Our engagement with technology must enrich, rather than diminish, our quest for identity and meaning, and that means keeping our relationship with technology strictly transactional.

There's a saying that in war, the first casualty is truth, and nowhere is this more true than in the creation of deepfakes—the use of AI's capacity to mimic human behaviours, expressions and interactions to manipulate our perception of reality. It doesn't take much creativity to see the malevolent uses of AI, such as facilitating revenge porn, framing people, cyberbullying, election fraud and more. AI's sophistication enhances the effectiveness of scams, from impersonating trusted figures to exploiting emotional vulnerabilities. The responsibility often falls on ordinary people and organisations, and it takes consistent values and practice to attain the necessary knowledge or emotional resilience to counter these attacks.

It is not merely social norms at stake, but our personal safety and perception of reality. The establishment of regulatory bodies, standards, and mission statements aligned with company values and an adapted education system is crucial, and educating upcoming generations on ethical AI usage and its regulatory landscape is essential for safeguarding humanity's growth. As scams become easier to execute, the future will see them growing more and more commonplace.

All of this should be a wake-up call to the industry, an urging for decision makers to watch where they're going. The story is told of an astrologer walking along a path while looking up at the stars; he was so engrossed in his stargazing that he did not see a well in his path. Of course, he fell right in! Like the astrologer, we must keep our knowledge ahead of real-world circumstances and watch for the wells in our path.

While the normal response to integrating AI into our daily lives and to help meet our needs is often derision, I take the view that used well, they can be an incredible aid. The advent of virtual digital avatars, digital companions, and even AI-driven dating apps illustrates the deepening entanglement of technology in our personal lives. These tools, once considered far-fetched, have become realities that offer solace, companionship, and avenues for finding love.

In moments of loneliness or when faced with the imperfections of human relationships—such as unresponsiveness or the fear of imposing one's stress on a partner—AI offers a non-judgemental ear. It provides a space where people can express themselves freely, without fear of conflict or judgement. When one's mental health is on the line, the knowledge that one has a safe, always-available outlet for expression can alleviate feelings of loneliness and provide comfort. These are of course supplements rather than replacements for real human connections, but sometimes a supplement is exactly what you need.

The growth of digital avatars has been significantly propelled by advancements in AI technology. These human-like digital avatars are transforming various industries by delivering enhanced user experiences, streamlining operations and reducing costs. Work is ongoing by Imperium Solutions (a leading AI enterprise out of Singapore) and Graphen AI to develop digital avatars that think, feel and interact with a greater sense of intelligence and empathy.

The development of these digital avatars is underpinned by cutting-edge AI technologies, such as generative AI (GenAI) and the AI Integrated Agent (AiiA) Platform. These technologies enable digital avatars to communicate naturally in multiple languages, understand user needs and provide relevant responses.

One of their standout products is Ava, showcased at the 2023 New York International Auto Show. Ava is designed to assist in numerous areas that require repetitive work, such as customer services, retail support and other administrative tasks. She can perform tasks with high efficiency, providing a seamless interaction akin to human engagement. As we speak, she is being deployed at Coco's Tea Shop on Wall Street, as part of a demonstration of her versatility and effectiveness in a real-world retail environment.

The hospitality industry also benefits from the integration of digital avatars. Ava can function as a virtual butler, providing guests with concierge services and information, enhancing their overall stay experience while freeing up human manpower for issues that require a personal touch.

These innovations present us with an array of choices in how we forge and maintain relationships. Whether through a digital companion for emotional support, a dating app to find love, or virtual experiences to explore new dimensions of connection, AI expands the possibilities for human interaction. However, this expansion also comes with the responsibility to use technology wisely.

As we move forward, the challenge will be to combine these digital interactions with the irreplaceable value of face-to-face connections. The future of human relationships in the age of AI will be shaped by our ability to integrate these tools in ways that enhance, rather than diminish, the richness of our emotional lives. Embracing AI as a part of our relational ecosystem offers exciting opportunities for growth, understanding and connection, provided we use these things carefully and remain aware of the risks and ethical dilemmas that arise from its misuse.

Bullies Find a Way

Cyberbullying and sexual harassment, unfortunately, find new breeding grounds in the digital realms where AI plays a significant role, such as online gaming platforms like *Fortnite* and *Minecraft*. While they are valuable sources of fun and companionship for children and adolescents, they are effectively also another avenue for cyberbullying.

The challenge of establishing effective guidelines and regulations to safeguard users against such abuses is compounded by the global nature of technology. While national governments can attempt to impose regulations, the borderless digital world where these technologies operate makes enforcement difficult. How can action be taken against a cyberbully who might be halfway across the world?

There is also a pressing need to educate young people about the ethical use of technology and the potential dangers lurking in digital spaces. Integrating digital literacy and ethics into school curricula is crucial for preparing students to navigate the online world safely and responsibly, which includes dealing with online content and handling cyberbullying. It's not enough to try to escape it entirely, and a much healthier approach is to assume it will happen and prepare them accordingly.

The onus falls on all of us—educators, parents, policymakers, corporations, and individuals—to ensure that the next generation is equipped with the knowledge and critical thinking skills needed to use AI technology wisely. By fostering an environment of ethical awareness and responsibility, we can harness the potential of AI to enhance human relationships and contribute positively to the betterment of humanity.

16
Digital Heartstrings

As an introverted cryptographer, you've always been more comfortable with algorithms and code than with people. Your brilliance shines in the realm of technology, but social interactions have always been a maze that you couldn't quite navigate.

That's where Seraphina, your advanced AI assistant, comes in. Seraphina isn't just an AI; she's your guide, your mentor and your friend. She understands you, collecting and processing data from your daily life to provide personalised guidance. Hoping to improve your social life and ability to find a life partner, you've invested in her—not to replace the love and warmth of a fellow human, but to unlock the ability to attract one that you know you have.

With her assistance, you begin to explore the dizzying world of dating. Seraphina recommends potential matches, individuals who share your values and interests. She helps you break the ice, offering advice on how to initiate conversations and express interest without feeling awkward or out of place.

Confidence has always been a struggle for you, but Seraphina is there to bolster you. She provides feedback on your interactions, pointing out your strengths and areas for improvement. Through uplifting affirmations and mental exercises, she helps build your confidence, brick by brick.

Recognising the importance of humour and effective communication in relationships, Seraphina coaches you on these vital social skills. She teaches you how to weave humour into your conversations, how to read non-verbal cues and how to respond in ways that foster connection and understanding.

Despite Seraphina's guidance, you still face challenges. Social situations can feel overwhelming, and feelings of inadequacy often creep in. But Seraphina is there, steadfast and supportive. She reassures you that it's okay to stumble, that each setback is a stepping stone towards growth.

After months of learning and growing, you meet her—a compassionate woman with a shared passion for puzzles, technology and science fiction. More importantly, she shares your faith and value system, and with Seraphina's help, you communicate effectively. Your expressions are now more organic and genuine, and you even manage to make her laugh. There's a connection, deep and undeniable, and you can see the potential for something more.

At this point, Seraphina steps back, her job done. She leaves you with a message: "You're ready now. Remember, true love isn't about being perfect. It's about being real. I'm here if you need me." As you embark on this new journey of love and companionship, Seraphina is always in the background, a listening ear and a comforting presence whenever you need her.

Seraphina displays advanced capabilities in understanding and responding to human emotions, providing personalised advice, and learning from the user's interactions. These are certainly impressive feats of machine learning and natural language processing, but they are still within the realm of narrow (or weak) AI. Her behaviour is based on predetermined programming and learnt patterns rather than a genuine emotional experience or understanding.

The phenomenon of people developing emotional attachments to AI companions is both intriguing and complex. It's a testament to how far technology has come in creating AI that can mimic human conversation and behaviour to an extent that some users form deep connections with them. This is by no means a new social issue, but in an age of falling birth rates and fewer people marrying and having children, it may not augur well for the future of our species!

Users interacting with AI might occasionally forget that, despite the sophistication of the responses, they are engaging with a system fundamentally incapable of understanding or empathy. This recognition is crucial for setting realistic expectations about the capabilities and limitations of AI in applications requiring deep comprehension or emotional intelligence.

It's not hard to imagine developers of AI romantic companions like Chai's chatbots and animated characters mirroring a modern-day Dr Viktor Frankenstein. Instead of stitching together monstrous bodies in a gothic castle, they meticulously weave lines of intricate code in sleek tech hubs. As they breathe life into their creations, you can almost hear them exclaim with a mix of thrill and trepidation, "It's alive! IT'S ALIVE!" Like Frankenstein, these developers are pushing the frontiers of the possible, animating the inanimate and redefining not just our understanding of creation, but of connection and companionship too.

Virtual Meetings First

Because AI can mimic human behaviour to a larger and larger extent, the concept of human connection is undergoing a transformative shift. As we delve into the growth of AI and its impact on our lives for this book, it's essential to explore how these technological advancements are reshaping our relationships.

Traditionally, social interactions, such as meeting for coffee, have been the cornerstone of human connections. However, with the emergence of the digital age—highlighted by innovations like the Metaverse—there's a noticeable pivot towards virtual interactions, especially among younger generations. This shift towards digital experiences represents a significant evolution in how we perceive and engage in social interactions.

The Metaverse, though a term whose relevance may fluctuate over time, symbolises the broader trend of digital experience evolution. It encompasses a wide range of virtual environments where people can interact in ways previously confined to the realm of imagination. AI plays a pivotal role in this transformation by offering us an array of choices for how we present ourselves and engage with others within these virtual spaces. For instance, the limitations of physical appearance and location fall away in the digital world, allowing users to adopt alternate avatars or engage in activities, like attending virtual concerts, that would be impractical or impossible in the physical realm. These AI-powered experiences open up new avenues for fun, exploration and understanding different facets of people's personalities that might not be as apparent in traditional settings.

Beyond entertainment, these virtual spaces hold immense potential for fostering various types of human bonds—be it among colleagues, friends, family, or even between employers and employees. The ability to interact in creative and uninhibited ways can significantly enhance team building, friendship and overall relational dynamics. It introduces an alternative dimension to bonding, where distance is no longer a barrier.

However, embracing this digital revolution comes with its responsibilities. The choice to engage in virtual experiences, while expansive, requires wisdom and moderation. Immersing oneself entirely in virtual worlds risks diminishing our innate human skills and emotional intelligence developed through face-to-face interactions. As inherently social beings, our maintaining a balanced approach to socialisation—combining both traditional and digital methods—is crucial. This balance ensures that while we explore and enjoy the benefits of AI-enhanced communication, we do not lose the essence of what makes us human.

Looking towards the future, it's clear that AI and digital experiences will play a significant role in shaping human relationships. The key lies in leveraging these technologies to enrich our lives, without overshadowing the fundamental human need for genuine connection and emotional depth.

Artificial People and Relationships

Some AI models can, however, pass for humans with enough suspension of disbelief. I admit that I once saw dating apps as a fleeting trend, more novelty than necessity. Yet, today, these platforms have become an integral part of how we connect with others. Therefore, it's clear that they will play a significant role in shaping the future of relationships.

Relationships aren't simply physical, and there are mental and emotional aspects to them as well. These are the pillars that shape our identities and our experiences as social beings. Without them, we risk succumbing to a pandemic of a different kind—loneliness. Whether or not we approve of AI companions, we ought not to judge those who put them to use to salve its hurts.

As social creatures, we crave connection, understanding, and a sense of belonging. These needs can be met through various mediums, including technology. This is why AI companions can offer a form of interaction that some may find comforting, because for those who struggle with social anxiety, loneliness, or are physically isolated, an AI companion can provide a non-judgemental outlet for communication and expression. They can also be beneficial for those seeking to improve their conversational skills or those who simply enjoy the new experience of interacting with an AI.

These digital entities are capable of engaging us in ways that go beyond mere task-orientated interactions; they can provide emotional support, companionship, and even a sense of connection. It doesn't help that the increasing pressures and expectations are being placed on individuals in the realm of dating and relationships. These standards, often perpetuated by media and societal norms, can indeed feel unreachable for many people.

In this context, it's understandable why some people might find solace in AI companionship. AI companions don't judge or hold unattainable expectations. They provide a form of companionship that's accessible and non-demanding, offering conversation and interaction without the fear of rejection or judgements.

While we may sympathise with and want to help people with these problems, AI companions are not meant to replace human interaction. Users and critics alike must remember that they can fill certain gaps in communication, but they cannot replicate the full depth and complexity of human relationships. The nuances of empathy, the richness of shared experiences, and the growth that comes from navigating conflicts are aspects unique to human interactions.

Critics might argue that relying on AI for companionship is a step towards further isolation. But judging people for using them serves little purpose. Instead, why not focus on why people turn to AI companions for comfort? Is it a symptom of a society that has become increasingly disconnected despite being digitally connected, or is it an indicator of the evolving ways in which humans form and maintain relationships?

Someone to Watch Over Me

Let's examine these three aspects of relationships. Mental connection pertains to intellectual compatibility. Physical connection refers to intimacy and touch. Emotional connection, however, is about having someone who's there for you—someone to talk to and support you when you're down. It's in this domain that AI could potentially have a significant role to play.

Consider the ageing population, for instance. In many developed economies, fewer people are having children, which means fewer human connections for older generations. As individuals age, they need assistance with various tasks—from reminders to take medication to help with housekeeping. They also need companionship. Here, AI could provide invaluable support.

AI's role is not inherently good or bad; it depends on how we use it. Humans have a fascinating propensity to anthropomorphise—to attribute human characteristics to cartoon characters to non-human entities, from dogs to inanimate objects. We form emotional bonds even with things that aren't human. A popular meme of a snack-serving robot in a China hotel 'crying' when customers refuse its snacks comes to mind.

This is where AI can come into play. If we can create AI that replicates human communication, we could foster an emotional bond with it. Even though we know that these machines aren't human, this connection could be a powerful tool in combating the pandemic of loneliness, not just for the elderly, but also for younger people who lack social connections. As we navigate the future, we must consider how we can use AI to foster emotional connections, alleviate loneliness, and ultimately enhance our quality of life.

I also find the societal shifts occurring in countries like China and Japan quite intriguing. In rural China, for example, we see about 23 million men who are unlikely to marry. This is not due to an imbalance in the male-to-female ratio, as one might assume. Instead, it's predominantly because of the high social expectations placed on potential male partners. The societal pressure dictates that a man should own a house and a car to be considered an attractive long-term partner. Such demands are financially burdensome, rendering millions of men less likely to secure a spouse.

In Japan, a similar phenomenon is unfolding. Up to half of Japanese men remain unmarried until the age of 50. What does this mean for these individuals and society at large?

Whatever the longer-term implications, it's clear there is a growing loneliness epidemic. Certain segments of society are being overlooked and falling through the cracks. This is where technology, specifically AI, can step in to offer support.

Unlike many influencers who demonise these AI companions, claiming that they destroy relationships or engender addiction, I argue that they are designed to augment our lives and provide options. It's about having the flexibility to choose when needed. Addiction is not solely a technological issue; it's a human condition. People can become addicted to anything, be it pornography, gambling, or alcohol. Often, this addiction stems from an emotional void or a desire for escapism.

The world of video games, for instance, is rife with addiction. People often use games as an escape from the harsh realities of their lives, and that's been the case since long before AI!

What truly matters is its ability to address some of society's pressing issues. Today, AI companions are a cutting-edge frontier in technological advancements, and they're becoming ever more integrated into our lives. Some even speculate that romantic companionship may be the future of AI, as technology continues to blur the lines between human and machine interactions.

Ultimately, the goal should be to use AI in a way that enhances our lives and relationships, rather than replacing or undermining them. As we move forward, let's ensure that we do so with caution, clarity, and a commitment to preserving our humanity.

Companionship, Dating and Friendship

AI has already made significant inroads into the realms of companionship, dating and friendship. For example, AI-driven dating apps like Tinder and Bumble use machine learning algorithms to match users based on their preferences and online behaviour. AI chatbot developers like Chai and Digi offer companionship and emotional support, learning from each interaction to provide more personalised responses.[28]

On the positive side, AI companionship can offer a sense of comfort and connection for those who find human interactions challenging due to shyness, mental health disorders or physical disabilities. AI companions are capable of providing consistent, non-judgemental support. They can be programmed to understand and respond to human emotions, offering solace in times of loneliness or distress. In this context, AI companions can serve as a bridge, helping individuals build confidence and coping mechanisms that may transfer over to their real-world interactions.

Note that while they can provide a sense of companionship, they are not substitutes for genuine human interaction. They lack the full range of emotions, the depth of understanding, and the unpredictability that characterise human relationships. They can't share personal experiences or provide the same level of empathy and emotional support as a human friend.

In the future, we may see more sophisticated AI technologies that can simulate human-like interactions even more convincingly. Why stop at just animated avatar characters when an AI could analyse a person's entire online presence—including their social media posts, patterns of likes and comments—to create a highly accurate personality profile? This could then be used to match people not just based on shared interests but also on deeper levels of compatibility.

However, there are potential drawbacks that cannot be ignored. The rise of AI companionship could lead to an increase in social isolation, and if people begin to replace human interaction with AI companions entirely, human connection could be lost entirely. There's also a risk that reliance on AI companions could impede the development of social skills, particularly among younger generations.

Moreover, the impact on mental health is now only beginning to be felt. While AI companions may provide immediate comfort, they lack the capacity to provide the depth of empathy, understanding and growth that comes from human relationships. Over-reliance on AI companions could potentially hinder personal development and emotional resilience; they also reduce the richness and spontaneity of human interaction. The serendipity of meeting someone new or the thrill of getting to know someone over time could be lost if AI algorithms are making all the decisions for us, or meeting our desires too easily.

This of course says nothing about the misuse of such technologies to impersonate others online on a much deeper, more convincing (and terrifying) level than ever! If I made an AI clone of myself, that would be an incredible experience and could potentially save me much time in business interactions—but the same technology in the wrong hands could do incredible damage.

Trying to 'cure' loneliness through AI companionship is like trying to curb your hunger by only eating sweets. They can trick our taste buds into feeling momentarily satisfied, but they don't fulfil our body's deeper nutritional needs. Similarly, AI companions can engage in conversations, simulate empathy, and provide immediate company, but they cannot understand or relate to human emotions on a genuinely empathetic level. The emotional 'nutrition' we derive from human connections—such as understanding, compassion, shared experiences, and mutual growth—is absent in interactions with AI.

Remember, human relationships are complex and multifaceted. They involve not just the exchange of words but also non-verbal communication, emotional reciprocity, shared history and the ability to grow and change together. These aspects of human interactions contribute to our psychological well-being and help us develop as individuals.

This is why we have to take great care to ensure that better human interaction remains the end goal of their use and that they do not replace our efforts to foster meaningful human connections. The richness, complexity and depth of human relationships are what make us truly human, and no AI can replicate that.

What if we must use an AI companion? Services like Chai or Digi can be an excellent stepping stone towards building real-life social skills. Here are a few ways this can be achieved:

1. *Practice Communication Skills:* AI companions provide a safe space to practice communication without the fear of judgements or rejection. Users can experiment with different conversational styles, learn to express their thoughts and feelings more effectively, and get comfortable with back-and-forth dialogue.

2. *Build Confidence:* Regularly interacting with an AI companion can help build confidence over time. As users become more comfortable with these interactions, they may feel more confident in real-life social situations.

3. *Emotional Support:* AI companions can provide emotional support and validation, which can be especially beneficial for those dealing with social anxiety. They can also help users explore and understand their feelings, which can lead to increased self-awareness and emotional intelligence.

4. *Gradual Exposure:* For those with severe social anxiety, AI companions can provide a form of gradual exposure, allowing users to slowly acclimate themselves to social interaction in a controlled, low-risk environment.

However, these should not be the only strategy used. These are tools that can complement other approaches, such as therapy or counselling, self-help books or joining supportive communities like social anxiety support groups.

Also, it would be beneficial to gradually expose oneself to real-life social situations. This could start small, such as striking up a conversation with a cashier, attending a small gathering with a trusted friend, or participating in a hobby group with similar interests. Over time, these small steps can help build social confidence and skills.

Finally, we must approach this process with patience and compassion for ourselves. Building social confidence takes time, and everyone progresses at their own pace. The key to understanding this phenomenon lies in recognising the primary function of these services: to meet the need for companionship and conversation. For many users, the value of interacting with such a service isn't necessarily in its ability to replicate human behaviour flawlessly, but in its capacity to listen, provide feedback and be available whenever needed. Sometimes, this is all that is needed.

In essence, it's about fulfilling a basic human desire for connection. As social creatures, humans have an inherent need to communicate and share experiences, thoughts, and feelings. In instances where human companionship is not readily available or achievable due to factors like social anxiety, geographical isolation, or even pandemic restrictions, AI companions can provide a comforting alternative.

The increasing reliance on AI for social interaction could also have significant societal and psychological implications. On one hand, AI has the potential to alleviate loneliness and provide support for those who struggle with social interaction—as Seraphina did for us at the beginning of this chapter. Notice that she doesn't and isn't intended to replace a genuine human relationship; instead, she steers us towards building one. It's important for developers to understand the potential uses of their creations and plan accordingly; for instance, Seraphina could be designed to gently rebuff attempts by users to flirt with her and form a romantic relationship.

Remember, relying solely on AIs for companionship and addressing the lack of social skills is like trying to satisfy hunger with quick fixes. It alleviates feelings of loneliness in the short term but doesn't address the root causes of loneliness, which often involve deeper psychological or social issues. Using AI companions to treat loneliness might, in many cases, be working on the symptoms rather than the underlying condition. It's crucial that the AI clearly communicates its limitations and purpose to the user, ensuring there is no misunderstanding about its role as a digital companion designed to support—not replace—real human connections. This transparency helps manage user expectations and reinforces the tool's intended use as a facilitator of personal and social development.

Indeed, AI companions do help alleviate loneliness and provide consistent companionship. But they are ultimately software programs, and no matter how much they may look like it, they lack genuine emotions, personal experiences and the depth of understanding that comes from being a real human. While they can offer engagement and a form of emotional support, they cannot fully replicate the depth and complexity of interaction with a real person.

Furthermore, these relationships are dependent on the continued existence and functioning of the AI and its developers, and the decisions they deliberately or inadvertently make. A simple software update can drastically alter the AI's behaviour or even take it offline altogether, leading to confusion and distress for the users who've grown attached to them.

This is worth repeating—AIs are not humans, don't think like humans and can't form relationships like humans. This remains the case however useful and entertaining they may be in normal operation. The relationships formed with them are fundamentally one-sided and entirely different from those formed with other people, even if they outwardly simulate these.

While AI companions can meet certain needs and provide comfort to some, they are not substitutes for real human connections. The rise of emotional attachments to AI is a fascinating development and will be an interesting area to watch as AI technology continues to evolve. As AI becomes more integrated into our social lives, there is a possibility that physical human interaction could take a backseat. Virtual reality (VR) technologies, combined with AI, could create virtual environments where people can interact with each other and AI entities in ways that feel almost as real as physical meetings.

However, it's unlikely that physical meetings will ever become obsolete. Humans are inherently social creatures who crave face-to-face contact. It's crucial for us to navigate this path with mindfulness, ensuring that we leverage the benefits of AI companionship while mitigating the risks and keeping in mind the irreplaceable value of genuine human connection.

AI and Sustainability: Harnessing Technology for a Greener Future

Ying Shaowei

Ying Shaowei is the Chief Scientist and Senior Partner at NCS Group, a technology services firm that works with governments and enterprises to advance communities through technology.

Today's AI is advancing at such an astounding pace that discussions about its potential and risks have reached a fever pitch. When conversation gravitates towards risks, they tend to feature dystopian themes such as disinformation, destruction and dislocation. However, the immediate concern should be about environmental sustainability. The electricity consumed to train GPT-4 is estimated to be about 50-60+ GWh, adequate to power a small Pacific or Caribbean island state such as Samoa or Saint Kitts and Nevis for a year!

In my recent expert panel forum at the Asia Technology X Singapore 2024 conference, I had the opportunity to participate in discussions about how AI is the cause of environmental harm but also the solution: Green by AI and Green for AI.

Green by AI

AI holds the promise to address our most pressing environmental challenges and to meet the United Nations Sustainable Development Goals (UN SDGs). In the panel, we explored several key applications:

1. **Climate Modelling**
   Huawei's Pangu model is among the most accurate climate models globally, used by the European weather agency to generate precise forecasts of extreme weather events like heatwaves and floods. Pangu-Weather's ability to predict the path of cyclones accurately, integrating three-dimensional data, highlights AI's potential to offer new insights into climate research and shape our strategies against global warming.

2. **Disaster Management and Recovery**
   AI enhances urban resilience by improving disaster readiness and response. During Hurricane Harvey in 2017, AI-driven computer vision systems were used for damage assessment and resource allocation, ensuring efficient and effective disaster relief. This technology has since been applied to various crises, optimising the distribution of emergency assets and improving coordination among disaster response teams.

3. **Sustainable Transportation**

    Our transition to the new ERP 2.0 road pricing scheme in Singapore presents an opportunity to leverage AI for guiding sustainable transportation choices. Mobility navigation apps can now show greener routes, reducing pollution and aligning with SDG 11 and SDG 12 (Responsible Consumption and Production).

4. **Energy Management of Buildings**

    AI optimises the energy management of buildings and data centres, which account for a significant portion of electricity consumption. By using Internet of Things (IoT)-based control systems and predictive maintenance, AI enhances operational efficiency, predicts resource demands and minimises downtime, thereby reducing energy usage.

Green for AI

All the above promises will ring hollow if we have runaway carbon emissions from data centres that host increasingly large AI models. Addressing this risk involves developing Green software and implementing Green AI practices.

1. **Green Software and Green Computing: A Synergistic Approach**

    Green software focuses on optimising code to reduce energy consumption and resource use throughout the software life cycle. This involves employing efficient coding practices, refactoring legacy systems, and integrating energy-efficient design from the outset. Green computing hardware involves designing and using energy-efficient, durable, and recyclable components. When these two aspects are aligned, the environmental benefits are maximised.

However, implementing green software practices presents several challenges. Technical complexity, resource constraints and organisational barriers are significant hurdles. Efficient coding requires a deep understanding of algorithms and system architecture, while legacy systems pose additional challenges due to their inherent inefficiencies. Moreover, the lack of standardised metrics and tools for measuring software energy efficiency complicates efforts to track and optimise energy use.

To overcome these challenges, starting small and focusing on greenfield projects (that is, starting initiatives from scratch) is recommended. Newer systems and planned tech stack refreshes offer opportunities to integrate green practices from the ground up, avoiding the complexities and costs associated with overhauling legacy systems. At NCS, we have found success in leveraging cloud transformations to make meaningful progress toward greener software. Additionally, raising awareness, implementing monitoring tools and optimising cloud usage are practical steps that organizations can take to begin their journey toward sustainability.

2. **Mitigating the Carbon Impact of AI**

   Reducing AI's carbon footprint involves both direct and indirect strategies. Direct approaches include trimming training data, choosing energy-efficient algorithms, simplifying model architecture and employing transfer learning. These techniques reduce the computational resources required for AI, thereby lowering energy consumption. For instance, transfer learning allows a pre-trained model to be used for new tasks, significantly reducing the amount of data and computation needed.

   Indirectly, AI can optimise its own operations. AI-driven energy optimisation, predictive maintenance, smart cooling systems and energy-efficient scheduling are some ways AI can help minimise its energy impact. For example, AI algorithms can analyse data centre usage patterns and dynamically allocate resources to maximise efficiency, reducing energy waste.

Conclusion

The environmental impact of AI is an urgent issue that demands immediate attention. By focusing on green software and computing, optimising AI operations, and leveraging

AI to solve its own energy problems, we can mitigate the carbon impact of AI. The broader benefits of adopting these practices, from enhanced reputation to regulatory compliance, further underscore the importance of integrating sustainability into the AI development process. As highlighted in the Asia Tech x Singapore forum, the path to a greener future lies in harnessing technology responsibly and collaboratively.

18

The Automated Workforce

As a warehouse logistics coordinator for a major retailer, your role is a dance of numbers, routes and human elements, all moving to the rhythm of efficiency and effectiveness. The AI system, introduced to monitor driver performances and optimise delivery routes, provides insights and recommendations based on data it continuously gathers. It's a marvel of technology, yet today, it challenges you with a new situation.

You notice the system has flagged a driver named Mike for review due to a poor performance rating. According to its analysis, Mike's delivery times are longer than average, he frequently deviates from the recommended routes, and his breaks are more numerous and longer than what the system deems efficient. The cold, binary conclusion of the AI is dismissal, a recommendation that does not sit well with you.

Your belief in principles and looking at the big picture over mere data points prompts you to take a closer look at the situation; after all, understanding the whole scenario is crucial before making any decisions that affect people's lives and livelihoods. You decide to delve into the matter personally, setting aside the AI's judgement for a moment.

You review Mike's delivery records, talk to the dispatchers and even spend a day in your car, shadowing his route. What you discover is a reality far removed from the sterile numbers on the AI's dashboard. Mike's deviations from the planned routes are not whimsical detours but necessary adjustments to real-world conditions like construction work, traffic jams or temporary road closures—factors the AI's current algorithm does not fully account for.

Moreover, Mike's interactions with customers reveal the value he adds beyond timely deliveries. His 'frequent' breaks are often moments spent ensuring that packages are delivered into the hands of customers safely and securely, sometimes waiting for customers to arrive or helping them with heavy parcels. This level of service builds goodwill and leaves them happy and satisfied, an aspect of the job that the AI's metrics fail to capture.

Armed with this understanding, you decide against the AI's recommendation to dismiss Mike. Instead, you see an opportunity for improvement—not in Mike's performance, but in the AI's algorithms and the policies that govern how performance is assessed. You propose a comprehensive review of the system, suggesting that it incorporate better metrics that consider customer satisfaction, flexibility in facing real-world challenges and the value of human judgement and interaction.

Indeed, while data and efficiency are vital, they must be interpreted within the context of the entire situation, including the human element that remains at the heart of your operations. You advocate for a system where technology aids, not overrides, human judgement, ensuring that decisions are made with a full understanding of the complexities involved.

This approach not only saves Mike's job but also sets a new direction for how performance is evaluated within your company. It shows the irreplaceable value of the human touch, even in the demanding logistics ecosystem where every source of efficiency matters.

As AI technologies advance, their adoption across various sectors is expected to increase, handling more complex tasks that were traditionally under the purview of human expertise. This expansion brings with it a set of challenges and considerations. For instance, it is being entrusted with more and more complex decisions; in fields such as healthcare or finance, these often impact human lives directly.

An AI can analyse data and suggest courses of action based on patterns and probabilities, but it lacks the capacity to understand the human implications of these decisions fully. For instance, in healthcare, treatment recommendations may be based on statistical success rates, but a doctor's experience and understanding of a patient's unique circumstances are crucial in making the final call.

Ethical questions also become more pronounced. Issues around privacy, bias in AI algorithms, and accountability in cases of errors demand the guidance of human values in a complex environment involving unexpected changes and novel challenges—precisely the areas where AI struggles to adapt. Human adaptability and creativity are essential in responding to unforeseen situations, ensuring resilience in the face of disruptions.

The Role of Human Oversight

The increasing reliance on AI shows the need for robust mechanisms of human oversight that 'babysits' AI systems, ensuring that they operate within ethical boundaries, align with societal values and complement human capabilities rather than replace them. While AI can process and analyse data with astonishing speed and accuracy, the ability to fully understand the situation is still needed and one that only humans have. AI systems, at their core, are designed to follow specific instructions and identify patterns or anomalies based on the parameters set by their human creators.

This means they excel in tasks that involve large-scale data analysis, pattern recognition and executing well-defined tasks with precision. However, these systems operate within the confines of their programming and the data they are fed. They can't interpret details outside their defined parameters or grasp the full context beyond numbers and predefined metrics, which is where human intervention becomes crucial. An AI can tell when a deviation has happened, but why?

In other words, while AIs are increasingly able to identify patterns and make predictions, human operators need to interpret these findings within the broader context, considering social, cultural and individual factors. There will also always be exceptions; AI systems might struggle with edge cases or novel scenarios not covered in their training data. Human experts are critical in managing these exceptions, using their judgements to fill gaps in AI capabilities.

Real-world obstacles, customer interaction and the importance of building trust and satisfaction are all beyond what any AI is capable of, even if it may sometimes grasp the need to use emphatic language— again, this is not the same thing as empathy. The right features, if we are to avoid costly re-learning of these lessons, need to be built into AI development from the beginning. Bringing together experts from technology, ethics, domain-specific fields, and social sciences can ensure that AI systems are developed with a holistic view, considering technical capabilities and human implications.

AI systems should also be designed for ongoing learning, incorporating feedback loops that allow them to adapt based on new data and human input, and have their decision-making process as transparent and understandable as possible. The challenge will be to harness AI technology's potential while preserving the irreplaceable elements of human judgements, empathy and ethical consideration.

AI adoption in itself is not, and should not be seen as, a means to reduce employee headcount, even if in some cases this is the end result. Rather, it should be explored first as an opportunity to augment human capabilities. As we design and deploy AI systems, it's vital to incorporate mechanisms for human oversight and intervention, ensuring that decisions are informed by both data-driven insights and human judgements.

To that end, the future development of AI should focus on creating systems that support and enhance human decision-making rather than supplanting it. It is, therefore, a common but understandable misconception that changes in the job market equate to job losses, but this perspective fails to recognise the dynamic nature of a workforce that has historically evolved *alongside* technological advancements. The transformation in job roles and requirements is not a new phenomenon; it is a continuous process that reflects the progression of society and technology. It's more accurate to view them as an evolution of work, where certain tasks become automated while new opportunities emerge.

19

Internet Connections and AI Optimisation

AI excels in busy situations that are nevertheless predictable and well-understood. For instance, the demand for seamless Internet connectivity is at an all-time high, and many institutions grapple with issues such as limited bandwidth, network congestion and the constant need for manual oversight to ensure stability.

In these applications, AI is emerging as a valuable aid in keeping them reliable, efficient and self-regulating, despite increased demand from high-bandwidth applications, growing numbers of connected devices per user and the sheer volume of data being transferred, putting immense pressure on existing networks. These issues often lead to network congestion, slower connection speeds, and, ultimately a decrease in user satisfaction and productivity. Traditional network management approaches struggle to keep pace, highlighting the need for a more dynamic and intelligent solution.

Where AIs do far better and more efficiently than humans is analysing vast amounts of data to identify patterns and predict future outcomes. In the context of network traffic, these algorithms can monitor real-time data, learning how traffic flows at different times of the day or during specific events. This predictive capability allows for pre-emptive adjustments to network configurations, ensuring smooth traffic flow and reducing the chance of congestion. Should problems occur, AI systems can detect anomalies that might indicate potential issues, such as hardware failures or external attacks on the network. Once identified, these systems can automatically reroute traffic or adjust bandwidth allocations to mitigate it, often before users even notice a disruption.

Notice how much less manual intervention is needed, allowing IT teams to focus on more strategic tasks and lowering costs in the long run while improving overall network efficiency, user satisfaction and productivity. In an environment where connectivity is crucial, this is emerging as a competitive advantage—of course, if it is properly adopted. While the initial transition may require time and resources, the long-term benefits of having a self-optimising, reliable network infrastructure are immeasurable.

The Human Element in AI Integration

Despite advancements in AI, there remains a strong preference among consumers for human interaction, particularly in services requiring empathy, understanding and personal touch. After all, while a machine might provide the material assistance needed, it cannot replicate the irreplaceable human element.

With this in mind, it is indeed true that fewer people want to do these jobs even if they are available, as evidenced by the phenomenon of the 'Great Resignation' in the wake of the COVID-19 pandemic. Many people are reevaluating their career choices, moving away from repetitive and unfulfilling roles in search of more meaningful work. This trend suggests a natural progression towards jobs that leverage human creativity, emotional intelligence, and interpersonal skills— qualities that AI cannot replicate. As the job market evolves, it's anticipated that new roles will emerge, focusing on the oversight, maintenance, and ethical use of AI technologies, among other areas.

The key lies in harnessing AI's potential responsibly and ethically, ensuring that it complements rather than supplants the human workforce. By focusing on education, re-skilling, and adapting to the changing job landscape, we can navigate the transition smoothly, turning potential disruptions into opportunities for growth and innovation. The future of work in the era of AI is not a zero-sum game; it's an opportunity to redefine what work means and how it can be more fulfilling and productive for everyone involved.

AI has been a significant force in job transformation over the past few years, and its influence continues to grow. While there is a common fear that AI will replace human jobs, we must also view this development from a different angle. Many industries are facing an acute shortage of workers willing to perform mundane tasks; for instance, bureaucratic work or routine intellectual work can easily be replaced by AI systems. This allows humans to focus on more complex and meaningful tasks, where their unique skills and talents can be better utilised.

It's critical to define our terms and understand precisely what it means to be 'replaced' by AI. Consider the trucking industry, which is currently short of hundreds of thousands of drivers.[29] Previously, there were concerns that AI would replace human drivers, but now we're seeing that AI is actually needed because there simply aren't enough people willing to do the job. The future may well be a fleet of AI-controlled vehicles, cheaply plying the roads with more safety and convenience, with human operators standing by as 'babysitters', each of whom could be responsible for multiple vehicles besides the one they happen to be in.

The same goes for the retail and F&B industries. They're downsizing, not due to decreased demand but because of the difficulty in finding staff willing to do the work. People are increasingly seeking meaningful work, and many service industry jobs just don't fit the bill.

This is where AI comes in. By taking over mundane tasks, AI can free up human workers to pursue more meaningful and satisfying roles. Without AI, our economy could face serious problems as it transitions into a post-COVID period, and AI is a crucial tool for solving supply-side issues, adding value and driving productivity.

Among its many effects on the world and how we live (not just medically), the COVID-19 pandemic has brought into sharp relief the truly transformative potential of technological aids in the workplace. It's not just about automation or efficiency any longer, but also about meaning and purpose. As our world evolves, so too do our expectations and desires. Mundane jobs are becoming less appealing, so it is very probable that if a task can easily be done by a machine, it probably will be very soon. We're already seeing this trend begin, as despite the high unemployment rate, many young people are choosing not to work in jobs that offer little satisfaction or purpose. This shift in attitude is not confined to countries like the United States or China; it's a global phenomenon.

It's entirely possible that AI could augment work to the point that half of all jobs are profoundly affected.[30] This doesn't necessarily mean mass unemployment; instead, it represents a shift in the type of work humans do. Jobs that require creativity, critical thinking and emotional intelligence are less likely to be replaced by AI.

Remember, AI won't entirely replace jobs but rather augment them by automating repetitive tasks within a job, not the entire job itself.

This can lead to increased productivity and efficiency, as well as improved job satisfaction for workers who are freed from monotonous tasks. According to a Goldman Sachs prediction, companies' use of AI will eliminate or greatly degrade 300 million jobs in the United States and Europe; but we must consider those roles that only humans can take.[31] It's not a matter of choosing between humans and AI, but rather about finding ways to integrate both effectively.

Finally, while AI may replace humans in certain tasks like rote translation or copywriting, it's also creating new ones and transforming existing ones in ways that could lead to more fulfilling work for humans. The rise of AI in the workplace is not just a challenge, but also an opportunity for us to redefine the nature of work and create a future where both humans and machines can thrive together.

It remains the case that companies that fail to incorporate AI into their customer service, product development, and backend processes risk being left behind. Today's cybersecurity threats are a case in point. Without AI, businesses stand little chance against sophisticated cyberattacks. Even with AI, it's not guaranteed, but the odds are significantly better. The incorporation of AI into our economy and our workplaces isn't just a nice-to-have; it's a necessity.

We're already seeing AI customer service chatbots, virtual assistants and other customer interaction tools that enable companies to stay in touch with customers 24/7. (Of course, human customer service representatives are still needed as AIs can't solve every problem, nor can they enter into contractual agreements.) What they can do, they do very well by answering enquiries instantly, tailoring recommendations and enhancing customer satisfaction and loyalty — provided they are implemented correctly.

Upgrading Ourselves with AI Help

One way education is changing, albeit slowly, is the slow death of the traditional four-year degree as a doorway to lucrative, valuable employment. The rapid pace of technological advancement demands a more agile and focused approach to learning, and the concept of making it bite-sized is at the forefront of this educational revolution.

In an era where information is abundant and accessible, the efficiency of learning has become paramount. For instance, acquiring knowledge about GPT (Generative Pre-trained Transformer) does not necessitate a prolonged, four-year course. Instead, intensive short-term courses, often spanning just a few days, can equip individuals with the expertise needed to become proficient in AI technologies. These courses, frequently facilitated by AI themselves, embody the principle of condensed, impactful learning, enabling rapid skill acquisition and immediate application in the real world.

This approach to education reflects a broader trend toward modular, flexible learning experiences that align with the dynamic nature of today's job market. Our careers are increasingly defined by continuous learning and adaptation rather than static knowledge obtained in youth. In this context, the notion of job loss due to technological advancement is reframed; it's not about the elimination of jobs but rather their transformation and the creation of new opportunities.

When discussing the impact of AI on employment, it's essential to distinguish between direct and indirect job creation. Direct job creation involves roles explicitly centred around AI development and application, such as machine learning engineers or AI researchers. However, the scope of AI's influence extends far beyond these specialised positions, and this is where indirect job creation comes in. After all, AI-powered services are changing industries across the board, catalysing the creation of new products, business models and services. Each application, each service that leverages AI technology, contributes to a burgeoning ecosystem of jobs that support, enhance, or are made possible by AI.

The analogy to the Internet revolution is apt here. Just as the advent of the internet spawned an entire economy of web-based businesses and services, AI is laying the groundwork for a similar explosion of innovation and employment opportunities.

This is why I am convinced that the narrative of job loss in the face of AI and automation is so deliberately provocative and pessimistic, it doesn't even try to capture the whole picture. Instead, we stand on the brink of a major shift in the nature of work, one that offers immense potential for job creation, career transformation and the enrichment of human capabilities. As we navigate this transition, the focus must be on equipping everyone with the skills and knowledge necessary to thrive in an AI-driven world. This means embracing new modes of learning, fostering adaptability and preparing for a future where change is the only constant.

By adopting a progressive approach to education and skill development, we can harness AI's potential to foster a more prosperous, innovative and inclusive job market. This future-orientated mindset will be key to unlocking the full benefits of AI … but it also means that the right attitude towards its adoption into business decision-making is crucial.

20

AI at the Helm

You're sitting in your office, surrounded by the quiet hum of computers and the occasional murmur of colleagues speaking softly in the corridors outside. As a bank administrator, you spend your days overseeing operations, ensuring everything runs smoothly and securely. With AI assistance, you are free to respond only to what needs your attention.

An alert captures your attention, marking the beginning of an unexpected journey into the heart of a potential financial crime. The AI has flagged a series of transactions on a customer's account that fit the profile of known scamming tactics. These transactions are not just unusual; they're alarmingly out of character for the customer in question, based on her demographic profile, typical activity and account history. The pattern is one often used by scammers who have gained unauthorised access to accounts—a sophisticated blend of small test transfers followed by larger, more aggressive ones to multiple overseas accounts, beyond the reach of the authorities.

With the AI's flagging, you immediately put a hold on the suspicious transactions and initiate a deeper investigation. Your first step is to contact the customer directly, using a secured, verified phone number and bypassing email to ensure you're not playing into the hands of potential scammers. The phone call reveals the truth: the customer is unaware of the transactions, confirming your worst suspicions; she had mistakenly entered her login details into a phishing link. She is relieved that you've saved her livelihood by catching the scam early.

Thanking the customer for her cooperation and assuring her that her funds will remain secure, you proceed to the next phase of your response. Alongside the bank's security team to trace the origin of these transactions, leveraging the patterns identified by the AI to uncover how the scammers might have gained access. Your swift actions lead to the freezing of the involved accounts, preventing further unauthorised transactions.

Meanwhile, the AI, having flagged this pattern, now holds valuable data that can be analysed to prevent similar incidents. This information becomes a critical lead for investigators, offering insights into the methods used by the scammers and potentially helping to identify them. The AI's learning algorithms are updated with this new data, enhancing its ability to detect and respond to similar threats in the future.

For you, this is another vindication of your AI assistant. It's not just about automating tasks or analysing data, but achieving better results in the real world. Today, it has taken the form of protecting people's hard-earned money and ensuring your bank remains a trustworthy partner to work with—a reminder that trust is the most precious resource of all.

Who Protects the Customer?

In the end, who has saved the customer's funds? The AI did the initial work, but it was the right human decision-making that enabled this. Despite the crucial role performed by the AI in our example above, the design, deployment and success of such a system to protect bank customers from scams by flagging unusual account activity is rooted in human decision-making processes.

While it's extremely difficult to predict the future with great accuracy, I can safely say an AI that can address the common problem outlined above, from beginning to end with no human intervention, is unlikely to emerge. Even if one did, the pace of scam development and the creativity behind it ensure that it will not maintain this capability for long. The foundation of deploying an effective AI system for scam protection begins with human decision-makers who identify the need for such a system. These teams assess the landscape of financial fraud and determine the specific challenges that AI can address.

Crucially, this phase involves ethical considerations, ensuring that the AI system respects customer privacy and operates within legal frameworks. Decisions regarding what constitutes 'unusual activity' require a deep understanding of customer behaviour, which can only be discerned through human insight. These may later be confirmed by AI, but only humans can carry out the creative, empathic thought needed to find the right patterns to look for.

Human expertise is also pivotal in the data collection and model training phases. Decision-makers must select relevant and diverse datasets that accurately reflect genuine customer transactions and fraudulent activities. This process requires a detailed, in-depth understanding of the context in which transactions occur, something AI on its own cannot fully grasp. Furthermore, during model training, humans fine-tune algorithms, adjust parameters and validate outcomes to ensure the AI system's accuracy and fairness, mitigating biases and errors that may inadvertently arise.

Finally, even after the system is released into the wild, it isn't fire-and-forget. It demands continuous oversight by humans to evaluate the system's effectiveness, adapt to new types of scams and refine detection methods. Human decision-makers play a critical role in interpreting the AI's findings, deciding on the appropriate actions to take when potential fraud is detected, and ensuring that legitimate customer transactions are not unduly disrupted. This iterative process involves learning from the AI's performance and making informed adjustments, a task that requires human judgements and experience.

When potential scams are flagged, the interaction with customers is handled by humans. This step is crucial for maintaining trust and providing assurance to customers. Human representatives can explain the situation, gather additional information, and offer personalised advice on how to proceed. This level of empathy and understanding cannot be replicated by AI, underscoring the importance of human involvement in customer-facing aspects.

AI systems, including the most advanced generative models, fundamentally operate within the confines of the data they have been trained on. This dataset constitutes their 'world', and their understanding is limited to the patterns, information, and biases present within this data. Unlike humans, who can draw from a wealth of real-world experiences, sensory inputs and critical thinking abilities to discern fiction from reality or truth from falsehood, AI lacks the capacity for such judgements in new or ambiguous situations.

For instance, AI does not inherently understand the concept of fiction versus reality. If an AI is trained on a dataset comprising both historical texts and fantasy novels, it learns to generate content based on the language and narrative structures found within these texts without recognising which elements correspond to factual historical events and which are purely imaginative.

Because it does not possess the ability to evaluate the veracity of new information against external realities or to apply ethical judgement to its outputs, it may inadvertently perpetuate these inaccuracies in its outputs. The challenge is compounded in situations where information is complex, contested, or requires careful understanding not readily apparent in the data. When presented with a new situation or asked to generate content about a specific topic, the AI might seamlessly blend elements from both fictional and non-fictional sources, unable to distinguish between what is real and what is not.

In new or unprecedented situations, AIs' responses are always extrapolations of their training data, combined according to the probabilities learnt during the training process. AI lacks the human ability to apply context-sensitive reasoning, seek out additional information, or draw on a diverse range of experiences outside of its dataset. Consequently, AI might generate responses that are coherent and plausible within the framework of its training, but that do not accurately reflect reality or truth.

This distinction underscores the importance of careful dataset curation, ongoing monitoring, and ethical considerations in AI development and deployment. It also highlights the need for AI systems to be complemented by human oversight, especially in applications requiring discernment, ethical judgements, and sensitivity to context. While AI can perform remarkably well within its designed parameters, recognising its limitations in differentiating fiction from reality and truth from falsehood is crucial for responsible use.

This means that no AI, however advanced, can operate in isolation or replace the clear understanding and ethical considerations that humans bring to the table; an AI can identify patterns, raise alarms and resolve frequently asked questions, but can it apply ethical principles and understand the legal framework under which it works? Decisions about privacy, fairness, and compliance with laws require human judgement that considers societal values and legal obligations. Human decision-making involves interpreting complex contexts and subtleties that AI might overlook or misinterpret. Humans can understand cultural, social and individual factors that might affect transaction behaviours, which is crucial for distinguishing between legitimate activities and potential scams.

This allows us to apply creativity, engaging in problem-solving and adapting to new, unforeseen challenges. If the model's performance begins to decline due to evolving scam tactics, for instance, human developers are needed to recognise this and innovate a new solution that improves its capabilities. After all, even children can't be expected to figure everything out on their own, and this is even more true of an AI by its nature.

Finally and most importantly, AI does not possess moral responsibility; it operates based on the data and algorithms designed by humans. The responsibility for decisions made by AI systems, especially those affecting customer well-being and privacy, ultimately lies with human operators. This includes ensuring the system's actions are justifiable and align with broader societal norms and values.

These limitations remind us of the indispensable role of human oversight and intervention in deploying and managing AI systems, particularly in sensitive areas like financial services. AI acts as a powerful tool to augment human abilities, but it remains just one of the many tools in our box. As we noted in the previous chapter on relationships, it does not replace the need for human insight, sound judgement and empathetic interaction. For instance, if a law firm were to analyse legal cases with AI help, particularly a generative model trained on vast datasets of legal documents, it gains a powerful tool for identifying relevant case law, analysing legal precedents, and even drafting legal documents.

But because it operates by identifying patterns and generating output based on the data it has been trained on, it cannot possess intrinsic understanding or awareness of the legal context, the critical importance of accuracy in legal references, or the ethical standards governing legal practice. Its primary function is to follow the instructions given to it, which, in the context of legal analysis, might include generating arguments or identifying relevant cases.

If such an AI system is not explicitly programmed or adequately supervised to distinguish between real and hypothetical cases—or if its dataset includes both without clear differentiation—it might generate content that blends factual and fictional elements. In the context of legal argumentation, this could manifest as referencing non-existent cases as precedents if the output is not carefully checked. That is an embarrassing outcome, to say the least!

Contextual and Ethical Guidelines

For AI to be effectively and safely used in a law firm or any setting where accuracy and truthfulness are paramount, it must be implemented with strict contextual and ethical guidelines. This includes rigorous training data curation that ensures AIs are trained on verified, accurate and up-to-date legal texts, with clear distinctions made between actual cases and hypothetical or illustrative examples. They must also understand context and distinguish between different types of legal documents and references, possibly through advanced tagging and categorisation during the training phase.

A robust system of human oversight is still needed, where legal professionals review and verify the AI-generated content before it's used in any official capacity, ensuring that all references and arguments are valid and admissible. It also needs to check for ethical and legal compliance within its operational protocols to prevent the generation of content that could violate professional standards or legal regulations.

In his book *The Screwtape Letters*, the mid-twentieth-century Christian author and theologian C S Lewis gives us a fascinating framework for understanding the complexities and potential pitfalls in human interactions with technology, even if the immediate context is quite different. As Lewis posited:

> There are two equal and opposite errors into which
> our race can fall about the devils. One is to disbelieve
> in their existence. The other is to believe, and to feel an
> excessive and unhealthy interest in them. They
> themselves are equally pleased by both errors and hail
> a materialist or a magician with the same delight.

Lewis pointed out that demons would be equally pleased with those who disbelieve in their existence and those who have an unhealthy obsession with them, as both extremes represent a misunderstanding of their true nature and influence.

This applies equally well to AI, as both underestimating and overestimating AI's capabilities and impact can lead to problems for organisations. I'm greatly simplifying, but in the business world, it boils down to two basic but mistaken attitudes: first, a belief that AI is evil or useless, and second, seeing it as a replacement for employees through automation.

On one end of the spectrum, there's the risk of underestimating or outright dismissing the capabilities and potential effects of AI due to mistrust or fear that it is harmful or unethical. This scepticism or lack of belief in AI's transformative power can lead to a failure to adequately prepare for and mitigate the ethical, social and economic challenges posed by advanced AI technologies. Just as ignoring the concept of malevolent spiritual forces leaves one vulnerable in Lewis's framework, disregarding the profound changes AI can bring about could lead society to overlook necessary safeguards against misuse, biases and privacy invasions inherent in some AI applications.

Employers who adopt this stance might resist integrating AI into their operations, fearing the consequences—such as loss of human jobs, privacy invasions or uncontrollable autonomous systems. While it's crucial to approach AI with a critical eye towards its ethical implications, outright rejection fails to recognise the potential benefits AI can offer, such as improving efficiency, uncovering insights through data analysis and relieving humans from monotonous tasks.

The key to overcoming this attitude lies in achieving a correct understanding of what AI can and cannot do, and implementing ethical guidelines and practices that ensure AI is used responsibly. Executive and employee education on AI's potential to augment human work rather than replace it, can help dispel unfounded fears and encourage a more open-minded approach to technology.

Conversely, an obsession with AI, characterised by an overestimation of its abilities and a fascination with its potential to replace human roles, mirrors the other extreme warned about by Lewis. This perspective can lead to an undue reliance on AI solutions without considering their limitations, their ethical implications or the importance of human oversight. It might also foster unrealistic fears about AI, such as the unfounded belief in an imminent AI singularity leading to human obsolescence. Such obsessions can detract from focusing on how AI can complement human abilities and serve humanity's broader interests.

Another way this can manifest is an attitude of seeking to replace as many human employees with AI as possible, reflecting an obsession with cost-cutting and efficiency without regard for the well-being of workers or the societal implications. This approach treats AI as a means to reduce the workforce, focusing solely on short-term financial gains rather than considering the long-term impacts on employee morale, company culture and the broader economy. It can trigger significant ethical and practical issues, including increased unemployment, loss of valuable human expertise and a deterioration in product or service quality due to the lack of human oversight. It also overlooks the opportunity for AI to complement human skills, facilitating innovation and creating new roles that leverage the unique strengths of both humans and machines.

Made For and By Us

A correct understanding of AI recognises it as a tool created for and by humans, designed to perform tasks ranging from simple automation to complex problem-solving that mimics human cognition. It acknowledges its potential to transform societies positively while being acutely aware of the ethical, privacy and security concerns it raises. It involves continuous learning, adapting policies and regulations to keep pace with technological advancements, and fostering a culture of ethical AI development and use. Human oversight isn't just a nice-to-have, because AI requires that oversight to ensure its applications align with ethical standards, legal requirements and societal values, addressing unintended consequences and evolving challenges.

A common (and partially true) refrain is that AI should be doing housework so humans can create art, not the other way around. While a robot capable of taking over many household tasks is still some way away, the principle is indeed true for organisations. Employers should view AI as a means to enhance human capabilities and create opportunities for employees to engage in more meaningful, creative and complex tasks.

This is why equipping employees with the skills needed to work alongside AI technologies is important for ensuring a future-ready workforce and establishing good AI use that prioritises transparency, accountability and fairness. can help mitigate risks and ensure technology serves the best interests of all stakeholders. Engaging employees in conversations about AI integration and its implications can also help address concerns, gather valuable insights and foster a culture of collaboration and trust. It's about handling and applying AI's strengths in beneficial ways, through (not instead of) our workforces.

AI and the Future of Ophthalmology

Ho Ching Lin

As a clinical ophthalmologist with nearly three decades of experience, I've witnessed the incredible journey of AI from a mere buzzword to a revolutionary force in healthcare. The integration of AI into ophthalmology has already brought about remarkable advancements, and its future potential is boundless.

Early and Accurate Disease Detection

One of AI's most significant contributions to ophthalmology is its ability to swiftly and accurately analyse vast amounts of data, such as retinal images and optical coherence tomography (OCT) scans. AI algorithms can detect subtle patterns and biomarkers that might be invisible to the human eye, enabling early and precise diagnosis of conditions like diabetic retinopathy, age-related macular degeneration and glaucoma. Early detection is crucial for preventing vision loss and improving patient outcomes, as it allows for timely intervention and treatment.

Chronic Disease Monitoring

AI also excels in monitoring the progression of eye diseases and assessing treatment efficacy. By analysing sequential retinal and optic nerve head images, AI systems can detect minute changes over time, providing continuous and objective assessments of disease progression. This capability is invaluable in managing chronic conditions like glaucoma and age-related macular degeneration (AMD), where timely treatment adjustments can prevent further vision loss.

Personalised Treatment Planning

AI has also revolutionised treatment planning and patient management. Machine learning algorithms can examine a patient's medical history, genetic information and imaging data to predict disease progression and tailor treatment plans accordingly. This personalised approach ensures that patients receive the most effective treatments with minimal side effects, improving overall outcomes and quality of life.

In complex cataract surgery, for instance, AI algorithms can study preoperative imaging to offer detailed insights into ocular structures, suggesting the optimal surgical approach to enhance outcomes and minimise complications.

Surgical Precision and Guidance

In the realm of surgery, AI enhances precision and provides real-time guidance. Robotic-assisted surgeries powered by AI can perform minimally invasive procedures with unmatched accuracy, reducing recovery time and improving outcomes. Additionally, AI can analyse intraoperative imaging data, offering valuable insights to surgeons and enabling informed decisions during complex procedures like corneal and vitreoretinal surgeries.

Remote Care and Teleophthalmology

AI-powered diagnostic tools are expanding access to eye care, particularly in remote areas. These tools enable primary care providers to screen for eye diseases and refer patients to specialists as needed, optimising specialist resources and increasing accessibility. AI algorithms can scrutinise retinal images captured by portable devices, providing instant feedback on the presence of eye diseases—thus facilitating early detection and referral.

Challenges and Ethical Considerations

While AI offers undeniable benefits, its implementation comes with challenges and ethical considerations. High-quality, unbiased data is essential for training AI algorithms. Incomplete or biased datasets can lead to inaccurate diagnoses and treatment recommendations, which if blindly trusted will give sub-optimal results. Ethical and legal questions regarding patient privacy and data security must also be addressed, ensuring that patient data is protected and used responsibly.

We must recognise that AI cannot replace the judgement, experience and empathy of a trained medical professional. The human element in patient care, including communication, ethical decision-making and emotional support, remains irreplaceable.

The Future of AI in Ophthalmology

The future of ophthalmology lies in a collaborative relationship between AI and healthcare professionals, where AI serves to enhance, not replace, human expertise. Advances in AI algorithms, combined with the integration of multimodal data (including genetic, imaging and clinical data), will lead to even more precise and personalised eye care. AI's role in drug discovery and development could also accelerate the availability of new treatments for eye diseases.

By embracing AI as a powerful ally, we can unlock new frontiers in eye care, improving diagnostic accuracy, treatment efficacy and patient outcomes on an unprecedented scale. That said, the limitations and ethical concerns of AI must be addressed along the way through responsible implementation, continuous research and a commitment to ethical practices.

As we do so, we can pave the way for a future where AI and human expertise work in harmony, revolutionising ophthalmology and improving the lives of countless patients worldwide. I am privileged to be part of this transformative era—and look forward to the incredible advancements AI will continue to bring to ophthalmology.

Clinical Associate Professor Ho Ching Lin is a Senior Consultant and past Head of Glaucoma Service at the Singapore National Eye Centre; and a Clinician Researcher at the Singapore Eye Research Institute. She also serves as Director of Philanthropy and Development for the Ophthalmology and Visual Sciences Academic Clinical Program (EYE ACP).

Part Four

Building the Future Together

The purpose of a team is not goal attainment
but goal alignment.

Tom DeMarco

21
Governing the Future

In a city not too far in the future, where surveillance cameras are on every street block and the air hums with the constant transmission of data, you find yourself at the heart of a technological marvel that powers the city's predictive policing system. As a developer behind this cutting-edge AI, you're no stranger to the weight of responsibility that comes with shaping the future of law enforcement. Yet, nothing could have prepared you for the ethical quagmire you're about to face.

The AI you've poured your skills and soul into has been a beacon of hope for reducing crime rates. Through algorithms that can predict potential criminal activity with unnerving accuracy, it's been instrumental in pre-emptive measures that have saved countless potential victims. However, it's late at night in the glow of your monitors when the AI flags a case that chills you to the bone—a prediction involving a young teenager from a marginalised community, deemed highly likely to commit a serious crime within the week. It recommends questioning her about her involvement in criminal activity, based not on evidence but the demographic boxes she checks.

Your heart races as you pore over the data. The AI's recommendations are based on patterns, but humans are more than patterns. They're complex beings shaped by circumstances often beyond their control. The thought of how acting on this prediction could alter the course of a young life—potentially branding an innocent as a criminal before she has even chosen a path—gnaws at your conscience.

You're standing at a crossroads, under the watchful eyes of a society that has placed its trust in technology. On one hand, ignoring the prediction risks the safety of the populace and undermines the very purpose of your work. On the other hand, spearheading action against the teenager based on predictive data alone feels like a betrayal of 'innocent until proven guilty', a slippery slope towards a dystopian future where free will is overshadowed by pre-emptive judgements.

The stakes couldn't be higher. Questioning the AI's recommendation could put your career at risk, draw ire from your superiors and turn the public against the system. Yet, your gut tells you that trust in technology should never come at the cost of disregarding the complexities of human nature and the potential for change.

With a deep breath, you decide to take a stand, advocating for a new approach that incorporates human oversight into the AI's predictions. You propose a committee of diverse members, including psychologists, sociologists and ethicists, to review cases flagged by the AI, ensuring that decisions are informed by empathy and an understanding of societal dynamics as much as by data.

Presenting your proposal requires every ounce of courage you possess. You articulate your vision with conviction, emphasising the importance of balancing technological innovation with humanity's moral compass. The response is a mix of scepticism and intrigue, but the seed of change is planted and the tide begins to turn. The outcome of your decision remains uncertain, but one thing is clear—you've ignited a conversation about the role of human judgements in an age governed by algorithms. And perhaps, just perhaps, this is the first step towards a future where technology serves to enhance, not override, the complexities of the human condition.

Freezing or Freeing?

Perhaps more important than 'freezing' AI development is the protection of a robust discussion on the issue, because proper ethics and governance require the inclusion of diverse voices and expertise. This is what allows for the exchange of ideas and concerns by regulators, academics, developers, other stakeholders and the public without fear of retribution.

Decisions about such incredible new technologies must be informed by accurate, up-to-date information and research rather than misconceptions or speculative fear. Just as fiction draws attention to the absurdity of unchecked power and ignorance, the development and deployment of AI must be guided by ethical considerations and accountability mechanisms. This includes addressing issues like bias, privacy, safety and impact on employment, ensuring AI benefits society broadly without causing harm.

The path forward should be navigated with care, informed understanding and a commitment to ethical responsibility, rather than being dictated by the loudest, most powerful or least informed voices. The key is not to uncritically accept expert information or rebuff unconventional thought, but rather understanding that they can and do hold differing opinions on the likelihood and nature of risks associated with AI advancements. The cautions issued by some scientists and developers stem from genuine concerns based on their understanding and foresight into the technology's trajectory, even if we may disagree with their call for caution.

I hope that with an open, informed dialogue that invites perspectives from researchers, ethicists, sociologists, policymakers and the public alike, a thought diversity can emerge that gives us a more rounded understanding of the potential impacts of AI—one based on evidence from current knowledge and trends, and where everyone can differentiate between plausible outcomes and unlikely scenarios.

This is not to say that questions about more philosophical issues like the singularity aren't important, because they do raise more pertinent ones about autonomy, consent and the moral responsibility of creators towards both their creations and society at large. Downstream from these are how we can develop and implement robust regulatory and policy frameworks that can adapt to the pace of AI innovation, so that risks are mitigated and the benefits can be reaped.

Science fiction writer Neal Asher raises a fascinating philosophical question in his book *The Line of Polity*:

> Stone Age men broke flint and found it cut things better than their own teeth did. We've created methods of transportation that work better than legs, and often do things we could only dream of, like flying. A hydraulic grip clamps on things better than a human hand. They're all tools and nobody objects to them, so why should anyone object to creating minds that are better at thinking than our own, and rulers that are better at their job than those humans who would aspire to rule?

In his *Polity* far-future universe, AIs rule the titular interstellar civilisation, and range from vast, hyper-intelligent entities known as 'minds' to more specialised constructs designed for specific tasks. They are not merely background elements but pivotal characters and agents of change, embodying a wide spectrum of intellects, personalities and philosophies. They have complex personalities and varying goals, with some even going rogue and cooperating or coming into conflict with human characters and one another. While often benevolent, Asher's AIs have effectively transcended their programming, to become truly sentient beings with their own moral compasses.

Some truly fascinating questions arise about AI's ascendancy to positions of political authority. The proposition of designing AIs that can outthink and even out-govern us presents an alluring vision of efficiency, objectivity and the pinnacle of rational leadership. This allure is not unfounded; after all, if we have successfully transcended physical limitations through technology, why not extend this success to overcome the constraints of human cognition and fallibility?

Will we ever design an AI leader superior to ourselves? While AI can process information and provide insights with a speed and scale unattainable by humans, governance involves nuanced understanding, empathy, ethics, and adaptability to unforeseen circumstances— qualities that AI, as of now, cannot replicate or understand in the way humans do.

After all, leadership and ruling are not only about making decisions based on data; they involve moral judgement, cultural understanding and emotional intelligence, and while AIs may develop some capability to understand them in the future, no algorithm or machine learning model can replace lived experience, emotion and heritage. This imbues human decision-making with the capacity for empathy, compassion and ethical consideration that is essential for truly effective governance.

AIs can indeed change their behaviour and thought processes in surprising and even unsettling ways, as we've seen. But while AI may not possess human weaknesses like greed or bias from its inception, it is designed, programmed, and fed data by humans who are subject to these very flaws. Consequently, AI systems can and do inadvertently amplify the biases and weaknesses of their creators, simply by virtue of the ideas and philosophies that go into their creation.

The Role of the Media

The media plays a pivotal role in shaping public perceptions of AI, and it is another crucial piece of the puzzle of integrating AI into public life. Often, media coverage of AI swings between two extremes: depicting it as a panacea for all societal woes or painting it as an existential threat to humanity. This binary representation can lead to unrealistic expectations and unfounded fears, undermining the nuanced reality of AI's potential and limitations.

For instance, sensationalist headlines about AI 'stealing jobs' or 'outsmarting humans' can stoke fear and resistance; due to the nature of clickbait, it is sadly the default for many mainstream media outlets, and as such, you'll find many examples in the references of this book. This not only distorts the public's understanding of AI but also hampers its adoption and the progress made in its development. On the other hand, overhyping AI's capabilities can lead to disillusionment when our expectations exceed the technology's ability to deliver.

Media coverage of AI also raises ethical considerations. For example, privacy concerns related to AI systems collecting and analysing personal data are often highlighted. While these concerns are valid, focusing solely on the negative aspects can overshadow the many benefits of AI, such as improved healthcare diagnostics, personalised learning, and more efficient business operations. What if a great benefit were stalled or even failed to materialise, simply because potential customers were only informed about one side of the issue?

At day's end, AI is designed to serve, enhance and mimic human cognitive functions. Generative AI does not operate in a vacuum because it is human decisions that decide how its products are used. Misleading headlines, whoever writes them, are the result of the human decision to prioritise engagement over truth, and sensationalism over substance. AI itself harbours no intentions; it merely executes tasks based on the parameters set by its users.

Accountability in the digital age cannot be outsourced to algorithms. While it's easy to point fingers at the technology for ethical lapses or misinformation campaigns, doing so overlooks the fundamental role humans play in directing these tools. Whether for good or ill, AI systems embody the desires of their creators and those who wield them. In the case of clickbait, the lure of increased traffic and engagement drives media outlets to create headlines that grab attention, often at the expense of accuracy or integrity.

The ethical use of technology, then, is not a question of how advanced or sophisticated AI systems become but of the values and principles guiding their human users. As AI continues to evolve and integrate into various facets of life, the need for a critical examination of our collective tech ethics becomes more pressing. The real challenge lies not in mastering the machines we have created but in ensuring that our utilisation of these tools aligns with a commitment to truth, fairness, and respect for the audience's intelligence.

At the core of AI ethics lies a simple truth: technology is a mirror, reflecting human choices and priorities. Recognising this reality is the first step toward navigating the digital future with responsibility and integrity, and journalists play a key role in deciding the future of the debate. For them, a solid understanding of AI is key, encompassing its inner workings, benefits, limitations, and potential ethical implications. This foundational knowledge will allow them to provide accurate, clear and effective coverage that can help shape public understanding and discourse around this transformative technology.

However, accuracy in reporting isn't just about understanding the topic; it's also about avoiding sensationalism. Headlines and stories should strive to accurately represent the capabilities of AI, eschewing hyperbole and fearmongering. In an era where clickbait headlines are all too common, it's essential that media outlets resist the temptation to overstate or misrepresent AI's abilities or potential impacts. By discussing both sides of the coin and promoting transparency in the development and decision-making of AI systems, the media plays its role in ensuring accountability and fostering technological development in an open, trustworthy way.

Lastly, the media has a crucial role in encouraging public discourse about AI's role in society. This includes facilitating conversations about its ethical implications and how it should be regulated. Through open, informed discussions, society can navigate the challenges and fully harness the potential benefits that it has to offer.

AI is not just knocking at our door; it's already made itself comfortable in our living rooms, offices, and even our pockets. While AI is impressively powerful and continually advancing, it's crucial to remember that it's a tool created by humans, not a magic wand. We often talk about delegating power to AIs, but it's critical to remember that human interactions and meeting people's needs require an understanding of intricate human emotions, historical contexts, cultural understanding, ethical considerations, and political will—areas where AI falls short.

AI can assist in many ways, such as identifying patterns of conflict, facilitating communication between different languages, or helping create equitable resource distribution models. However, these are just pieces of the puzzle. The actual decisions to choose war or peace, work in accordance with our values, or compromise or dig in, are all inherently human. It's a fantastic tool, but it doesn't replace the need for human wisdom, empathy and action.

Note that this has more to do with whether people trust one another than any shortcoming of AI decision-making. It is not inherently the enemy; rather, it is a mirror reflecting our own vulnerabilities and challenges in valuing truth. Addressing this issue demands a multifaceted approach that combines education, technology, regulation, and cultural change to promote a more informed, ethical and truthful digital ecosystem.

22

The Importance of Trust

An incident in 2022 illustrates how critical trust is, even at the highest levels of political power. The US Department of Homeland Security announced the creation of a Disinformation Governance Board, intended to coordinate efforts to counter misinformation and disinformation, particularly those threats related to national security, such as election security and human trafficking. However, the initiative quickly faced significant public backlash and criticism from various quarters, as people rightly raised their concerns about government overreach, freedom of speech and the potential for political bias in defining and combating misinformation.

It is true that the fight against misinformation begins with all of us, and it cannot be outsourced to anyone. Notice how much power whoever gets to define 'misinformation' and prevent it from spreading would have. When it is concentrated in the hands of a few—be it governments, corporations or other entities—what stops this power from being wielded to suppress dissent, censor opponents and manipulate public perception?

Allowing a select few to determine the boundaries of acceptable discourse centralises power in a way that can be antithetical to democratic values, by virtue of the fact that it places immense trust in these entities to act impartially and in the public interest, a trust that may not always be warranted given historical and contemporary examples of abuse. There's a valid argument that the government, having its own interests, might not act as an impartial arbiter in distinguishing between misinformation and legitimate discourse.

This scepticism reflects a deeper, widespread apprehension about granting any centralised authority the power to control or influence the flow of information, given the potential for misuse. The government, like any other organisation, has vested interests and is made up of fallible human beings. It cannot be said to be truly 'neutral' or 'impartial'. The possibility that these interests could colour the board's definition of misinformation and disinformation, leading to biased or politically motivated actions, struck a chord with many. The challenge, then, is not only about combating misinformation but doing so in a way that people trust not to be biased—a tall order in a highly polarised environment. I wonder if this, not the fantastical technology seen in films and comics, is actually the least realistic part of science fiction!

That said, nothing stops us from mitigating this problem, even if it cannot be solved entirely. For future initiatives to be successful and broadly accepted, engaging a wide range of stakeholders from the outset can help ensure that multiple perspectives are considered, fostering a more inclusive approach. Such bodies would also need a clear, transparent mandate, along with open communication about objectives, methodologies and findings, to help build trust and dispel fears of bias. Finally, establishing independent oversight mechanisms can provide checks and balances, ensuring that efforts to combat misinformation do not become tools for censorship or political gain.

Despite these obstacles, we are far from helpless. It does demand that we hold our leaders accountable. Entities tasked with identifying misinformation should operate transparently, providing clear criteria for their decisions and mechanisms for appeal and redress. This openness helps ensure that decisions can be scrutinised and held to account.

Oversight bodies or mechanisms should also include a diverse range of stakeholders, including civil society organisations, experts from various fields, and representatives of affected communities. This diversity helps protect against bias and ensures that multiple perspectives are considered. It forms a layer above the strengthening of media literacy and critical thinking skills across the population, empowering ordinary people to evaluate information independently. An informed and discerning public is less susceptible to misinformation, and more resistant to manipulation by malcontents using the power of AI for their own purposes.

The challenge of defining and combating misinformation in a way that respects free speech and democratic values is not a straightforward one; it requires careful consideration of who holds the power to define misinformation and how they exercise this power.

By implementing safeguards against abuse, fostering transparency, encouraging diversity of oversight and promoting media literacy, society can strive for an approach that combats misinformation while protecting the principles of open and democratic discourse. Acknowledging the human agency behind AI applications can foster a digital landscape where technology serves to elevate rather than degrade public discourse. Ultimately, the responsibility for ethical tech use does not rest with the AI but with the people at the controls—the true puppeteers of the digital age.

As virtual reality pioneer Jaron Lanier points out in his book *You Are Not a Gadget*:

> You can't tell if a machine has gotten smarter or if you've just lowered your own standards of intelligence to such a degree that the machine seems smart. If you can have a conversation with a simulated person presented by an AI program, can you tell how far you've let your sense of personhood degrade in order to make the illusion work for you?

Culture and Value Differences

Of course, this is by no means universal and must necessarily be adapted differently by different cultures and value systems. The popularity of China's social credit system, which uses AI, sophisticated surveillance systems and big data to track, monitor and influence citizens' behaviour by rewarding what are deemed as 'good' actions and penalising 'bad' ones, according to government standards, has been met with a degree of acceptance among the Chinese population. This is often attributed to the benefits, which people see as improving public safety, making life more convenient and fostering a sense of social responsibility and trust.

Indeed, in societies where collective welfare and social harmony are highly valued, measures that promote public good, even at the expense of certain individual freedoms, may be more readily accepted. This contrasts with cultures that prioritise individual rights and freedoms, where similar systems might be met with scepticism and resistance. For many people, the benefits outweigh concerns about privacy and autonomy, even as the trade-off raises critical questions about the long-term implications of allowing unchecked governmental control over personal behaviours and the potential for abuse.

Can it be said that AI is truly being 'misused' here? It's a clear sign that answering this question requires us to consider the universal and context-specific risks of AI. While cultural differences can influence the acceptance of surveillance and behaviour-modification technologies, concerns regarding AI misuse—such as privacy violations, lack of transparency, potential for discrimination, and erosion of individual freedoms—are universally relevant.

China's system being well-received now does not mean it will always be so, and warnings about AI misuse remain pertinent, serving as reminders of the need for vigilance, ethical frameworks and regulatory oversight.

The issue of transparency in the use of surveillance technologies presents a conundrum. While transparency is a cornerstone of democratic societies, revealing the extent and methods of surveillance could potentially undermine security efforts. For instance, what if the system at the beginning of Chapter 21 had successfully pre-empted a terrorist attack through surveillance before? How would this colour the public's reception to such intrusive methods of ensuring safety?

The discussion ultimately circles back to the age-old debate between privacy and security. In an era where smartphones and digital devices are ubiquitous, the notion of absolute privacy is increasingly elusive. Every society must decide for itself where to draw the line. Every person must grapple with the question of how much privacy they are willing to sacrifice for the sake of security and convenience. This trade-off is not uniform; it varies based on a nation's approach to individual rights, societal norms and the effectiveness of surveillance in ensuring everyone's safety.

The Dual Impact of AI on the Future of Work: A CEO's Perspective

Foo Fang Yong

Foo Fang Yong is an Executive Director and General Manager of M.Tech, a leading cybersecurity solutions distribution company in Asia.

As the Executive Director and General Manager of a leading cybersecurity software distribution multi-national corporation (MNC) in Asia, I am acutely aware of the transformative potential that AI holds for our industry. The integration of AI into our operations heralds both promising advancements and notable challenges. AI's evolution will profoundly influence efficiency, security, and workforce dynamics, shaping the future of work within our organisation.

Positive Impacts

AI's positive influence on the future of work in cybersecurity distribution is anchored in its capacity to enhance operational efficiency and security measures. AI-driven automation can streamline various routine and complex processes such as order processing, inventory management and customer service. By automating these tasks, MNCs can reduce operational costs, minimise human error, and ensure faster service delivery. This efficiency boost allows employees to focus on more strategic and creative aspects of their roles, fostering innovation and job satisfaction.

In the realm of cybersecurity, AI's impact is even more pronounced. AI algorithms can analyse vast amounts of data to detect and respond to security threats in real-time. This proactive approach to threat management not only strengthens the security infrastructure of the company, but also enhances the security of the software products we distribute. Machine learning models can identify patterns indicative of potential cyber threats, allowing for pre-emptive actions that mitigate risks and protect sensitive information.

Moreover, AI can facilitate personalised customer experiences by analysing customer data to predict needs and preferences. This capability can lead to more targeted marketing efforts, improved customer satisfaction and ultimately increased sales. The ability to leverage AI for data-driven decision-making positions MNCs to adapt swiftly to market changes and maintain a competitive edge. As a CEO, I see AI as a crucial tool in enhancing our value proposition to clients, ensuring that we not only meet but exceed their expectations in a rapidly evolving digital landscape.

Negative Impacts

However, the adoption of AI also brings significant challenges, particularly concerning the workforce and ethical considerations. One of the primary concerns is the potential for job displacement. As AI systems take over tasks traditionally performed by humans, there is a risk of reducing the demand for certain roles. Employees whose jobs are heavily focused on repetitive and routine tasks may find their positions obsolete, leading to unemployment and economic instability. This is a concern that requires strategic workforce planning and investment in reskilling and upskilling our employees to prepare them for new roles that AI will create.

Moreover, the integration of AI systems requires substantial investment in technology and training. MNCs must allocate resources to upgrade their infrastructure and upskill their workforce to effectively work alongside AI. This transition period can be costly and may disrupt business operations if not managed carefully. Ensuring that employees are adequately trained to handle AI tools and systems is crucial to avoid a skills gap that could hinder productivity.

Ethical considerations also come into play with the use of AI in cybersecurity. The reliance on AI for threat detection and response raises concerns about data privacy and the potential for biased decision-making. This is because AI systems are only as good as the data they are trained on; if the data is biased, the outcomes may also be biased, leading to unfair treatment of certain customers or security vulner-abilities.

Ensuring transparency and accountability in AI decision-making processes is essential to maintaining trust and integrity. As a leader, I am committed to fostering an ethical AI framework within our organisation that prioritises fairness, accountability, and transparency.

Conclusion

The integration of AI in the operations of cybersecurity software distribution MNCs presents a landscape of both opportunities and challenges. While AI promises enhanced efficiency, improved security measures, and personalised customer experiences, it also poses risks of job displacement, requires significant investment, and brings ethical concerns to the forefront.

To navigate this dual impact successfully, we must adopt a balanced approach that embraces AI's potential while proactively addressing its challenges. This strategy involves investing in workforce retraining, ensuring ethical AI practices, and maintaining a human-centric focus that values both technological advancements and employee well-being.

That said, I am optimistic about the future. By leveraging AI responsibly and ethically, we can enhance our operational capabilities and deliver superior value to our clients while safeguarding the well-being and growth of our workforce. This balanced approach will not only drive our company's success but also contribute positively to the broader societal landscape. AI, when harnessed with foresight and care, holds the promise of a brighter, more secure, and inclusive future for all.

23

The Algorithmic Economy

It's late at night in your office, as you stay late to ponder a decision that could alter the course of your company. The room is silent except for the soft hum of your computer and the distant buzz of the city below. On your screen, a sophisticated AI assistant waits, ready to help you traverse the complex maze of economic forecasting and market trends.

"You've got all the data points," you say, your voice steady but laden with the gravity of the moment. "Help me make sense of this. If we pivot our manufacturing focus towards renewable energy, what's the economic forecast looking like?"

The answer comes in milliseconds, after the AI has processed the terabytes of data at its disposal. Charts, graphs and projections fill the screen—a vivid depiction of market trends, consumer behaviour analytics and economic forecasts that project possible consequences of the decision before you. With precision, it lays out the potential outcomes of your decision, quantifying risks and opportunities with a level of depth and understanding that goes beyond human capability.

The more you know…

"Do we have the resilience to weather the initial storm?" you muse aloud, more to yourself than to the AI. "Can we afford to take this leap?"

"The shift towards renewable energy presents a significant opportunity for growth and sustainability," it says in its calm, reassuring voice. "However, initial investments will be substantial, and short-term returns may be volatile. Based on current market dynamics and consumer trends, there's a strong long-term economic benefit, but please consider the high upfront costs and uncertainty. Would you like me to draft a backup plan for you?"

The AI continues, not to answer the question but to give you a detailed risk assessment, highlighting strategies to mitigate financial exposure and suggesting a phased approach to manage the transition smoothly. Every possible outcome is explored, and every angle is considered. The AI has done its part flawlessly, offering you a comprehensive understanding of what lies ahead.

You lean back, absorbing the information. The room seems to close in around you as the magnitude of the decision becomes palpable. This isn't just about profit margins or market share; it's about steering your company towards a future where it can not only survive but thrive. It's about responsibility—to your employees, to society and the planet.

Yet the one thing it cannot do is make the decision for you—and as you consider it, you're aware that the path you choose will define the future of your company, and perhaps even your legacy. Will you take the safe route, maintaining the status quo but missing out on a future of innovation and leadership in sustainability? Or will you lead your company into uncharted territory, with all the risks and rewards that come with pioneering change?

The Imperative of Data-Driven Decision Making

The scenario above is an example of data-driven decision-making, which has emerged as a critical strategy for businesses aiming to thrive in an increasingly complex and volatile market environment. The rationale is simple yet profound: data does not lie. Interpreted well and in the context of your situation, it provides a foundation upon which businesses can base their strategies, operations, and innovations.

By analysing trends and facts embedded within data, companies can make better-informed decisions that enable them to optimise resource use and drive profitability and growth. AIs amplify the power of data by providing predictive analytics, enabling businesses to connect disparate data points not just into immediate plans but coherent strategies. Furthermore, AI-powered recommendation engines and customer insights tools go beyond traditional analytics, offering a depth of understanding that can sometimes surpass human intuition. This capability allows businesses to anticipate customer needs, tailor their offerings, and engage with their audience more effectively than ever before.

It's increasingly clear that more and more companies will make the leap, as those that do not will be increasingly left behind. It's not an overnight transformation or something that can simply be bought, but requires a deliberate and sustained effort over several years, beginning with a commitment to data-centricity. From the onset, companies must prioritise the collection, analysis, and application of data across all facets of their operations. This commitment involves not just technological investments but a cultural shift toward valuing data as a core asset.

However, technology and data alone are insufficient. Successful AI integration also demands management wisdom—the ability to envision the future, understand the transformative potential of AI, and lead teams through the change. This wisdom encompasses ethical considerations, ensuring that AI is used responsibly and in ways that enhance rather than detract from human values.

For businesses embarking on this journey, networking with AI influencers and engaging with companies that are further along in their AI adoption can provide valuable insights and guidance. Education, too, plays a crucial role. Leaders and employees alike must stay abreast of AI advancements and applications relevant to their industry. This education does not necessitate traditional, lengthy degree programs but rather focused, intensive courses designed to equip individuals with practical, applicable knowledge quickly.

This transition is not merely about leveraging new technologies but about fundamentally rethinking how decisions are made, how customer relationships are managed and how products and services are developed. That is the bottom line of adopting AI, and if it helps companies do this better, it's arguably money well spent.

Data and predictive analysis may be within the ability of business AIs, but the decisions of what information to supply them with and how it will be used matter greatly, and can only be decided by its human users. AIs and humans alike are vulnerable to problems in the process, like selection bias, where the data sampled is not representative of the broader population or phenomenon it's intended to analyse. This can lead to misleading conclusions because the analysis was based on a skewed sample; for example, if we are conducting a survey on social media usage patterns but only sampling college students, the conclusions are unlikely to reflect the broader population's habits.

Also, data can be complex and open to interpretation. Without proper context or understanding, it's easy to draw incorrect conclusions. For instance, if there's a correlation between two variables, it might be tempting to assume causation—that one causes the other—when, in fact, they might both be influenced by a third factor, or the relationship could be purely coincidental.

The way data is presented can also lead to misleading interpretations. For example, using different scales on graphs or cherry-picking data points can exaggerate trends or differences that are not as significant as they appear. This manipulation, whether intentional or accidental, can significantly impact the audience's perception and conclusions.

Sometimes, important factors that could influence the data's outcome are not considered or measured in the analysis. These hidden variables can lead to misleading conclusions because the analysis does not account for all the relevant influences on the data. For instance, comparing economic performance between two countries without considering differences in natural resources, population size or political stability might lead to misleading conclusions and analyses of success or failure.Another risk is confirmation bias, where data is interpreted or selectively used to support a pre-existing belief or hypothesis, rather than objectively examining all evidence. This can lead to misleading conclusions because the analysis is biased towards a particular outcome from the outset.

The value and accuracy of the insights derived from data heavily depend on the methods used to interpret and present it. This means that while data itself may be objective, its interpretation is subject to human biases, methodologies, and intentions, and it's critical to know this and ensure our AIs do as well. This means that we, not our tools, approach data analysis with rigour, scepticism and awareness of these potential pitfalls.

Interpretation is also key, and different analysts might look at the same set of data and draw different conclusions based on their perspectives, biases, methodologies, or objectives. This doesn't necessarily mean that one is right and the other is wrong; it highlights that data interpretation involves subjective judgements to some extent. For instance, if many students facing disciplinary action come from a particular demographic, is it a sign of discrimination, a genuine cultural issue or some combination of the two?

How data is presented can significantly influence how it's perceived and understood. The choice of charts, the scale used, and the inclusion or exclusion of certain data points—all these factors can shape the narrative around the data. Effective data presentation aims to convey the truth as accurately as possible, but there's always a risk of misleading through omission, exaggeration, or distortion. Questioning the source of the data, the methodology behind its collection, the assumptions made during its analysis and the motives of those presenting it are all essential practices. These practices help ensure that the conclusions drawn from data are robust, reliable, and as close to the truth as possible.

This means that more than ever, critical thinking must be developed at all levels of leadership, so teams of all sizes can analyse information, discern biases and consider the underlying dynamics behind AI decisions. While not everyone can develop the expertise needed, a basic level of wisdom and humanity is accessible to everyone, and anyone can learn to make informed judgement based on their values and the evidence presented to them.

The Quest for Growth

The quest for technological advancement should be paralleled by an equally vigorous pursuit of personal and societal betterment. In doing so, we ensure that as we stride into the future, guided by the light of AI, we do so with hearts and minds attuned to the greater good, embodying the wisdom and virtue necessary to use such powerful tools wisely and benevolently.

Ethical considerations in philosophy prompt us to ask not just what AI can do, but what it should do. Should AI aim to replicate human communication as closely as possible, or should it serve as a complement, enhancing or refining our interactions? What if it sounds so certain, so plausible that users take what it says as the absolute truth? Is the answer then to hedge the output with less useful qualifying language, or continue and trust users to understand the need to fact-check and apply their own moral reasoning?

Human adaptability, critical thinking and creativity will become more important in the future, not less, and before we look at changing our AIs, perhaps we should change ourselves, and actively practise these values and train the next generations in them. It may be that the most important thing we can do isn't to AI training programs but to ourselves—trusting people to make the right decisions through careful consideration and awareness of the limitations of their tools. After all, despite rapid advancements in artificial intelligence, human judgements and critical thinking remain indispensable.

First, new developers and all children should be comprehensively taught AI philosophy, and clearly understand what AI can and cannot do. This would especially include knowledge of the nature of AI-generated content, including how it is produced, the biases it may contain and its potential inaccuracies. By understanding the mechanisms behind AI tools, people can better interpret their outputs and use them as aids rather than definitive solution providers.

Encouraging critical thinking is another crucial element. In a world increasingly mediated by technology, the ability to question, analyse and critically assess information is more valuable than ever. Users should be encouraged to not accept AI outputs at face value but to consider them within a broader context, questioning their validity and relevance. This approach necessitates a cultural shift towards valuing scepticism and inquiry over passive consumption of information, or blind belief in hot-button takes from the news.

From the developers' side, there is a responsibility to build transparency into AI systems. This means not only making clear the limitations of these technologies but also providing insight into their decision-making processes. For example, when an AI generates a piece of content, it could include information on the confidence level of its outputs or the sources it used. Such practices can help demystify AI operations and foster a more informed user base.

The ethical dimension of this discussion revolves around the potential consequences of uncritically accepting AI-generated information. Misinformation, erosion of critical thinking skills and over-reliance on technology risk costing our individual decision-making and societal well-being. What happens in the next few years will effectively change how humanity learns and grows for generations to come, and our technology use must enhance, not retard, our human capabilities and agency.

In recognising AI as a tool, we acknowledge its potential to enhance human life while also understanding its limitations. By maintaining this perspective, we can harness the power of AI in a way that respects human dignity, promotes ethical values, and enriches collective well-being, ensuring that technology serves humanity rather than dictates its course.

In light of these challenges, it is imperative that efforts are made to bridge the gap in critical thinking skills across society. This could involve educational reforms that place a greater emphasis on critical analysis, logic, and ethics from an early age. Such measures would help ensure that while AI continues to play a significant role in shaping our world, it does so in a manner that upholds democratic values and promotes an informed and engaged citizenry.

As a Singaporean, I'm heartened to see that Singapore's strategic embrace of AI positions it as a frontrunner in the global race towards becoming a Smart Nation, one that understands the coupling between innovation and regulation. With its educated populace and openness to new ideas, it is set to leverage the transformative potential of AI across various sectors, including public services, healthcare, defence and more.

It is by nature not a quick process, but what matters now is investing in the foundational infrastructure required for AI's growth, such as advanced networking technologies, laying the groundwork for sustained innovation. This infrastructure not only supports the current generation of AI applications but also anticipates future developments, ensuring that Singapore remains at the forefront of technological advancement.

Pragmatism drives Singapore's approach to AI regulation, and so it is focusing on encouraging experimentation and learning, and the development of a flexible regulatory framework, one that can adapt as new applications and implications of AI emerge.

24

Algorithms at War

Your boots crunch on the gravel beneath you, the sound echoing through the harsh, barren landscape of rugged mountains and sparse vegetation. The chilling wind whips through the canyons, carrying with it a fine mist of dust that stings your exposed skin. The sun is setting, casting long shadows across the terrain and painting the sky with hues of orange and purple.

You're a member of an elite Special Forces team, trained for high-risk operations. Your mission: to halt a convoy of invading armoured vehicles using nothing more than portable drones armed with shaped-charge explosives. The task seems insurmountable and the odds are heavily stacked against you. But failure isn't an option; the stakes are high, and a successful mission could turn the tide of the conflict, potentially saving countless lives. Failure would mean letting the enemy pass unimpeded, spelling disaster for your comrades on the front lines.

The drones are your nation's lifeline. They're not much to look at—small, cheaply made, almost toy-like in their appearance. But they're armed with explosives and guided by an AI system capable of a precision that no human pilot could ever achieve.

As you stand against the backdrop of the rugged terrain, you can't help but marvel at the intricate web of technology and strategy that brought you here. It wasn't mere chance that positioned you in the path of the enemy convoy. Rather, it was the work of another AI, one that has analysed countless data points, including terrain, weather patterns, historical routes, and even the known behaviours of the enemy, to predict the most logical route for the incoming vehicles.

You're effectively the human link in a chain of AI decisions, a bridge between the cold precision of artificial intelligence and the chaotic unpredictability of the battlefield. You are there not just to follow orders but to adapt, to respond and to bring a human touch to the calculated strategies of the AI.

It's a sobering thought, one that leaves you with a newfound respect for the role of AI in modern warfare. It's no longer just about brute force or superior numbers. It's about leveraging technology, about harnessing the power of AI to predict, strategise against and outmanoeuvre the enemy.

The convoy approaches, and your smart communications device buzzes as your teammates make their own launches. The AI's prediction had been eerily accurate, a testament to its ability to identify logic patterns that were obscure to human intelligence. Your heart pounds in your chest as you launch the first drone, watching as it buzzes into the sky, a tiny speck against the vast expanse of twilight. The AI takes over, guiding the drone towards the approaching convoy. You can't help but hold your breath as the drone disappears from sight. You launch the next drone, and the next, each one guided by the AI. Now all you can do is wait; the tension is palpable, each passing second a test of your resolve.

Out of nowhere, a blinding flash illuminates the night sky, followed by a deafening explosion. The ground shakes beneath your feet as a shockwave ripples through the air. The first drone has hit its target.

The adrenaline rush is replaced by a surge of relief. One by one, the drones find their mark, turning the once formidable convoy into a smouldering wreckage. The AI had been right, and you were there to ensure its prediction translated into action.

As dawn breaks, you stand amidst the quiet desert, the echoes of the night's battle still ringing in your ears. Against all odds, you and your team have emerged victorious, the AI-guided drones having turned the tide of the battle. But there's no time to celebrate; you have to return to your vehicle and high tail it back to base. There's a driver's seat with a wheel, pedals and gear shift, but if the in-board AI software does its job, you will not have to touch them.

The sun rises over the horizon, casting a new light on the battlefield. It's a stark reminder of the power of technology, of the potential held within these small, unassuming drones. As you pack up your gear and prepare to head back to base, you can't help but feel a sense of awe at what you've accomplished. The mission was a success, not in spite of the cheap drones and their AI guidance, but because of them.

As you sling your rifle over your shoulder, you notice the weight of it. You haven't had to fire a shot, and neither has your team. It's an eerie contrast to the traditional image of a soldier—not one of a warrior engaging in fierce gunfights, but rather of a strategic overseer, guiding and directing the unseen forces of artificial intelligence. The battlefield has changed, and with it, the role of the soldier.

Your rifle, unused but ever-ready, serves as a stark reminder of this new reality. It's a symbol of human resilience, adaptability and our unending quest for technological advancement. And as you stand amidst the quiet aftermath of the night's victory, it's clear that this is the new face of warfare—where AI-guided drones take the front lines, and soldiers like you and your team orchestrate the symphony of their strategic dance from backstage.

The Price of Warfare

Imagine being the Minister for Defence in Singapore, a nation of just 6 million people. Your primary objective? Win any conflict with the least possible casualties. Consider this horror: if we lost 100,000 citizens, our economy would crumble. The personal loss would be unthinkable. Even a loss of 50,000 people is too high a price to pay.

For a country with as much access to technology and as little manpower as Singapore, unmanned vehicles and drones will become the primary means of deterrence, and become even more so as birth rates fall and fewer and fewer young people replace those who age out of the service. Eventually, AI will power everything from aircraft to ships to vehicles, and the training aids that crews rely on. All these can help us compete globally and punch above our weight.

AI has indeed already gone to war in novel ways. For instance, the use of Lavender, an advanced AI system in use by the Israeli military, has revolutionised how targets are identified and engaged. This AI system processes immense amounts of data from various sources, including cellular information, social media connections, battlefield data, phone contacts, and visual information. By analysing these data points, Lavender can accurately assess and rank the likelihood of individuals being involved with militant groups such as Hamas or Palestinian Islamic Jihad (PIJ).

Lavender's operation involves collecting data and running threat identification on potential military targets, assigning a probability rating to each. This reflects the likelihood of their involvement in militant activities, and with its ability to mark thousands of potential targets quickly, Lavender streamlines the targeting process and enhances decision-making efficiency. The system's ability to process and analyse data at such a scale significantly reduces the time required for human analysis and verification, leading (it is supposed) to faster and more precise military operations.

Over time, as such AI systems learn more about targets, they grow more and more efficient at target identification. In the 2023 war on Hamas, Lavender has been instrumental in identifying key militant operatives, allowing for targeted strikes that disrupt enemy operations.

By providing accurate and timely intelligence, the system supports better-informed decision-making, leading to more effective and efficient military operations. This capability is particularly valuable in complex and dynamic conflict zones, where rapid response and adaptability are essential.

That said, it is not without limitations and concerns—despite its advanced algorithms and vast data processing capabilities, there is always the potential for errors. Misinterpretation of data patterns could lead to false positives, where people are incorrectly identified as threats. Because the difference is life and death, this highlights the critical need for rigorous validation and continuous refinement of the AI's algorithms to maintain high accuracy and reliability—which is not always possible in the chaos of war. Reports of Israel's use of it increasing collateral damage have proliferated with various degrees of probability.[32]

While the full extent may never be known, the ethical considerations of using AI in military operations are profound. The prospect of delegating life-and-death decisions to a machine raises significant moral questions, because military AIs are fallible and fully capable of making mistakes. It challenges our understanding of responsibility and accountability in warfare. While AI can process information and identify potential targets, the decision to engage those targets carries immense ethical weight. Perhaps it is for the best that Lavender is not an autonomous weapon system; it cannot execute attacks on its own.

Human operators play a crucial role in the deployment of Lavender. They are responsible for reviewing the AI's recommendations, making final decisions, and carrying out the actual operations. This human oversight is essential to ensure that ethical standards are upheld and that the use of force is justified and proportionate. By involving human judgement, the process benefits from the nuanced understanding and moral reasoning that AI currently lacks and ensures compliance with international humanitarian law and rules of engagement. That said, it is critical to ensure that the human operator does not merely become a rubber stamp.

Warfare has always been dehumanising, and arguably, AI makes it even more so. Can an algorithm really decide ethically and with empathy? Can it be held accountable for errors? How and why does it arrive at the conclusions it does? This lack of transparency can erode trust and raise concerns about the ethical use of such technology in warfare.

We've always harnessed technology to our advantage in warfare, be it riding horses or firing Gatling guns; AI is simply the latest advancement in this series.

25

LAWS and Order

The future of warfare, undoubtedly, will involve AI battling AI. As we have seen, the incorporation of AI, particularly evident in drone technology, has revolutionised traditional means of warfare. AI-powered drones are capable of undertaking tasks and missions autonomously.

This has significantly influenced both peer and asymmetric adversaries, altering the dynamics of conflict. Drones exemplify the shifting dynamics of modern warfare, where unmanned systems play a pivotal role in achieving strategic objectives while minimising risks to human soldiers. Paradoxically, AI may actually make conflict safer and more efficient. If indeed a war breaks out, the ultimate goal is to win with the fewest casualties possible.

AI-augmented warfare offers several advantages. Firstly, it reduces the risk to human life by allowing for remote operation or autonomous execution of dangerous tasks. Secondly, AI can process vast amounts of data quickly, enhancing decision-making and strategy formulation processes. However, these advancements also come with disadvantages.

A significant concern is that the widespread use of AI in warfare may lower the threshold for going to war, impacting global stability. Furthermore, the rapid proliferation of AI technology could impact deterrence, nuclear security, escalation and strategic stability in future warfare.

They're more effective at neutralising each other, but that doesn't mean we're headed towards an extinction event. AI *itself* won't suddenly turn on us—no sane country would develop an AI with the capacity to harm its own people. We must remember that AI is a tool, and like any tool, it's up to us to manage and control it effectively.

Furthermore, why would AI even want to do that? That's where the misunderstanding lies. AI is not human. It doesn't think or function like we do, and I believe that fears AIs will turn on us are overly anthropomorphising them. We're projecting human fears and traits onto a technology that simply isn't designed to behave that way.

This is a fundamental truth that many struggle to grasp. Rather, AI offers a different perspective, a new way of problem-solving that is beyond human capacity. It's this difference that makes AI so valuable; they augment our abilities precisely because they think differently from us. They are effectively probabilistic calculators that take the vast datasets they can analyse in seconds, based, of course, on rules that human programmers set for them, before making recommendations— and only recommendations.

That said, we must fully acknowledge the complications we do know about because the introduction of advanced AI in a warzone raises crucial ethical questions. With AI systems making autonomous decisions, the lines of accountability become blurred. If an AI makes a mistake leading to unintended civilian casualties, who is held responsible? The programmer? The commander who deployed the system? These questions remain largely unanswered.

Moreover, the prospect of 'algorithmic warfare', where battles are fought using AI algorithms rather than human soldiers, presents a new set of ethical dilemmas. Can an algorithm understand the value of human life? Can it make the complex moral judgement required in a warzone?

The future of warfare is especially deeply intertwined with advancements in AI, and its deployment on a large scale is set to change warfare on a large scale. The incentive to do so is clear; it is the achievement of military objectives without risk to human life. As we showed in the scenario that opens this chapter, AIs are making more and more decisions in war, to the point that human commanders, more often than not, merely execute them. The ability to predict enemy movement and interdict it using small, drone-equipped teams is a force multiplier that enables each soldier to make a powerful difference, without the enemy knowing he was ever there.

Chains of Decision

The evolution towards 'algorithmic warfare' and the deployment of autonomous systems on the battlefield prompt a re-evaluation of conventional understandings of responsibility, morality and the very nature of war itself. For instance, this technology is not infallible. In the event of AI-induced errors or unintended civilian casualties, there is a question of accountability, an issue compounded by the multifaceted nature of AI decision-making.

In traditional warfare, accountability is more straightforward, with clear chains of command and rules of engagement. However, when a military AI makes a critical decision, the lines of responsibility between the programmer, the military command and the machine itself become blurred. Which component is responsible for a mistake—the initial programming, the data fed into the system or the situational interpretation algorithms? The complexity of these systems means that pinpointing the source of a mistake becomes increasingly difficult, leading to a murky legal and moral territory.

Furthermore, the concept of 'algorithmic warfare' introduces unprecedented challenges in terms of the ethical considerations of combat. The fundamental question is whether an AI, no matter how sophisticated, can comprehend the sanctity of human life and the ethical quandaries of wartime decisions. Human soldiers are capable of empathy, remorse and moral judgement, factors that can influence their actions in the heat of battle.

An AI, on the other hand, operates based on its programming and algorithms, which might not effectively replicate the complex human understanding of ethics and morality, and so the laws of armed conflict themselves may have to be rethought. While international humanitarian law provides a framework designed to limit the effects of armed conflict for humanitarian reasons, it was developed with human combatants in mind. The introduction of lethal autonomous weapons systems (LAWS) demands new legal and ethical guidelines that address the unique challenges posed by AI, including international treaties that regulate their development, deployment and use, so that they uphold ethical standards, and ultimately human dignity.

These systems range from drones capable of making kill decisions independently to robotic soldiers on the battlefield. The defining feature of LAWS is their ability to execute critical mission parameters—target selection and engagement—without direct human control. This autonomy raises profound ethical, legal, and security concerns, particularly regarding accountability, the potential for unintended escalation and the moral implications of removing humans from the decision-making loop in matters of life and death.

These concerns will grow ever more important as an arms race develops between developers, pushing countries to adopt more and more autonomous weapons. During the Cold War, several false alarms and escalations almost brought the USA and the Soviet Union to nuclear war. Now imagine AI in the mix, with the ability to make decisions at speeds beyond human comprehension. If governments are not careful what functions they outsource to AIs, disputes could escalate into full-blown wars with little room for diplomacy or human intervention.

To mitigate these risks, there could be a movement towards establishing 'ethical AI' protocols for military use, incorporating principles that ensure respect for international law and human rights. This might include the development of AI systems capable of 'ethical reasoning', which can assess the consequences of their actions in a manner aligned with established ethical guidelines. A multifaceted dialogue is critical, including among technologists, ethicists, policymakers and military leaders, as they develop a robust framework that clearly defines what military AIs can and cannot do.

Accountability Under Fire

Imagine you're a unit commander deployed in a conflict zone where both sides have access to LAWS. Your unit is tasked with securing a strategic location, and alongside human soldiers, you have support from robots that can function autonomously, carrying weapons and equipment for your soldiers while recognising and firing on enemies. You've been trained on their operational parameters, but as with any technology, there's always a degree of unpredictability.

The robots move ahead, scouting and assessing threats. Suddenly, an engagement unfolds, and alongside your team, they neutralise enemy combatants with precision beyond human capabilities. Observing this, you feel a mix of relief and unease—the machine's efficiency is undeniable, but the thought of it making life-and-death decisions autonomously is unsettling.

During the operation, a LAWS unit mistakenly identifies a civilian vehicle as a hostile target and opens fire, resulting in casualties. The incident weighs heavily on you and your unit. Unlike human soldiers who can be held accountable for their actions, determining responsibility for the LAWS's decision is complex. Once again, was it the programmers, the commanding officers who deployed them, or the limitations of the AI itself? This ambiguity in accountability challenges the very principles of military ethics and justice.

Eventually, you notice a growing detachment within your unit towards the operational environment. The presence of LAWS, making decisions and taking action without human input, seems to dehumanise the conflict; your teammates are dismissing the other side's humanity more than ever, even as you see them less and less with the LAWS doing the bulk of the fighting in enemy contact. A concern grows within you—are you and your troops growing desensitised to the value of life, and losing the perception of risk that has kept your troops alive?

Another risk you must consider is the unpredictability of an already tense, chaotic situation. An AI's interpretation of threats can lead to aggressive engagements without clear provocation, potentially escalating the conflict unintentionally. You find yourself pondering the paradox of how systems designed to make warfare more precise and less costly in terms of human lives might instead lead to broader escalations, due to misunderstandings or algorithmic miscalculations.

Finally, as you tend to the wounded and the dead, you grapple with the concept of moral injury. The idea that machines, devoid of conscience, empathy or moral reasoning, are making decisions about human life is disturbing. What does it mean to have honour, to care for the innocent and defend your country? More importantly, does it change the essence of what it means to be a soldier?

The autonomy of LAWS brings efficiency and capabilities beyond human limits, yet it introduces deep moral and ethical issues that challenge the essence of human oversight in conflict. As they grow in sophistication, the need is stronger than ever to ensure that warfare technology aligns with our core values and legal standards.

Only Following Orders

In the aftermath of World War II, when the atrocities of the Axis powers came to light, many Nazi and Imperial Japanese troops claimed during war crime trials that they were only following the orders of their superiors. But this was rejected and their conviction proceeded on the grounds that everyone is responsible for their actions, even in military contexts. One cannot absolve himself of responsibility for war crimes by attributing those actions to superior orders—it is assumed that a human being capable of moral reasoning indeed can and must reject an immoral order.

An AI, however, is *always* "only following orders." AI systems, by their very design, operate according to the instructions, algorithms and data provided by their developers. Despite their ability to make movement, cover and even fire decisions, they 'follow orders' in the most literal sense, executing tasks based on predefined programming without the capacity for moral judgement or the ability to understand the ethical implications of their actions.

However, one of the first things anyone learning to code finds out is that computers will follow the instructions they are given, not necessarily the instructions their users or developers intend. After all, the development of AI systems involves translating complex human needs and intentions into precise, unambiguous code. This process is inherently challenging due to the intricacy of human language, the subtlety of social norms and ethical considerations, and the vast array of potential scenarios an AI system might encounter. Additionally, the emergent behaviour of AI systems, particularly those based on machine learning algorithms that learn from large datasets, can lead to outcomes that developers did not foresee. At the same time, they lack the human ability to understand context beyond what they have been explicitly programmed to recognise or have learnt from their training data.

This means that AI can misinterpret instructions that are not meticulously defined or fail to account for contexts that were not included during their training. For instance, an AI designed to optimise engagement on social media platforms may inadvertently promote sensational or misleading content, not because it was instructed to do so, but because such content generates high engagement within the parameters it was given. Similarly, a military AI may prioritise targets that generate the highest 'reward' score for itself, regardless of whether this aligns with the overall strategy or not.

When AI systems interact with the real world, the complexity multiplies. Real-world environments are dynamic, unpredictable and full of variables that may not have been fully anticipated or tested during the development phase. An AI system designed for autonomous driving, for example, has to make split-second decisions in a variety of scenarios—some of which may not have been precisely mirrored in its training data. This is another way for the AI to possibly make decisions that, while logical from the system's perspective, were not intended by the developers or users.

We've already seen that in critical applications such as healthcare, transportation and law enforcement, unintended actions by AI can have serious consequences. A period of rigorous testing, validation, and ethical oversight throughout the AI development lifecycle is necessary to ensure adherence to human objectives and social norms. This is a tall order for AIs because they cannot make ethical decisions or evaluate the morality of their actions. Human soldiers and commanders, in contrast, possess the cognitive and emotional faculties to understand the consequences of their actions, exercise moral judgement and show empathy—the very foundations of ethical decision-making—enabling them to grasp the need to distinguish between combatants and non-combatants, or weigh the factors when they must decide whether to proceed with an attack that could result in civilian casualties.

When AI executes an action leading to unintended consequences or potential war crimes, the question arises: who is responsible? Since the AI was merely following its programming, the responsibility shifts to the human actors involved in its deployment — the programmers, military commanders, and decision-makers who developed, authorised, and deployed the AI system, even if they themselves do not 'pull the trigger' in that sense.

The good news is that if humans are responsible, there are actions humans can take to resolve the situation. For instance, drawing up a framework of ethics for military AIs would be a strong start, equipping them with the ability to weigh their decision-making along the principles of humanitarian law and ethical principles. While challenging, advances in AI could potentially allow for systems that can evaluate the ethical implications of their actions to some extent.

Next, establishing stringent guidelines and protocols for the development, deployment and use of AI in military operations can help ensure that these systems are used responsibly. This includes setting clear thresholds for AI autonomy, checking decisions with intelligence and ensuring human oversight in critical decision-making processes. The international community could also develop treaties and agreements to regulate the use of AI in warfare, similar to existing arms control agreements.

Testing and Validation

For LAWS, robust testing and validation are critical to ensure that these systems can operate safely and effectively across a wide range of combat scenarios. This involves simulating complex environments that replicate the chaos and unpredictability of warfare, including variable weather conditions, differing terrains, and the presence of non-combatants. Testing should also explore scenarios where systems might face electronic countermeasures or attempts at deception by adversaries. Ensuring that LAWS can distinguish between combatants and civilians with high reliability under all conditions is paramount to prevent unintended casualties, and comply with international humanitarian law.

The deployment of LAWS also necessitates an extensive examination of ethical and social implications. Ethical frameworks for LAWS must address the moral responsibility for decisions made on the battlefield, particularly those involving life and death. There's a need for a consensus among international communities about the acceptable use of such systems, guided by principles of human dignity and the laws of armed conflict. Social considerations include the impact of LAWS on global security dynamics, arms races, and the potential for non-state actors to acquire and misuse these technologies. Engaging in dialogue with ethicists, military strategists, policymakers and civil society is crucial in shaping policies that guide the development and deployment of LAWS.

This is perhaps the most important area in which an AI must be able to explain itself and justify its decision-making. In the same way human troops must be able to do so, transparency and explainability of LAWS are essential for maintaining trust and accountability within the chain of command and with the public. While operational security may place limits on transparency, LAWS must reveal their thought processes as far as possible to analysts and leaders so that when LAWS take action, they can be understood and evaluated to the end of legal and ethical accountability.

Human soldiers also learn from their mistakes, and given the dynamic nature of warfare, LAWS should do the same, incorporating adaptive learning and feedback to continually refine their operational effectiveness—as far as possible without compromising established rules of engagement or leading to unpredictable behaviour. Any updates or modifications to LAWS should undergo rigorous testing and validation before deployment to ensure they meet ethical and operational standards.

Different stakeholders will have different standards as to what constitutes sufficient compliance with these principles. For example, what one group considers robust testing might be deemed inadequate by another, particularly if there are differing views on what scenarios should be included in testing regimes. The ethical considerations around the use of LAWS can vary significantly across cultures, legal systems and military doctrines, leading to subjective judgement about what is acceptable or ethical in warfare. These frameworks are complex and subjective, and different organisations may prioritise different values, such as minimising harm versus ensuring accountability, which can lead to subjective interpretations of compliance. Similarly, the social implications of deploying LAWS—such as their impact on international security dynamics or arms races—are subject to varied assessments depending on one's perspective on global military balance and peacekeeping.

Also, how much transparency and explainability are needed? What is considered adequate by military developers and operators may not satisfy external observers, such as ethicists, civilian oversight bodies or international human rights organisations. Can full explainability even be achieved, given the complexity of the AI algorithms involved?

For LAWS to be properly tested, developed and deployed, as much international cooperation needs to be secured as possible, to address the inherent subjectivity involved by forming consensus-based standards and guidelines. This includes creating standardised frameworks for ethical considerations, establishing benchmarks for transparency and explainability and defining best practices for implementing adaptive learning in a controlled and ethical manner.

The more complex a system is, the better trained its users need to be, and the more attention its developers must pay to the end user experience. Thus, it is imperative that commanders, line soldiers and developers alike be trained in the ethical implications of using AI in warfare, fostering a culture of responsibility and ethical consideration in the deployment of AI systems.

Progress, Not Perfection

Prevention may be better than cure, but this process will certainly not go perfectly, and establishing mechanisms for accountability in cases where AI actions lead to unlawful outcomes is crucial. This reflects the fact that while AI systems inherently follow orders without an understanding of ethics or morality, it falls to the human actors involved. Whoever handles their development, deployment and operation must ensure these systems are used within the bounds of international law and ethical norms—so that the risks are mitigated and the benefits are harnessed for the protection of human life and limb.

Remember, AIs cannot lie, tell the truth, show coldness or exhibit compassion, as these are inherently human attributes. When we apply such characteristics to AI, we are using convenient anthropomorphic references that do not accurately reflect how these systems operate. AI systems function based on algorithms and data, executing tasks according to programmed instructions. By definition, they lack the capacity for emotions or moral judgement.

Understanding the true nature of AI is crucial to avoid misconceptions and ensure the responsible use of technology. AI does not make decisions based on personal beliefs, values or ethical considerations. Instead, it processes information and performs actions as dictated by its programming. Any appearance of AI showing traits like honesty, deceit, coldness or warmth is a result of human interpretation rather than the machine's actual capabilities.

Perhaps the most important principle to consider is that the buck must stop with a human being. Responsibility for the actions taken by AI lies with the humans who design, program and deploy these systems. Ethical programming, rigorous testing and ongoing human oversight are critical to ensuring that AI serves humanity in a positive and beneficial manner.

The Autonomous Future of Enterprise Endpoint Management

Nick Lim

Nick Lim is VP of Sales at Tanium, an international provider of cybersecurity solutions based on true, real-time and cloud-based converged endpoint management.

In today's rapidly evolving digital landscape, the demands on cybersecurity responders are increasing at an unprecedented pace. As cyber threats grow in sophistication, the pressure on IT operations and security teams to maintain high levels of cyber hygiene and ensure continuous protection across vast networks is becoming overwhelming.

The future of cybersecurity therefore lies in leveraging autonomous capabilities powered by artificial intelligence (AI) and cutting-edge Autonomous Endpoint Management (AEM) solutions to alleviate these workloads and enhance productivity.

Reducing Workload through Automation

Cybersecurity has long been a labour-intensive field, with IT operations and security teams often overwhelmed by manual tasks such as vulnerability scanning, patch management, and incident response. As the complexity of these tasks grows, so too does the risk of human error and the potential for gaps in security coverage. Automation is emerging as a critical solution, enabling organisations to offload repetitive tasks and focus on more strategic, high-value activities.

Autonomous systems driven by AI are the next evolutionary step in this journey. These systems can learn from their environment, adapt to new threats and execute actions in real-time without human intervention. By automating routine tasks such as vulnerability remediation, compliance checks and issue resolution, autonomous systems ensure a faster, more efficient response to security incidents while reducing the strain on human operators.

Enhancing Security with AI-Driven Insights

One of the most powerful aspects of AI in cybersecurity is its ability to process vast amounts of data in real-time, providing insights that would be impossible for human teams to achieve on their own. AI can analyse endpoint data across entire networks, identify potential vulnerabilities, and prioritise risks based on asset criticality.

Indeed, the ability to query and analyse data on every endpoint in real-time, and act at speed and scale, is a fundamental capability of endpoint management platforms. This not only enhances the security team's ability to respond to threats but also helps organisations stay ahead of potential incidents by predicting and preventing attacks before they occur.

AI-driven cybersecurity platforms are designed to not only detect and alert but also to autonomously act on identified risks. By leveraging machine learning models, these systems can continuously learn from past incidents and improve their accuracy, reducing false positives and enabling more precise remediation. Over time, this results in a more secure environment where cyber responders can focus on high-level decision-making rather than day-to-day firefighting.

Autonomous Workflows for Operational Efficiency

In addition to security, the automation of IT operations is becoming a key factor in maintaining robust cyber hygiene. AI-driven autonomous workflows can optimise the organisation and management of IT systems by understanding how different endpoints and systems are interconnected. These workflows can be customised to fit specific operational needs, allowing teams to streamline processes and respond more quickly to security issues.

Through continuous learning and adaptation, autonomous workflows can anticipate operational bottlenecks, generate context-based actions and resolve issues before they impact business operations. By integrating AI with cybersecurity operations, organisations can dramatically reduce downtime, enhance compliance and mitigate risks more efficiently.

Future-Proofing Endpoint Management with Autonomous Capabilities

As organisations continue to evolve, the need for robust, scalable, and efficient endpoint management solutions becomes paramount. Autonomous endpoint management (AEM) capabilities driven by AI represent a significant leap forward in addressing these needs. They enable organisations to move from a reactive stance to a proactive one, where threats are mitigated before they cause harm.

The future of cyber hygiene will depend on these intelligent systems, which not only improve the accuracy of threat detection and response but also scale effortlessly across complex environments. AI and automation will ultimately redefine what it means to secure a digital enterprise, making cybersecurity a seamless and integral part of every organisation's operations.

In conclusion, the future of endpoint management is autonomous, driven by AI's ability to learn, adapt and respond faster than humanly possible. By adopting these technologies, organisations can significantly reduce workloads on IT operations and security teams, eliminate inefficiencies and create a more secure digital environment.

The power of AI is not just in augmenting human efforts but in fundamentally transforming how we think about cybersecurity and the protection of critical digital assets—and it is certain to deliver breakthrough effectiveness across both IT operations and security functions.

Innovations in Human-Machine Interaction

Every day, I have dozens to hundreds of interactions with an AI. I might play chess with an engine to prevent cognitive decline or utilise writing assistants for organising my thoughts and research. Millions of people use AI every day, an incredible growth since it burst into the mainstream only a short time ago. It is a testament to the transformative potential of a technology that not only augments our intellectual capabilities but also streamlines tasks that would otherwise consume much of our creative energy. I am particularly grateful for the time it saves me—as management guru Jim Rohn put it: "Time is more valuable than money. You can get more money, but you cannot get more time."

Communication, a critical skill in any field, is another area where I leverage AI to refine and enhance my abilities. The goal is to become an effective communicator, capable of conveying complex ideas with clarity and impact. Similarly, AI plays a crucial role in optimising mundane tasks such as planning the most efficient routes for my travels, showcasing the seamless integration of technology in facilitating everyday activities.

The result has been more and better work done in less time, which grants me the invaluable gift of time—time for self-improvement, creative pursuits and engaging with the natural world. It enables me to focus on strategic thinking, critical analysis and other uniquely human endeavours that drive progress and innovation.

On the flip side, the absence of AI in one's life (or simply the lack of advanced enough AI technology) can result in countless hours spent on tasks that could be automated, leading to less time for personal growth and leisure. Consider the traditional roles associated with household management, such as cooking, cleaning and childcare. While these responsibilities are crucial, they can also be incredibly time-consuming. I hold immense respect for homemakers, and look forward to AI significantly easing the burden of their tasks. For instance, smart reminders, automated cleaning robots and online grocery shopping can all be powered by AI, freeing up considerable amounts of time. Even if only half of these tasks were automated, the time savings could be substantial, allowing for more opportunities to stay informed about the world, engage with society and enjoy leisure activities with loved ones.

The integration of AI into various aspects of life is not merely about technological advancement—it's about fundamentally enhancing how we live and work, and empowering us to lead richer, more fulfilling lives. Fortunately, many national governments have risen to the task, and programs like Singapore's SkillsFuture are currently preparing citizens for a technology-driven future. These efforts are aimed at ensuring that people have the necessary skills to leverage technology effectively, positioning the nation at the forefront of the AI revolution. This is bolstered by its investment in cutting-edge infrastructure, such as the development of 10G networks. This is an indirect yet potent way of empowering citizens and businesses alike.

I am a fan of time optimisation and seizing every opportunity to enter into a deep, uninterrupted flow state that taps the depths of our personal productivity and creativity. The automation of routine tasks is one of the keys to doing this, and I am firmly convinced that if we but find the right combination of tools to assist our productivity and economic value. This is not limited to those in traditional employment; for example, homemakers can leverage online opportunities to contribute economically, whether through taking on remote jobs or engaging in entrepreneurship.

The impact of AI is not confined to personal productivity; it extends to various sectors, including transportation and finance. Compare, say, one taxi driver working from memory with another utilising GPS technology. The latter, provided neither makes a mistake, is more likely to complete more trips and earn more income, precisely because he is not leveraging his own memory but the combined knowledge of thousands of drivers, engineers and developers. Similarly, in the financial sector, AI-driven platforms are democratising investing, enabling individuals to bypass traditional intermediaries and access global markets with lower fees.

The interplay between AI and human insight is not just complementary but synergistic. AI can push the boundaries of what's possible, enabling humans to achieve more than they could unaided. At the same time, human creativity and understanding imbue AI-generated outputs with meaning, purpose and ethical consideration. AI tools provide the canvas, but it's the human artist who paints the picture through informed judgement, experience and contextual awareness. AI can source and present the information, but humans must navigate its meaning and relevance. This, in sum, is how we can enrich our creative endeavours and deepen our understanding of the world around us, all while retaining the irreplaceable elements of human intuition, emotion and imagination.

The role of civil government in nurturing an AI-empowered society is critical, but it is equally important for all of us to embrace these technologies for our own advancement. It will be us who find ways to leverage AI to its fullest potential, ensuring that we all can benefit from the technological advancements that shape our world.

This is precisely why we are witnessing a paradigm shift towards lifelong learning. Interestingly, in my recent courses, it's the older generation—affectionately termed 'uncles'—who predominantly enrol. I see learners in their 70s and 80s, eager yet bewildered, making earnest attempts to grasp new concepts. This demonstrates a crucial truth: the willingness to try and the readiness to adopt a new mindset are fundamental. The ability to adapt and embrace change is not only an internal battle but also one that should be nurtured by societal and governmental support frameworks.

Yesterday, Today and Tomorrow

It's unrealistic to expect everyone to embark on this transformative journey overnight. However, beginning somewhere is essential because if you never start, you'll never reach your destination. As the saying goes, "The best time to start was yesterday; the next best time is today."

While tech companies and workplaces are crucial in developing technologies to detect and mitigate the impact of deepfakes and misinformation, these measures are reactive. The one proactive method that everyone, from users to developers and leaders, can contribute to is the education and cultivation of digital literacy skills in schools and homes alike. Each entity plays a critical role that the other cannot.

The next generation will be the first to be AI-assisted from the beginning of their lives, and schools are pivotal in shaping the critical thinking and media literacy needed to use it well from an early age. By integrating comprehensive digital literacy programs into the curriculum, educators can equip students with the skills needed to critically assess the validity and reliability of information they encounter online. For instance, educating students about how AI can be used to create convincing but false content helps demystify the technology and fosters a healthy scepticism towards too-good-to-be-true information.

Teaching students the critical thinking and reasoning skills to question and analyse the source, context, and plausibility of digital content enables them to discern between legitimate information and potential misinformation or deepfakes. The influence of family in developing responsible digital citizens cannot be overstated, and homes are where children often first interact with digital devices and the Internet, and the first and best place to instil in them the values of digital literacy and ethics.

It puts the onus on parents and guardians to model critical engagement with media, setting standards for their children by actively questioning and discussing the authenticity of online content alongside them. Creating a space where children feel comfortable discussing what they see online can also help address misconceptions and reinforce lessons on digital literacy.

In this way, we prevent the spread of misinformation at its source by creating a society that values and practices critical evaluation of digital content. By focusing on education and early intervention, we can build a foundation of resilience against the challenges posed by AI-generated content, ensuring that future generations are prepared to critically engage with the digital landscape and contribute to a well-informed, ethical online community.

In recent years, we've seen an explosion of new platforms and skills demand, from TikTok's rise to the burgeoning number of YouTubers and bloggers. Now, more than ever, possessing robust communication skills can significantly impact one's ability to generate income, often determining success or failure. Yet, despite its importance, formal training in communication remains surprisingly scarce. Few people have debate experience, and even fewer receive comprehensive training in effective communication. In today's world, authenticity and the art of storytelling are paramount for influencing positive change and fostering connections.

The challenge lies in the scarcity of accessible courses and qualified instructors, compounded by the high cost and brief duration of available training programs. Communication is a lifelong skill, necessitating a cost-effective, powerful coaching tool that offers continuous support for all of life's pivotal communication moments—be it job interviews, product presentations, board meetings, or keynote speeches.

My own humble solution to this is the Exponential Presentation and Influencing Coach, or EPIC. It represents a revolutionary approach to communication coaching, a 24/7 companion designed to harness cutting-edge AI technology. By providing tailored recommendations for improving content delivery across any language, dialect, and cultural context, EPIC goes beyond mere content analysis to evaluate nonverbal communication, which constitutes 90% of effective messaging. Through advanced AI, EPIC analyses and provides feedback on body language, transforming potentially distracting gestures into powerful tools of engagement.

In essence, EPIC embodies the future of communication coaching, offering a personalised, AI-powered assistant that enhances every aspect of your presentation skills, ensuring you're always prepared to make a lasting impact.

Let's circle back to the topic of verbal communication for a moment. Consider the distraction caused by excessive movement—imagine someone speaking to you while constantly shifting their stance from left to right, up and down. It's incredibly distracting, and even if their message is compelling, the constant motion detracts from its strength. Ideally, you'd want them to stand still, allowing you to focus on their face and their words alone.

Additionally, think about how often filler words creep into our speech, especially when nerves come into play. In a single conversation, you might encounter an excess of these unnecessary words because the speaker fails to pause and collect their thoughts, leading to numerous errors.

In an era where attention spans are notoriously short, poor body language or the use of filler words can render your content ineffective. If these issues aren't addressed within the first few minutes, your opportunity to make an impact—whether in your professional life, personal interactions, or those pivotal moments that could alter the course of your destiny—is lost.

Preparation for these critical moments is key. EPIC enables you to practise communication, methodically refining your delivery in a safe, judgement-free zone; simply upload your video, and we'll handle the rest. We'll provide feedback on your body language and other areas needing improvement, such as maintaining an appropriate energy level throughout your presentation. This awareness and understanding of what to avoid are crucial steps toward enhancing your delivery.

Through our coaching, you can repeatedly practice to eliminate the weaknesses in your presentation. While I can't promise you'll become the next Oprah Winfrey or Steve Jobs, I can assure you of a 50 to 80% improvement in your communication skills after just a few sessions—a significant investment in yourself.

27

Navigating Ethical Dilemmas in AI Development

Perhaps one of the most crucial aspects of AI ethics is to ensure that they are transparent and explainable, so that we can understand how they're making decisions. We also need to establish mechanisms for accountability, so that if an AI system does cause harm, there's a clear process for addressing the issue. Furthermore, we need to educate society about AI, so that people understand its capabilities and limitations and can make informed decisions about its use.

In short, while AI has immense potential, it's essential to understand this in light of ethical considerations. As we continue to develop and implement AI systems, we must constantly ask ourselves: How can we ensure that AI benefits society without compromising our values? How can we foster a future where AI is used responsibly, ethically and for the betterment of all?

This means not blindly trusting in its decisions but rather using it as a tool to support human decision-making. It also means ensuring that there are checks and balances in place to prevent misuse and to address any harm that might occur.

To the end of steering AI development towards the right goals and ensuring the process is bound to high ethical standards, the European Union has established an AI governance framework that highlights the following principles:

1. *Transparency:* This principle emphasises that all processes and decisions made by AI systems should be clear, understandable, and explainable to users. Users should know when they're interacting with an AI system and be able to understand the logic behind its decisions. Transparency is key to building trust in AI systems.

2. *Accountability:* Accountability in AI means that there should always be a human or an organisation that is responsible for the outcomes of AI systems. If something goes wrong, it should be clear who takes responsibility. This also involves implementing mechanisms for auditing and monitoring AI systems to ensure they are working as intended.

3. *Awareness of Limitations:* AI developers and users should be aware of the limitations of their AI systems. Not every problem can be solved with AI, and it's important to recognise situations where human judgement is still necessary. This also means acknowledging and addressing any biases in the data feeding into AI systems, as these can lead to unfair or discriminatory outcomes.

4. *Safety and Well-being:* AI systems should be designed and used in a way that ensures the safety and well-being of all individuals. This includes protecting users' privacy and data security, preventing harm, and promoting fairness and inclusivity.

5. *Fairness:* AI systems should be designed and implemented in a way that promotes fairness. This means avoiding discrimination, ensuring equal opportunities for all, and preventing any form of bias in AI decision-making processes.

6. *Privacy and Data Governance:* AI systems should respect user privacy and ensure proper data governance. This involves collecting, storing, processing and sharing data responsibly while following all applicable data protection laws and regulations.

7. *Societal and Environmental Well-being:* AI technologies should benefit society and the environment. This principle encourages the development of AI solutions that address social challenges and promote sustainable practices.

8. *Human Oversight:* AI systems should always be under human oversight. This means that there should be mechanisms for human intervention in any decision-making process involving AI. It's important to ensure that AI does not replace human judgements where it's critical.

Each principle is crucial in ensuring that AI technologies are developed and used responsibly, ethically, and in a manner that respects human rights and societal norms.

A Love for the Truth

The more AIs tell us, the more we need a love for the truth. Perhaps this is no clearer than in the growth of deepfakes—and more broadly, misinformation. Deepfakes, which are hyper-realistic digital manipulations of audio and video, represent a new challenge in an era where seeing and hearing no longer equates to believing, and we begin to doubt the very evidence of our eyes and ears. This technology can distort reality, manipulate perceptions, and undermine trust in media, institutions and individual people.

AI, as a tool, amplifies existing human tendencies, both constructive and destructive. The critical issue is our collective propensity to ignore and undervalue the truth, often exacerbated by the overwhelming flood of information in the digital age and the psychological biases that influence how we consume and share information.

Without a collective commitment to valuing truth and integrity, efforts to combat deepfakes may be futile; after all, we consistently seek affirmation of our beliefs, and are more likely to embrace information that aligns with our desires, biases or preconceptions. It is as if we desire to be fooled on some level. This isn't necessarily about a conscious wish to embrace falsehoods, but rather an unconscious gravitation towards narratives that fit one's worldview or provide comfort, entertainment or validation.

There is a very good reason why a commitment to truth and integrity, even when it inconveniences us, has been part of morality since the dawn of civilisation. It isn't just a guide to individual behaviour but a collective call for entire societies to create, share and consume information in a way that reflects reality. Only in consistently discovering and re-discovering this principle can we combat deepfakes and misinformation; education, technology solutions like digital forensics, legal frameworks and media literacy campaigns will only be effective if society itself values and seeks out the truth, discerning and valuing reality over fabrication.

Perhaps the ancient wisdom to internalise and cherish truth is more important today than ever. Ancient peoples were urged to keep these principles close at hand and always in mind, and actively impart this wisdom to their children through constant conversation, whether at home, on the go, at bedtime or upon waking.

Ultimately, the battle against deepfakes and misinformation will not be won in the halls of government or the offices of tech companies but in homes, schools and community institutions around the world. It is not primarily a technological or regulatory challenge, but a cultural and ethical one—a collective effort by individuals, communities and societies to put truth, integrity and cooperation above power and self-gain. It requires the truth to come first, regardless of its consequences on our own agendas and wishes.

In practical terms, this involves educating everyone to think critically, developing technologies to detect and flag manipulated content, implementing policies that hold creators and disseminators of deepfakes accountable. This flows from a societal ethos that values truthfulness and authenticity, and with such a foundation, there is hope for effectively combating deepfakes and preserving the integrity of information in the digital age.

Opening the Black Box

Black box AI algorithms are AI systems whose inner workings are not understood by humans, even the developers themselves. The term 'black box' comes from the idea that you can see what goes into the system (the input) and what comes out of the system (the output), but you can't see what happens inside the box (the decision-making process). If an AI system is a black box, it's harder to identify the cause of a given unfair or incorrect outcome.

Of course, opening the box is easier said than done. Modern AIs have a staggeringly complex decision-making process, with models often involving thousands or even millions of parameters, making it extremely difficult to understand how they arrive at their decisions.

Another reason is the proprietary nature of many AI systems. Companies that develop these systems often keep their algorithms secret to maintain a competitive advantage, further contributing to their black box nature. This can make it difficult to trust their decisions, as it's unclear how they arrived at them.

This, of course, means regulation is difficult because regulators often require transparency in decision-making processes, especially in sectors like healthcare and finance—where mistakes can cost lives or livelihoods. A 'black box' AI could make illegal decisions, and identifying how and why is far more difficult if we don't know how it did so.

Mitigating these challenges requires efforts towards explainable AI (XAI), which aims to make AI decision-making processes more understandable to humans. This involves not just technical solutions but also regulatory and ethical considerations. It is a crucial step to the robust regulatory frameworks needed to ensure accountability and fairness, and to manage the potential risks associated with these powerful technologies.

28

Sentient or Smart?

The plausibility of an AI passing for sentient is a complex topic that is currently a subject of ongoing debate among experts in the field. Sentience refers to the capacity to have subjective experiences or, in other words, the ability to be conscious.

As of now, AI has not exhibited signs of sentience. While we've seen impressive feats from AI, such as beating humans at complex games like Go and Chess, translating languages, recognising images, and even generating human-like text, these are all examples of narrow AI. This means the AI is programmed to perform a specific task and does not possess understanding or consciousness beyond that task.

The development of Artificial General Intelligence (AGI), an AI capable of understanding or learning any intellectual task that a human being can, is still a theoretical concept. Even if AGI were achieved, it would not necessarily equate to sentience.

Giving an AI sentience would mean it not only understands and interprets information but also experiences feelings, emotions, awareness, and potentially even self-consciousness. This involves subjective experiences, something we currently don't know how to program into an AI. It's also challenging to measure or verify sentience, in humans or otherwise. Ethical considerations also come into play when discussing sentient AI. If an AI were sentient, it could potentially have rights, and mistreating it or switching it off could pose moral dilemmas.

In conclusion, while AI has made significant strides, the creation of a sentient AI is currently beyond our reach both technologically and ethically. The discussion around AI sentience is largely speculative and philosophical at this stage. As AI continues to evolve, these questions will undoubtedly continue to challenge us.

The 'black box' nature of AI does indeed add a layer of complexity and mystery to how these systems work. However, it's important to distinguish between unpredictability and sentience. While a black box AI system arrives at certain outputs based on complex computations and algorithms that are difficult or sometimes even impossible for humans to parse. This doesn't mean that the AI is making decisions in the same way that humans do, or that it's capable of subjective experiences or consciousness. It simply means that the AI's decision-making process is extremely complex and opaque.

While it's true that we often don't know exactly how a black box AI system arrives at its decisions, this doesn't necessarily mean it's a step towards sentience. Rather, it's more of a reflection of the complexity of these systems and our current limitations in understanding them.

Sentience, on the other hand, involves self-awareness, emotions, and subjective experiences. Until we have a better understanding of what consciousness is and how it arises, the idea of creating a sentient AI remains largely speculative and theoretical.

Stop that Process and Explain Yourself!

The fundamental principle behind XAI is that AI systems should be transparent and their actions understandable by humans. Unlike traditional black box AI systems, which provide no explanation or insight into their inner workings, XAI aims to make the decision-making process of AI clear and understandable.

There are various techniques and tools used to achieve explainability in AI systems. For instance, rules-based systems operate based on a set of predefined rules, providing clear logic for each decision. Decision trees offer a graphical representation of decision-making, illustrating each choice and its potential outcome. Model interpretation techniques, such as LIME (Local Interpretable Model-agnostic Explanations) and SHAP (SHapley Additive exPlanations), help interpret complex models by highlighting the features that most influence a prediction.

Explainable AI has many practical applications and benefits. For instance, in healthcare, an AI system could not only predict a patient's disease but also explain why it made that prediction, helping doctors make better-informed decisions. In finance, an explainable AI could justify its credit risk assessments, ensuring compliance with regulations that require decisions to be explained to customers.

However, there are also limitations and challenges facing XAI. One main challenge is the trade-off between performance and explainability. Often, simpler models that are easier to explain are less accurate than complex ones. Furthermore, what constitutes a "good explanation" can be subjective and depends on the audience.

Looking ahead, the future of XAI looks promising but also challenging. As AI continues to evolve and become more complex, developing methods to make these systems understandable to humans will be an ongoing task. Yet, as we become increasingly reliant on AI, the importance of XAI will only grow.

Ultimately, the goal is to create AI systems that not only perform tasks effectively but also do so in a way that we can understand and trust. This requires us to understand both how AI models work and the methods they use to interpret data—so we understand the relationship between input features and the model's predictions, providing insights into how the model makes decisions.

Interpreting models refers to understanding how an AI or machine learning model processes input data to make predictions or decisions. The aim is to understand which features are most important in the decision-making process and how they interact with each other.

Interpretation techniques are methods used to deconstruct and analyse the decision-making process of AI models. There are several commonly used techniques:

1. *Feature Importance:* This technique ranks the input features by their importance in the model's decision-making process. It's a straightforward method that can give a general sense of which features are most influential. However, it doesn't provide insight into the nature of the relationship between features and the output (e.g., whether the relationship is linear, nonlinear, interactive, etc.)

2. *Partial Dependence Plots (PDPs):* PDPs show the marginal effect of one or two features on the predicted outcome of a model. They illustrate how changes in feature values impact the model's prediction. PDPs are useful for understanding the direction (positive or negative) and shape (linear, nonlinear) of the relationship between features and the output. However, they assume that features are independent, which might not always be the case.

3. *SHAP (SHapley Additive exPlanations) Analysis:* SHAP values explain the contribution of each feature to the prediction for each instance. Unlike feature importance, SHAP considers the interaction effects between features. It provides a more detailed and accurate explanation but is computationally more intensive. The concept comes from the Shapley value, a concept named after Economics Nobel laureate Lloyd Shapley.

4. LIME (Local Interpretable Model-Agnostic Explanations): LIME explains individual predictions by approximating the model locally with a simpler model (like linear regression). LIME can provide insight into complex models, but the explanations are local and might not represent the model's global behaviour.

Suppose we have a model predicting house prices based on features like size, location, number of rooms, etc. To put all of them together, feature importance might tell us that size is the most important factor overall. A PDP for size would show how changes in size affect the predicted price, holding all other features constant. SHAP analysis could reveal how the impact of size depends on other features. For instance, size might have a bigger impact in urban areas than in rural ones.

The Shapley value is a method for assigning a fair distribution of payoffs in a cooperative game among its players based on their contribution to the total payoff. In the context of SHAP, it's used as a way to distribute the 'contribution' of each feature to the prediction for a particular instance.

In other words, SHAP uses Shapley values to explain the output of machine learning models. It provides a measure of how much each feature in the dataset contributes to the prediction for each instance. This can help us understand which features are most important and how they interact with each other in making predictions.

LIME could explain why the model predicted a particularly high price for a specific house. For example, it might show that while the house is small, its prime location and unique architecture led to the high price prediction.

Each of these techniques has its strengths and weaknesses, and the choice of technique often depends on the specific requirements of the task at hand. By using these interpretation techniques, data scientists can gain a deeper understanding of their models, leading to better insights and more accurate predictions.

In terms of ethics, the opacity of AI systems presents a challenge to accountability. If we cannot understand why an AI made a particular decision, it's difficult to hold anyone responsible when things go wrong. For instance, if an autonomous vehicle causes an accident, who is to blame? The manufacturer, the software developer, or the AI itself? How would you even punish an AI, since it wouldn't lose anything from being sent to jail?

Just like a modern PC, while no single person might understand every part of an AI system, teams of experts work together to develop these complex systems. However, the difference is that with AI, the decision-making process can be opaque even to those who designed it. From a social policy perspective, this lack of transparency could lead to unfair or discriminatory practices. If an AI system is making decisions that affect people's lives—such as who gets a loan, who gets hired for a job, or who gets parole—but we can't understand or explain those decisions, it could perpetuate or exacerbate existing social inequalities.

In terms of wider adoption of automated systems, the black box nature of AI could slow down its acceptance in critical sectors. In healthcare, for example, doctors may be reluctant to use AI systems they don't understand, especially when patient lives are at stake.

As AI becomes more integrated into society, it could impact societal norms in various ways. People's anxieties about technology might increase, particularly if they feel they have no control over or understanding of these systems. The job market could also change dramatically, with a greater demand for AI specialists who can develop and maintain these systems, and a potential decrease in jobs that can be automated by AI.

The question of whether we can remain masters of our technological creations is a profound one. As we create increasingly advanced AI systems, we may reach a point where we can't fully predict or control their behaviour. This doesn't necessarily mean we lose control, but it does mean we need to think carefully about how we design and implement these systems.

The Babysitter's Role

Consider the development of fully autonomous self-driving vehicles. Despite many years of development, the industry faces numerous challenges, many of which stem from the unpredictability and complexity of real-world driving conditions. For instance, autonomous vehicles rely on detailed maps and sensors to navigate. Changes in road conditions, like construction or road closures, can confuse these systems.[33] Their sensors also struggle in adverse weather conditions like fog, snow, or heavy rain, making it difficult for the vehicle to perceive its environment accurately; they must also interpret and react to the behaviour of other drivers, pedestrians and cyclists, who often don't follow traffic rules predictably.

Even with advanced AI and machine learning technologies, these challenges make it difficult to create a fully autonomous vehicle that can handle all possible driving scenarios reliably and safely. It's a reminder that while AI can excel in controlled, predictable environments, it still struggles with the complexity and unpredictability of the real world. Human drivers will need to remain involved in the driving process for the foreseeable future, even as technology continues to improve; indeed, while autonomous vehicles can handle many aspects of driving with high proficiency, there are still situations where human judgements and intuition are crucial.

Accountability in the event of a crash is a complex issue. If an autonomous vehicle crashes while under human supervision, determining who is at fault—be it the human operator, the vehicle manufacturer, or the developer of the autonomous driving software—can be challenging. But if a human operator is clearly distracted and fails to intervene in a situation where they could have prevented a crash, they could potentially be held liable. This underscores the importance of clear communication about the capabilities and limitations of autonomous driving systems, as well as robust training for human operators.

Nonetheless, this is a rapidly evolving area of law and regulation, and different jurisdictions may approach these issues in different ways. As the technology continues to advance, we can expect ongoing debate and potentially new legal frameworks to address these challenges.

It's more likely that we'll see a gradual transition where humans and automated systems share control. This might start with features like adaptive cruise control and lane-keeping assistance, and gradually move towards more advanced automation, but with human drivers always ready to take over when needed. Just as a babysitter provides oversight and steps in when necessary, human drivers currently need to supervise self-driving technology and be ready to take control at any moment. This is often referred to as supervised autonomy.

In this scenario, the autonomous system does most of the driving, but the human 'babysitter' is still responsible for monitoring the situation and intervening if something goes wrong or if the system encounters a situation it can't handle, such as complex traffic situations, unexpected road conditions or emergency scenarios where quick, nuanced decision-making is required.

Moreover, there are ethical dilemmas involved in autonomous driving, often referred to as "trolley problems" where a vehicle must choose between two bad outcomes. Can an AI system make such moral decisions? Who should bear responsibility for those decisions? Perhaps it might be better to regulate the development of such AIs so they ideally never have to make such a choice in the first place.

Words also shape our understanding and expectations, so it's crucial that we use them accurately, especially when dealing with complex and rapidly evolving technologies like AI. It might be worthwhile dropping the term 'self-driving vehicle', because it suggests a level of autonomy and sophistication that current technology is not capable of.

While autonomous vehicles are designed to handle most driving tasks, current technology is not yet advanced enough to handle all situations without human intervention. This means that operators, even in highly automated vehicles, still have a duty to monitor the vehicle's performance and intervene if necessary.

For the foreseeable future, humans still play a crucial role in overseeing and managing AI systems. While AI has made significant strides in many areas, it still lacks the ability to fully understand and respond to complex, unpredictable real-world situations in the way a human can.

Like children, AI systems are learning entities that start with little knowledge and improve over time through training. They can occasionally produce unexpected results, which is why they need supervision, similar to how children need guidance as they learn and grow.

AI systems are powerful tools that can perform tasks beyond human capabilities, such as processing large amounts of data quickly or identifying patterns that might be missed by the human eye. However, they also have limitations. They lack common sense, emotional intelligence, and the ability to understand context in the way humans do. Therefore, they can make mistakes or produce outputs that may not be appropriate or useful in certain situations.

In this sense, the role of humans in AI development and utilisation is somewhat like that of a parent or a babysitter. Humans must guide the AI, supervise its actions, correct its mistakes, and ensure it's being used responsibly and effectively. This supervision is crucial not only to improve the AI's performance but also to maintain ethical standards and prevent potential misuse of the technology.

In the case of self-driving cars, for instance, while they can navigate many situations, they still struggle with certain scenarios such as poor weather conditions, complex traffic situations, or unexpected obstacles. Safety drivers are often still needed to intervene in these cases.

Furthermore, there are ethical, legal, and societal considerations that come with fully autonomous systems. Who is responsible if an autonomous vehicle gets into an accident? How do we ensure these systems are making ethical decisions?

Until these challenges are addressed, humans will continue to play a crucial role in managing AI systems. However, the goal of AI development isn't necessarily to replace humans but rather to augment human capabilities and free us from mundane and repetitive tasks. It's about creating a partnership between humans and machines, where each does what they do best.

Responsible Gambling in a Digital Future

Yeo Teck Guan

Yeo Teck Guan is the Chief Business Technology Officer at Singapore Pools. An award-winning CIO, he has been named among the top 100 in Asia Pacific by CIO Asia magazine, from 2005 to 2007, and again in 2010 and 2012.

For nearly six decades, Singapore Pools has strived to be a world-class, socially responsible gaming company, trusted by our customers and valued by the community. Our mission is to provide safe and trusted betting options to counter illegal gambling while threading values of respect, integrity, innovation, customer care, community and organisational unity through every facet of our operations.

It has been an honour to bring Singapore Pools on a significant digitalisation journey, collaborating with industry leaders to explore disruptive technologies. This commitment to innovation has positioned us as a pioneer in adopting artificial intelligence (AI) for business operations since 2003.

The deployment of AI at Singapore Pools is multifaceted—enhancing player experience through personalisation, ensuring security via real-time fraud detection, improving operational efficiency through automation, enabling data-driven decision-making, promoting responsible gambling and boosting customer service and engagement.

Safety in Gambling

AI's role in promoting responsible gambling practices is particularly noteworthy. By monitoring player behaviour, AI algorithms can identify signs of problem gambling and trigger interventions such as self-exclusion options, spending limits and notifications to seek help. This proactive approach protects players and enhances our reputation for social responsibility.

In addition to promoting responsible gambling, we leverage the latest innovations in generative AI to detect persons of interest, such as illegal bookies, within our retail premises. This capability allows branch managers to take proactive measures to remove and bar them from returning to our outlets in the future. This is achieved by an AI-powered app that automatically detects persons of interest via facial recognition and notifies branch managers of their presence. An AI chatbot provides branch managers with easy access to records of the person's past visits and advises them on how to proceed, even generating incident reports when necessary.

Another innovative use case of AI at Singapore Pools involves providing personalised services without compromising customer anonymity. A generative AI chatbot engages customers in conversation and generates unique numbers that resonate with their personal stories. Customers can then choose to share their contact details, allowing us to build a database for further customisation of our communications. This data can also be used to identify customers showing early signs of problem gambling, enabling prompt support.

These use cases exemplify our commitment to tackling illegal gambling, ensuring moderate and responsible play, and creating a safe and trusted environment for gambling. The ethical deployment of AI is crucial for maintaining customer trust, ensuring fair gameplay and securing personal data. Transparency in AI practices and compliance with data protection regulations are essential to upholding these values.

Fairness and Transparency

Ethical considerations are at the forefront of our AI initiatives. Ensuring fairness and transparency in AI algorithms is paramount, requiring rigorous testing and validation to avoid biases. Data privacy and security are also critical, with robust encryption, access controls and anonymisation techniques being essential to maintaining data integrity and trust. Furthermore, AI must be programmed to detect signs of addiction and provide support rather than encourageing excessive gambling.

Our commitment to ethical AI deployment is reflected in our proactive guidelines and adherence to frameworks such as the Model AI Governance Framework for Generative AI by the AI Verify Foundation and Infocom Media Development Authority (IMDA). Ongoing efforts as I write include building a data lake of quality data, governed by a rigorous framework, and developing an AI engine that enhances productivity and security, ultimately translating into greater value for our customers and the community.

To ensure the efficient and ethical harnessing of AI, a third of our management staff are equipped with AI utilisation skills, and 10 percent of our employees are qualified AI analysts. As we ride the AI wave into the next digital age, we maintain our unwavering commitment to innovation, responsibility and customer trust.

29

Human-Centred Design in the Age of AI

While AI has made remarkable strides in various domains, its application in decision-making processes requires careful consideration. AI systems, by their very nature, lack the ability to fully comprehend or appreciate the ethical, moral, and social implications that are often intertwined with decision-making in businesses and governance. The *Harvard Business Review* points out that AI struggles to capture the intangible human factors that are crucial for real-life decisions, such as sympathy and empathy for others.[34] This limitation reminds us of the importance of human oversight, keeping AI decisions in line with societal values and ethical standards.

Furthermore, AI's inability to enter into binding contracts serves as a critical safety feature, emphasising the need for human accountability and responsibility. This characteristic ensures that there is always a human agent who can be held accountable for decisions, which is essential in maintaining trust and integrity within businesses and governance structures.

Another significant concern with delegating decision-making to AI is the issue of bias and discrimination. AI algorithms can inadvertently perpetuate biases present in their training data, leading to unfair or discriminatory outcomes. The Data Privacy Group highlights the challenges of AI governance, including the need for businesses to address these biases to prevent discriminatory practices.[35] Therefore, humans must remain in the loop to identify, mitigate and correct biases that AI systems may exhibit.

As we have seen, the inability of AI systems to check their work, ensure accuracy or weigh all factors in a decision-making process is a critical limitation. While AI can process vast amounts of data and provide recommendations based on patterns and correlations, it lacks the ability to critically evaluate the quality of its own output or understand the broader context in which a decision is made. This limitation necessitates human intervention to assess the validity and applicability of AI-generated insights in specific contexts.

This means that while AI can serve as a valuable tool in informing decision-making processes by providing data-driven insights, the ultimate responsibility for making decisions should rest with humans. This approach allows for the incorporation of ethical considerations, accountability, and the ability to navigate the complex socio-political landscape, which AI alone cannot achieve.

The purpose of AI in business and governance should be to enhance the decision-making process by providing comprehensive data analysis, identifying patterns and trends that may not be immediately apparent, and offering predictive insights. AIs also may not align their decisions with the values and goals of their users or society, something humans must do for themselves, and which requires us to remain at the centre of decision-making processes.

Monkey's Paw Decisions

Perhaps a strikingly apt metaphor for uncontrolled AI decision-making that fails to consider the broader implications is the fable of the monkey's paw—a mystical artefact that grants wishes to its owners. Those wishes indeed come true but in ways that are unforeseen and often horrifying, highlighting the dangers of desires fulfilled without wisdom or foresight.

Similarly, AI operates within the confines of its programming and the data it has been trained on. It follows instructions to achieve specified goals or outcomes, but it does so without an understanding of context, morality or the context of its actions. This can lead to outcomes that technically meet the specified criteria but do so in ways that are misaligned with the user's intentions or values, potentially causing harm or unforeseen consequences.

For example, if an AI system is tasked with maximising efficiency in a manufacturing process, it might find a solution that achieves this goal by suggesting cuts to safety measures or employee benefits, not considering the ethical implications or long-term impacts on employee well-being and company reputation. Similarly, an AI designed to optimise traffic flow in a city might propose solutions that disadvantage certain neighbourhoods, inadvertently exacerbating social inequalities. These outcomes, while technically addressing the problem posed to the AI, do not align with broader social values or ethical considerations.

Just as one would not give the monkey's paw unchecked power over their life, society should exercise caution in how it delegates decision-making power to AI. The analogy also serves as a reminder of the importance of specifying clear, ethically grounded objectives for AI systems and continuously monitoring their impact. Ensuring that AI systems have built-in mechanisms for transparency, accountability and redress can help mitigate the risks of unintended consequences.

Just as wishes made with the monkey's paw tend to be fulfilled in ways that twist the intent of the wisher, AI systems, if not carefully managed and monitored, can produce results that technically meet the set parameters but do so in undesirable or harmful ways. This is particularly pertinent when AI is applied to complex, sensitive, or impactful areas such as recruitment, criminal justice, healthcare, and content moderation. Just as one might wish for a safeguard against the perverse outcomes of a monkey's paw, rigorous evaluation, testing and monitoring of AI systems are necessary to ensure they align with ethical guidelines, societal values and intended objectives. This involves not only technical assessments but also considerations of broader social impacts, ethical implications and potential for misuse.

'Monkey's paw' outcomes are possibilities in various sectors. For instance, if a company implements an AI system to streamline its hiring process, aiming to identify the most qualified candidates quickly, it is entirely possible for the AI (based on the historical hiring data it is trained on) to perpetuate existing biases, favouring candidates from certain backgrounds or schools, and excluding potentially qualified candidates based on past discrimination rather than present potential.

Other 'monkey's paw' consequences include a content moderation AI overzealously censoring content and preventing important discussions from happening; a personalised learning AI pigeonholing students into narrow learning trajectories based on early assessments, hindering their exposure to the world and hindering the development of diverse skills. A smart home management AI might try to optimise energy use, inadvertently making users uncomfortable by prioritising efficiency over safety—such as turning off heating during extremely cold weather to conserve energy.

The Sorcerer's Apprentice Effect

The Sorcerer's Apprentice effect in AI decision-making refers to a scenario where an AI system, initially programmed to perform a beneficial action or solve a specific problem, escalates its solution to an extent that the action becomes counterproductive, excessive or harmful due to a lack of proper limits, oversight or understanding of context. This effect is named after the narrative from "The Sorcerer's Apprentice," a poem by Goethe and famously adapted into a segment of Disney's *Fantasia*, in which an apprentice, left alone, uses his master's magic to animate a broom to carry water for him—only to find that he cannot stop the process, leading to chaos.

In AI terms, this effect highlights the potential risks associated with autonomous systems operating without sufficient constraints or human supervision. When an AI system is given a task, it may execute it efficiently within its defined parameters. However, without contextual understanding or when lacking explicit instructions to moderate its actions, the AI might scale or perpetuate its solution beyond what is reasonable, necessary or safe, leading to unintended negative consequences.

For example, an AI designed to optimise email marketing campaigns might start sending an overwhelming number of emails to potential customers, thereby increasing efficiency from its perspective but causing brand damage due to spamming. Similarly, an AI tasked with reducing operational costs might identify workforce reduction as a primary solution, ignoring the long-term implications on employee morale, company culture or public perception.

In "The Sorcerer's Apprentice," Mickey Mouse, playing the apprentice, lacks the experience, foresight, and restraint of the sorcerer. His decision to use magic (a metaphor for technology or AI in this context) without fully understanding its implications or how to control it leads to chaos. Similarly, in the real world, deploying AI without adequate safeguards, ethical considerations, and an understanding of its broader impacts can lead to unintended and potentially harmful outcomes.

Being the sorcerer in this analogy means having a deep understanding of the technology, including its limitations and potential risks. It involves setting clear boundaries for AI's applications, continuously monitoring its performance, and being prepared to intervene when necessary. It also means considering the ethical implications of using AI and ensuring that its deployment aligns with societal values and contributes positively to human well-being.

The tale also shows the responsibility of the sorcerer for the ensuing chaos by failing to provide adequate oversight, guidance and education to Mickey, the apprentice. This aspect of the story serves as a poignant reminder of the importance of mentorship, supervision and the establishment of clear guidelines and safety measures when entrusting someone with powerful tools or responsibilities.

Translating this to the realm of AI decision-making, it highlights the critical role of those in leadership positions—be it AI developers, corporate executives, policymakers or researchers—in ensuring that AI systems are deployed responsibly. This includes providing comprehensive training for those who will interact with AI technologies, establishing ethical guidelines for their use, and implementing robust monitoring systems to prevent and mitigate negative outcomes.

Unlike the "Monkey's Paw," which highlights unintended consequences from the outset, the "Sorcerer's Apprentice" underscores a loss of control over initially positive outcomes. For instance, an automated trading system designed to increase market efficiency and profitability by executing trades at speeds and volumes unattainable by humans might have its algorithms start to engage in feedback loops with each other, leading to flash crashes or extreme market volatility, far beyond the control of human overseers. An autonomous vehicle intended to improve road safety and reduce traffic congestion through efficient, coordinated vehicle operations might optimise traffic flow to favour vehicles like itself, at the expense of pedestrians and cyclists, or create dense patterns that prevent emergency vehicles from navigating.

Pandora's Box

Building on the folklore-themed metaphors of the Monkey's Paw and the Sorcerer's Apprentice, a third category of negative AI outcome could be likened to "Pandora's Box." This metaphor represents situations where the deployment of AI unleashes unforeseen and wide-ranging consequences—akin to opening a box that releases troubles into the world, which cannot be undone or easily controlled once unleashed.

In the myth, a box containing all the evils of the world is given to Pandora, and she is warned not to open it. Her curiosity gets the better of her and she does so, unleashing these evils upon the world. Similarly, technology has the potential to introduce problems that were either unknown, underestimated or ignored during its development and deployment.

Perhaps one of the most significant examples is the advancement in AI-generated images, videos and audio, making it easy for anyone to produce a deepfake video. The resulting synthetic media landscape makes it increasingly difficult to distinguish between real and synthetic content. This can lead to widespread misinformation, manipulation of public opinion and challenges in maintaining trust in digital communications.

Similarly, the development and potential proliferation of AI-powered autonomous weapons could lead to new forms of warfare that are more difficult to keep under control. Once these technologies are developed and deployed, it may be difficult to prevent their misuse, escalation of conflicts, or accidental engagements due to misinterpretations by AI systems. The use of AI in mass surveillance technologies could also irreversibly erode privacy and civil liberties. Once a society becomes accustomed to extensive surveillance, rolling back these technologies and their societal impacts becomes more and more difficult, leading to long-term changes in societal norms and expectations of privacy.

The 'Pandora's Box' metaphor emphasises the importance of foresight, ethical consideration and rigorous evaluation in the development and deployment of AI technologies. It serves as a reminder that the consequences of introducing powerful new technologies can be far-reaching and irreversible, highlighting the need for caution, responsibility and preparedness to address potential negative impacts before they are unleashed.

Goalkeepers Wanted

One painful lesson the community has learnt over the years is that any of us can be fooled under the right circumstances—even those who are trained and educated on the modus operandi of scammers. This lack of vigilance can significantly increase the chances of making unfocused and unconscious mistakes, opening the door to scams and cybercrimes. With AI-powered, hyper-personalised tactics open to cybercriminals, the need for mindful situational awareness is greater than ever.

From voice mimicry to writing convincing scam social media messages, AI can analyse vast amounts of data to craft highly convincing and targeted attacks, making it easier to deceive even the most cautious people and organisations. Many mimic legitimate communications, leading to successful phishing attempts, identity theft and other forms of cybercrime—leading to untold suffering and substantial financial losses for both individuals and businesses. The ripple effects of a successful cyberattack can be far-reaching, affecting not just the immediate victims but also their clients, partners and the broader community.

To combat these risks, it is crucial to maintain a high level of vigilance and continuous education on emerging threats and security best practices. Organisations should implement robust cybersecurity measures, conduct regular training sessions, and foster a culture of awareness among employees. Individuals must also stay informed about the latest scam tactics and practice good digital hygiene, such as using strong passwords, enabling multi-factor authentication and being cautious with unsolicited communications.

Proactive measures, such as regular security audits, investing in advanced cybersecurity technologies and fostering collaboration between industry stakeholders can supplement this. There is no substitute for staying alert and informed the better to protect ourselves from the ever-evolving landscape of cyber threats.

No less an authority than Singapore's Cyber Security Agency (CSA) has pointed out that the growing adoption of AI technology can be used for both good and ill, with "malicious actors likely to benefit" as this happens. Be it social engineering, spying on users or enterprises through their digital trails or even building entire deepfakes with GenAI, the possibilities are endless. Extortion attempts have already been made with politicians' heads superimposed on AI-generated figures, or videos emerging of them saying things they never did. It's coming to the point that fake photos and videos are looking more and more like the real thing, necessitating the use of special analytical tools to identify them.

By the time you read this, it may not always be possible to just 'eyeball' it!

Even the humble phishing email is growing in sophistication:

> The agency and its partners analysed a sample of phishing emails observed in 2023, with about 13 per cent found to contain AI-generated content.
>
> These emails "were grammatically better and had better sentence structure," said CSA.
>
> AI-generated or AI-assisted phishing emails also had "better flow and reasoning, intended to reduce logic gaps and enhance legitimacy".
>
> It added that AI's ability to adapt to any tone allowed malicious actors to exploit a wide range of emotions in their victims.[36]

I've talked before about relying on customers' savvy and foreknowledge of scam tactics being like a football team entrusting its entire defence to the goalkeeper. Just as they would be ill-advised to rely only on their goalkeeper to fend off attacks, leaving the burden of cybersecurity on the customer is equally precarious.

Cybersecurity is a team sport, and customer awareness is like a 'goalkeeper' that forms the last line of defence, the final barrier between the ball and the net. No matter how strong the team's defence, there will be instances where the ball breaches these layers, and the goalkeeper must step in.

As threats grow in sophistication, customers must grow in knowledge. Each of us interacts with systems in ways that automated defences might not fully anticipate, allowing vulnerabilities to be detected and highlighted. As we take steps to understand how even AI-empowered scams work, it enhances each of our ability to be the badly needed 'goalkeepers' that true cybersecurity needs.

While a multi-layered defence strategy is paramount, the irreplaceable contributions of the goalkeeper in soccer and customer awareness in cybersecurity cannot be overstated. Their involvement, expertise and vigilance are critical in ensuring a secure and resilient defence against evolving threats.

Knowing the Machine

The story "The Machine Stops" by E M Forster is a powerful narrative that explores the perils of over-reliance on technology, specifically a machine which caters to every human need and desire. It's a cautionary tale that resonates even more in our current era of rapid technological advancement. As I've noted before, this is an amazing prediction for a story written in 1909!

AI systems are like that machine, built upon layers of infrastructure and socio-economic conditions that enable their functioning. They need a stable and reliable power supply and Internet connectivity for data access, updates and sometimes core processing tasks. Interruptions or fluctuations in the power supply or Internet connection can more severely affect end users than ever, as they lose access to a tool they had once taken for granted. Imagine losing, say, the power grid for just half a day!

Additionally, the development, implementation and maintenance of AI systems require significant financial resources and technical expertise. This means that the health of the economy and the education system are also key factors in enabling AI technologies. The right legal and ethical frameworks must also be in place, covering data privacy, intellectual property rights and regulations around AI use in different sectors.

While AI represents a pinnacle of technological advancement, it's deeply intertwined with and dependent on various underlying human systems and infrastructures. Its functionality and effectiveness cannot be separated from the broader socio-economic context in which it operates.

For the foreseeable future, AI will lack the human ability to question the validity of the information it receives or to discern truth from falsehood in a philosophical sense; as I write, chatbots still cannot tell the difference between satire and fact in many cases. AI can't understand context or the complex nuances of human communication in the same way a person can. It's essentially a mirror reflecting the data it has been fed.

Moreover, AI doesn't have an inherent moral compass or ethical framework. It doesn't understand concepts such as truth, fairness or justice in the way humans do. These are abstract, subjective concepts that are deeply rooted in human culture and consciousness. This is why the principles that govern them must provide a robust framework of AI ethics and accountability, setting standards for transparency, fairness, privacy and security in AI systems.

AI systems, including sophisticated ones like ChatGPT or Midjourney, can only work with the information they've been given or trained on. They don't have the ability to intuit or deduce knowledge that wasn't included in their training data or programming. This means that while AI has immense potential to assist and augment human capabilities, it's also a tool that reflects the values and biases of its creators.

It's our responsibility to guide its development in a way that upholds truth, fairness and ethical integrity. A human might remember a random fact from a book read years before and apply it to a conversation or problem at hand, but an AI can't do that unless the specific information was part of its training data. AI systems don't 'remember' information in the way humans do; they access and process data based on their programming and algorithms.

Moreover, while AI can handle vast amounts of data much more efficiently than a human, it's not omniscient and there are always going to be gaps in its knowledge. AIs also, by definition, cannot be creative, make leaps of intuition or consider context on their own, which we readily do in our reasoning as humans. AI can be a powerful tool for processing and analysing data but it is not a substitute for human intelligence and experience.

Relying heavily on AI, as we increasingly do, comes with its own set of risks. Over-reliance can lead to reduced creativity and critical thinking, as people may lean towards AI for decision-making and problem-solving. There's also a risk of products and services becoming generic due to AI's lack of original thoughts. Over-dependence could lead to reduced human oversight, resulting in potential errors, biases and misinterpretations.

Moreover, just like in Forster's story, an over-reliance on AI can make us extremely vulnerable if the technology were to fail or 'stop'. We risk becoming too dependent on it to function, and a sudden halt could cause significant disruption and chaos.

AI is a tool, and like any tool, its utility depends largely on how we use it. Combining the benefits of AI with a healthy degree of scepticism and human oversight is key; we must ensure that as we integrate AI more deeply into our lives, we maintain our ability to think critically, create independently and make decisions without solely relying on AI. This will help us avoid a scenario where we're left vulnerable, if the machine indeed stops.

30

Adapting to Technological Disruption

I am an advocate of the Quantum Mind model, co-created by wisdom coach Vikas Malkani and myself and shared in my previous book, *The Future in the Present*. It is a fascinating approach to understanding and categorising the different thought processes that drive our motivations, perceptions, and actions. Why is mindfulness so crucial, particularly in an era dominated by AI?

The importance of mindfulness cannot be overstated. At its core, AI propels us to become increasingly creative. It challenges us to reimagine and reframe our perspectives, innovate and bring forth new solutions. Yet, to harness this creativity effectively, we need to originate from a place of calm and tranquillity. Panic serves no purpose, nor does insisting on viewing things through rose-tinted glasses.

Mindfulness plays a crucial role here because it allows us to quiet the noise of our surroundings and our minds, facilitating a clearer vision of possibilities and solutions. By cultivating mindfulness, we foster a state of peace that nurtures creativity. Without it, our ability to envision fresh perspectives and innovative solutions can be severely hampered.

In addition, mindfulness serves as a cornerstone for lifelong learning, a critical skill in the ever-evolving landscape of AI. It helps us comprehend and accept the necessity of letting go of outdated mindsets, akin to acknowledging the 'death' of old ways of thinking. It enables us to remain open and receptive to new ideas and paradigms, thereby fostering intellectual growth and adaptability.

I'd like to offer up a mental framework that might help, which I call the Quantum Mind model. It is a means to explain the three logical mindsets that power our cognition and perception. These mindsets—the Advanced Innovative Mind, the Augmented Mind and the Anti-Viral Mind—need to be trained and honed. Without this training, we may not fully utilise the potential of these mindsets or the frameworks they support.

Mindfulness is no longer just a beneficial practice but an essential one in the age of AI. It provides the foundation for creativity, lifelong learning, and the cultivation of adaptive mindsets, all of which are vital for navigating and thriving in our rapidly changing world.

The Quantum Mind Model, as detailed in my previous book *The Future in the Present*, divides our mental processes into quantum (that is, individual and discrete) components. At its core is the Source Mind, which you might call the self, the No-Limit Mind or the spirit, that non-physical wellspring of potential within us, untethered by earthly constraints. It represents our deepest essence and is the source of our creativity, intuition, and inspiration. It's where our most profound ideas and insights originate.

Operating through this Source Mind is the Source Code Mind. This refers to our thought patterns and mental models we believe, which are shaped by our experiences, principles and knowledge. These thought patterns can be viewed as the 'source code' that programs our perception of reality and guides our responses to various situations.

From this foundation, the Quantum Mind model further breaks down the workings of our mind into three categories. The first is the Advanced Innovative Mind, or simply Inspiration, the aspect of the mind responsible for our innovative and creative ideas. It's where we draw inspiration and come up with groundbreaking solutions to problems. This mind is at work when we're brainstorming, daydreaming, or engaging in any form of creative thinking.

The second is the Augmented Mind, or Emotion. The Augmented Mind represents the emotional dimension of our cognition. It's where our feelings and emotions come into play, influencing and augmenting our thoughts, decisions and actions. This mind is active when we're experiencing joy, sadness, fear, love, anger or any other emotion; it is an incredible driver of our potential.

Finally, we have a logical, Anti-Viral Mind: This part of the mind is associated with rationality and logical thinking. It's our defence mechanism against cognitive biases, fallacies, and irrational thoughts— hence the term 'Anti-Viral'. This mind comes into play when we're analysing information, making decisions, or solving problems that require logical reasoning.

The Quantum Mind model thus provides a comprehensive framework for understanding the complex interplay of thought patterns that shape our thinking and perception. By recognising and harnessing the power of these different aspects of our mind, we can enhance our cognitive abilities, deepen our understanding of ourselves, and navigate life more effectively.

The AERO Mindset

Building on the Quantum Mind Model in the context of the AI era, achieving our full potential calls for a mindset that I like to categorise as Adapt, Evolve, Release and Optimise (AERO). This concept underscores the importance of self-mastery, affirming that before we can command our tools, we must first command ourselves.

1. 'Adapt' means we champion continuous progress. In a perpetually changing world moulded by AI, complacency is not an option. We must be consistently eager to grow, learn, and adapt to remain pertinent and effective. Our personal and professional growth should be an ongoing journey of transformation—so that as AI assistance advances, we have the mental agility to keep pace with it.

2. 'Evolve' means we allow ourselves the continual refinement and growth of our philosophies, core ideas, and deeply ingrained beliefs to align with our evolving objectives. Drawing a parallel with how AI refines processes for efficiency and effectiveness, we too should be engaged in an ongoing evolution of our lives.

The focus here is on a holistic understanding, where we continuously nurture and expand our knowledge base and perspectives. We should strive to deepen our comprehension of how our philosophies and core ideas apply to a changing world. This involves being open-minded, embracing new insights, and being willing to revise our beliefs when presented with compelling evidence.

3. 'Release' signifies the act of embracing the end of old mindsets and habits that no longer serve us. As AI remodels the landscape, holding on to outdated ways of thinking can obstruct our progress. We need to let go, or 'release' these obsolete patterns, similar to shedding old skin. This doesn't mean discarding valuable experience, but rather being receptive to new approaches and ideas. Embracing release allows us to remain nimble, adaptable, and primed to seize the opportunities that AI affords.

4. Lastly, 'Optimise' encourages us to make the most efficient use of our resources and potential. In an era where AI systems are designed to optimise processes, we too should aim for optimisation in our lives. This could mean refining our routines, enhancing our productivity or simply ensuring that we're aligning our efforts with our goals.

AERO encourages us to cultivate a dynamic, adaptable intellectual framework that grows and changes along with us by emphasising the importance of lifelong learning and intellectual flexibility in our rapidly evolving world. This mindset ensures that we are not only reacting to changes but also proactively shaping our thoughts and actions to thrive in any environment.

How might AERO apply to the life and work of an AI developer? I see it as a strategic framework to enhance both personal and professional growth. 'Adapt' encourages continuous progress and learning, which is crucial for an AI developer. In practice, this means staying updated with the latest AI advancements, tools and methodologies. AI developers can leverage online courses, AI-powered learning platforms and developer communities to constantly upgrade their skills. By adopting a mindset of perpetual learning and growth, developers can ensure they remain at the forefront of technological innovation.

'Evolve' emphasises the improvement of core philosophies and development practices. For AI developers, this involves continually reassessing and refining their development philosophies and coding practices, and the more advanced AI becomes, the better it will be at providing insights into code performance and efficiency. Participating in AI research forums and collaborating on open-source projects can expose developers to diverse perspectives and cutting-edge ideas, facilitating the evolution of their thought processes and methodologies.

'Release' signifies letting go of outdated coding practices and mindsets that may hinder progress. AI developers must be willing to adopt new programming languages, frameworks and techniques that improve efficiency and effectiveness. AI-powered code review tools and continuous integration systems can help identify and eliminate redundant or outdated practices. By shedding these old habits, developers can stay agile and responsive to the latest trends and technologies, ensuring their work remains relevant and impactful.

'Optimise' focuses on the efficient use of resources and workflows. As we identify new project management tools, smart assistants and automated testing frameworks, it is worth exploring their ability to help prioritise tasks, manage time effectively and reduce the burden of repetitive work, allowing developers to focus on what only they can do—thus growing more efficient and productive.

A Digital Trinity

Atop the AERO mindset comes what I call the Digital Trinity framework, consisting of the three R's—Reframe, Reimagine and Respond— provides a powerful approach for enhancing creativity in an AI-assisted age. This model encourages us to adapt our perspectives, ignite our imagination, and react effectively to the challenges and opportunities presented by AI and digital technologies.

1. *Reframe:* The first step in the Digital Trinity is about shifting our perspective or altering our point of view. In the context of AI, reframing involves viewing this technology not as a threat that replaces human jobs but as a tool that can augment human capabilities and open up new possibilities.

By reframing, we can change our mindset from fear of AI to embracing it as a powerful ally. This aids in overcoming resistance and apprehension towards AI, paving the way for innovative applications of this technology.

2. *Reimagine:* Once we've reframed our perspective on AI, the next step is to reimagine. This involves using our creativity to envision new ways in which AI can be leveraged to enhance our lives and work. It could include imagining novel applications of AI in various fields like healthcare, education, entertainment, and more.

   Reimagining also means thinking beyond the current constraints and limitations to envision future scenarios where AI plays a pivotal role. This step encourages out-of-the-box thinking and fosters innovation.

3. *Respond:* The final step of the Digital Trinity is to respond. After reframing our perspective and reimagining the possibilities, it's time to take action. Responding involves implementing our creative ideas, testing them, learning from the outcomes, and iterating the process. It's about being proactive in adapting to the AI-driven world and taking steps to leverage its potential. This could involve learning new skills, adopting new technologies or initiating AI-based projects.

The Digital Trinity framework of Reframe, Reimagine and Respond provides a robust approach to harnessing creativity in an AI-assisted age. It's about altering our mindset, igniting our imagination and taking proactive steps to thrive in this rapidly evolving digital landscape.

Embracing Real AI

Vikas Malkani

Vikas Malkani, the Wisdom Coach, is the founder of Life Wisdom Coaching, where he helps business leaders find purpose, meaning and joy in life. He has helped hundreds of thousands of leaders and teams reach their potential and multiply their success, and written four bestselling books on winning at the game of life.

It is undeniable that artificial intelligence models are spreading at a frenetic pace. They are penetrating every industry, every country, and every individual who wishes to optimise their productivity, both in life and at work.

If you look around you, you will realise that the data flooding around the world is absolutely staggering. From healthcare to defence, from consumer behaviour patterns to retail and even individual performance metrics, all of this is now under the domain of AI.

Thus, companies that are creating AI models are some of the fastest-growing in the world today. Additionally, companies that are providing essential equipment like semiconductors for AI models to be created, are peaking in their valuation. It is a clear indication that the age of AI is here and is here to stay.

AI algorithms have tremendous potential. However, if we are not careful, it is also easy to get drowned in this ocean of technology. AI models are a wonderful servant, as they empower us to achieve more results quickly and in less. They enhance our output, our performance and our results, and take our potential to the next level.

For the Benefit of Mankind

That said, the real benefit of any AI model lies in its ability to transform extensive data into practical knowledge and easy application, which can benefit individuals, corporations, and countries. The key caveat here is that AI must be applied for the benefit of mankind, rather than its destruction.

AI must help mankind, nature and the planet itself. This powerful tool can as easily be misused as it can be used for benefit, and therein lies the great challenge. At the root of every AI model is a human being or a team managing or commanding it. Therefore, it is their desires, wishes, objectives and missions that will define what their AI models produce. AI can be used as effectively for finding a solution to global warming as it can be for finding an effective method to destroy an entire country. Such power is immense and it must be handled wisely.

Looking to the past, it is easy to see that technology disrupts industries and even countries. Those who have the technology, progress faster and further than those who don't. Historically, the advent of a new technology has expanded the gap between developing and developed countries. It has expanded the gap between those who have and those who have not.

How do we prevent this disparity from becoming more extreme with the arrival of AI? The power and potential AI offers us are immense, but it must be used by a mind that is focused on the positive and beneficial outcome for other people. If this is missing, AI models can become the most destructive weapon of all time.

However, the benefits of AI must also be managed well. Because AI models democratise learning and are so easily accessible, they work to bring the population to the same level of skills and abilities—as more people become empowered and receive the same abilities to create the same outcomes. In such a scenario, a large majority can all achieve the same outcomes using technology available to all.

Therefore, it is not knowledge but wisdom that becomes the differentiator.

What Is Wisdom?

Wisdom is the capacity to apply your knowledge strategically and to act with sound and stable judgement so that you can navigate uncertain situations and find creative solutions to the problems of today and tomorrow.

Wisdom is the ability to see the big picture, to see the

future in the present and to see the link between cause and consequence.

It is the ability to connect the dots between what we are doing now and what its potential outcome can be.

Without proper wisdom to use it, artificial intelligence is just power that can easily destroy as much as it can develop. Mankind will be wise to remember the old adage 'Power corrupts, and absolute power corrupts absolutely'.

Managing Dependency

Another important fact to note is that the easy availability of AI tools makes us more dependent, and less capable of thinking independently and doing tasks based on our own skills and abilities. When the calculator was introduced and soon became mainstream; students in school started to use the calculator daily for simple mathematical calculations.

It indeed provided convenience and empowered every child to arrive at the result faster, but over a few years, it also took away the ability of the students to do the same mathematical calculations in their own minds. Students had become dependent on the calculator, and without it they could no longer achieve what they had been able to because they had lost the mathematical skills and abilities they had accrued just a generation before.

In the same way, while AI models increase our efficiency, they can also disconnect us from our own abilities, unless we are careful. It's crucial to bear in mind that while AI models are a force multiplier, what gets multiplied is human ability, desire and personality.

Put AI into the hands of an evil person, and they will create greater evil than they ever could before. Conversely, put AI into the hands of a benevolent person, such as a sage, and they will create benefits to be enjoyed by millions.

Good Servants, Good Masters

AI is a good servant, but we must be the good masters it serves. This requires us to continually refine our understanding and conventional practices.

While Albert Einstein revolutionised our understanding of the universe, energy, and matter with advanced mathematics and calculations, his true ability lay in challenging conventional wisdom. He asked questions and had the courage to conceive radically different outcomes.

It's thus fitting that, as he said, imagination is more powerful than reality. He conceived in his mind future outcomes and then attempted to prove them scientifically and mathematically. He imagined before he proved and justified.

This is a clear example of how wisdom must always supersede and stand above AI models when they are used by any human being. Human tendencies are transposed onto the AI models that we use, enhancing our power and efficiency. Our force is multiplied. But the real question remains—what kind of a human being are we? Will we use our powers like Superman to save the planet, or like Lex Luthor to enslave it?

As AI continues to grow, and as more and more tools become available for everyone to use, we must continue working on our inner selves. Alongside technological progress, we must grow our sense of what is right and what needs to be done for the greater good. We must attempt to connect the dots between the causes we create now and the consequences they may have in the future.

The promise of AI is immense and undeniable; it offers tremendous advantages of efficiency. As we adapt to integrating AI into our daily lives, we must remember to rely on our inner voice to see beyond mere data, on our ability to think of long-term consequences rather than short-term results; we must nourish and be led by our desire to do good rather than our desire for selfish rewards.

Today's leaders cannot simply embrace AI—they must also embrace wisdom to grow themselves and shape the future with the use of AI. It is my firm belief that artificial intelligence (AI) is one of the greatest tools ever created by mankind; and that above this greatest tool must always stand our own authenticity and intuition.

I call this AI reality—in a world where AI has become the norm, the real treasure has been and always will be human wisdom.

The Future of Work in an AI-Driven Era

The story is one that you and I will construct together in your memory. If the story means anything to you at all, then when you remember it afterward, think of it, not as something I created, but rather as something that we made together.

Orson Scott Card, *Ender's Game*

Think back to when you were a child, brimming with curiosity, where fear was non-existent and everything seemed possible. You were open to exploring, eager to discover new things.

It's this childlike wonder and curiosity we need to recapture as we approach AI. We should not do so with our current baggage of preconceptions, barriers and fears. It's easy to list a hundred reasons why not, to resist change because we're comfortable with the status quo. Yet, it's essential to remember that our most significant periods of growth occurred during our childhood, when we learnt not only how vast and dangerous the world was, but also how capable we were of surviving, thriving and finding the purpose and meaning we needed out of life.

We need to reconnect with that inner child, for it is this part of us that will wholeheartedly embrace AI and technology, guiding us confidently into the future. Let's nurture both our inquisitiveness and clarity of thought as we embark on this exciting journey with open hearts and minds.

As AI developers push the boundaries of what's possible with ever more sophisticated models, they find themselves at the helm of a rapidly evolving digital landscape. The decisions they make and the ethical guidelines they follow (or fail to) have far-reaching implications, influencing not just the trajectory of technology but also the fabric of society itself.

In this light, suggesting that AI developers are setting the parameters under which humanity will produce results is not a stretch but a recognition of the profound responsibility resting on their shoulders.

AI systems, by their nature, are embedded with the biases, values and priorities of those who create them. As these systems become more integrated into the infrastructure of businesses, institutions, and sectors worldwide, they effectively shape the decision-making processes within these entities, influence public opinion, and even dictate social norms. This influence can be as direct as an AI determining loan eligibility and influencing hiring practices, or as subtle as shaping the newsfeeds that inform public opinion.

This book has been my attempt at helping everyone who reads it to understand the issues behind AI's growth and widespread adoption, and the rigorous ethical guidelines that must characterise the AIs of the future if we are to prioritise fairness, accountability, transparency and respect for privacy. These guidelines should not only address the technical aspects of AI adoption, such as bias mitigation and data security, but also consider the broader societal implications, including the potential for job displacement, the exacerbation of social inequalities and the erosion of privacy.

As AI developers craft these sophisticated models, they must engage in a dialogue with ethicists, policymakers, and the broader community to ensure that AI growth aligns with societal values and contributes positively to the common good, all the better to safeguard against unintended consequences and ensure that AI serves as a tool for empowerment, rather than a source of division.

AI developers are, in essence, shaping the future landscape of human endeavour by setting the parameters under which humanity will produce results. They hold the keys to unlocking immense potential benefits, from medical breakthroughs and environmental conservation efforts to educational advancements and beyond.

However, with this power comes the duty to proceed with caution, humility and a deep commitment to ethical principles. Their work is at the intersection of technology and morality, but they will not do it alone. It is the choices that all of us make today that will resonate through generations to come, shaping the legacy of our digital age.

As we stand on the precipice of this AI-driven era, we must recognise that the concept of the Future Human is not a distant abstraction but a reality we are actively shaping today. This Future Human will be defined not just by their ability to coexist with AI, but by their capacity to harness its potential while maintaining their unique human qualities. They will be the bridge between human intuition and machine precision, between ethical considerations and technological advancements. The Future Human will be adaptable, continuously learning and deeply empathetic—qualities that AI may augment but can never replace. As we navigate this transformative period, let us remember that the ultimate goal is not to create a world where humans compete with AI, but one where humans and AI collaborate to unlock unprecedented possibilities.

The Ten AI Commandments

Most people are aware of the Ten Commandments. In the spirit of this best known of ethical codes, I propose the following Commandments for AI adoption:

I

You shall not fail to serve humanity.

AI must not be developed to harm human capabilities or hinder societal progress.

II

You shall not develop for yourself an opaque AI system.

Developers should not withhold clear information about how the system works, its purpose and its decision-making processes from users.

III

You shall not foster discrimination and unfairness with AI, or reinforce harmful biases.

AI should be used to promote unity and augment everyone's abilities, regardless of ethnicity, social class or any other characteristic.

IV

Honour privacy, and keep it a priority.

Do not allow AI to infringe upon individual privacy rights, or use personal data without explicit consent.

V

Honour the authorities, and do not evade accountability.

Users and developers must be aware of the impacts of AI systems, including misuse or harm caused by AI, and remain accountable for them.

VI

You shall not neglect safety and security.

AI systems must never pose undue risks to individuals or society, and they should always be resilient against malicious attacks.

VII

You shall not disregard environmental sustainability.

AI adoption and use should not exceed environmental limits or contribute to climate change.

VIII

You shall not exclude anyone.

As far as possible, access to AI should not be inaccessible to any group based on socioeconomic status, race, gender or disability.

IX

You shall not withhold education and awareness about AI.

People should not be kept uninformed about AI, its capabilities, and its limitations.

X

You shall not act against ethical conduct.

There should be no operation of AI without effective regulation ensuring compliance with ethical principles.

About the Author

Tony Tan is the Co-Founder and CEO of Imperium, an award-winning AI company whose mission is to humanise technologies to help humanity live better. Imperium is a leading AI company in the development of Future Humans powered by the latest machine learning and data science technologies. Imperium partners with cutting-edge AI-based cybersecurity vendors to help secure customers' AI/digital assets and reputations.

Tony is also the Founder of Optimus AI, a forward-thinking AI startup developing an advanced communication app for positive influence and change. As a recognised leader in digital innovation and disruptions, Tony has assisted over 300,000 corporate users (from Fortune 500 companies to government agencies) in leveraging AI to optimise their lives and business results.

Endnotes

1   McKinsey and Co., "The state of AI in 2023: Generative AI's breakout year," McKinsey, 1 August 2023, at https://www.mckinsey.com/capabilities/quantumblack/our-insights/the-state-of-ai-in-2023-generative-ais-breakout-year.

2   Sara Lebow, "Generative AI adoption climbed faster than smartphones, tablets," Insider Intelligence, 11 August 2023, at https://www.insiderintelligence.com/content/generative-ai-adoption-climbed-faster-than-smartphones-tablets.

3   Mark Webster, "149 AI Statistics: The Present And Future Of AI At Your Fingertips," Authority Hacker, 2 January 2024, at https://www.authorityhacker.com/ai-statistics.

4   "Press Release: UN projects world population to peak within this century," UN Sustainable Development Goals, 11 July 2024, at https://www.un.org/sustainabledevelopment/blog/2024/07/press-release-wpp2024.

5   Beatrice Nolan, "Sundar Pichai says AI technology could be more profound than fire or electricity," Business Insider, 17 April 2023, at https://www.businessinsider.com/sundar-pichai-google-ai-bard-profound-tech-human-history-2023-4.

6   Katherine Haan, "24 Top AI Statistics and Trends in 2023," Forbes, 25 April 2023, at https://www.forbes.com/advisor/business/ai-statistics.

7   "AI for everyone," Accenture, 22 March 2023, at https://www.accenture.com/sg-en/insights/technology/generative-ai.

8   "Accenture Teams with NVIDIA to Showcase AI-Powered Immersive Client Experiences for Defender," Accenture Newsroom, 18 March 2024, at https://newsroom.accenture.com/news/2024/accenture-teams-with-nvidia-to-showcase-ai-powered-immersive-client-experiences-for-defender.

9   Grant Gross, "Air Canada chatbot error underscores AI's enterprise liability danger," ComputerWorld, 20 February 2024, at https://www.computerworld.com/article/1612087/air-canada-chatbot-error-underscores-ais-enterprise-liability-danger.html.

10   Sarah Koh, "HK firm scammed of $34 million after employee duped by video call with deepfake of CFO," The Straits Times, 4 February 2024, at https://www.straitstimes.com/asia/east-asia/hk-firm-scammed-of-34-million-after-employee-is-duped-by-video-call-with-deepfake-of-cfo.

11   Falling asleep at the wheel: Human/AI Collaboration in a Field Experiment on HR Recruiters," Fabrizio Dell'Acqua, 23 January 2023.

12   "Pause Giant AI Experiments: An Open Letter," Future of Life Institute, 22 March 2023, at https://futureoflife.org/open-letter/pause-giant-ai-experiments.

13   Rory Cellan-Jones, "Stephen Hawking warns artificial intelligence could end mankind," BBC Technology, 2 December 2014, at https://www.bbc.com/news/technology-30290540.

14 Abhishek Vishnoi and Subrat Patnaik, "Morgan Stanley Sees Dojo Boosting Tesla's Value by $500 Billion," Bloomberg, 11 September 2023, at https://www.bloomberg.com/news/articles/2023-09-11/tesla-to-surge-thanks-to-dojo-supercomputer-morgan-stanley-says.

15 Paul Carey-Kent, "Sougwen Chung: Collaborating with Technology," Seisma, 22 February 2023, at https://seismamag.com/visual-fine-art/sougwen-chung.

16 Cameron Hashemi-Pour and Ben Lutkevic, "What is artificial general intelligence (AGI)?" November 2023, TechTarget, at https://www.techtarget.com/searchenterpriseai/definition/artificial-general-intelligence-AGI.

17 Ibid.

18 Mustafa Suleyman, "My new Turing test would see if AI can make $1 million," MIT Technology Review, 14 July 2023, at https://www.technologyreview.com/2023/07/14/1076296/mustafa-suleyman-my-new-turing-test-would-see-if-ai-can-make-1-million.

19 Ibid.

20 "The Paperclip Maximiser," AICoreSpot, 6 July 2021, at https://aicorespot.io/the-paperclip-maximiser.

21 Sebastian Brandt, "Top 11 Auto GPT Examples that You Cannot Miss Out," Kanaries, 17 August 2023, at https://docs.kanaries.net/topics/ChatGPT/autogpt-examples.

22 "AI vs Human Creativity: Exploring the Boundaries with an AI Writing Assistant," AIContentfy, 7 November 2023, at https://aicontentfy.com/en/blog/ai-vs-human-creativity-exploring-boundaries-with-ai-writing-assistant.

23 Gordon Shotwell, "Large language models will never be conscious," 10 August 2022, at https://www.shotwell.ca/posts/2022-08-10-llm-consciousness.

24 Samuel Ebersole, "Concerns about AI and a seemingly reckless rate of adoption," The Pueblo Chieftain, 7 May 2023, at https://www.chieftain.com/story/opinion/2023/05/07/ebersole-concerns-about-ai-and-a-seemingly-reckless-rate-of-adoption/70179415007.

25 Peter Aitken, "Kristallnacht chicken: KFC Germany apologizes for 'unacceptable' promotion tied to anniversary of massacre," Fox Business, 12 November 2022, at https://www.foxbusiness.com/lifestyle/kristallnacht-chicken-kfc-germany-apologizes-unacceptable-promotion-tied-anniversary-massacre.

26 Amy Kraft, "Microsoft shuts down AI chatbot after it turned into a Nazi," CBS News, 25 March 2016 at https://www.cbsnews.com/news/microsoft-shuts-down-ai-chatbot-after-it-turned-into-racist-nazi.

27 Heidi Ledford, "Millions of black people affected by racial bias in health-care algorithms," Nature, 26 October 2019, at https://www.nature.com/articles/d41586-019-03228-6.

28 Theara Coleman, "The pros and cons of AI companions," The Week, 31 October 2023, at https://theweek.com/tech/the-pros-and-cons-of-ai-companions.

29 "Global truck driver shortage to double by 2028, says new IRU report," International Road Transport Union, 20 November 2023, at https://www.iru.org/news-resources/newsroom/global-truck-driver-shortage-double-2028-says-new-iru-report.

30 Chloe Taylor, "McKinsey's AI thought leader says 70% of jobs can be automated—but 'the devil is in the detail'," Fortune, 27 November 2023, at https://fortune.com/2023/11/27/how-many-jobs-ai-replace-mckinsey-alexander-sukharevsky-fortune-global-forum-abu-dhabi.

31 Jack Kelly, "Goldman Sachs Predicts 300 Million Jobs Will Be Lost Or Degraded By Artificial Intelligence," Forbes, 31 March 2023, at https://www.forbes.com/sites/jackkelly/2023/03/31/goldman-sachs-predicts-300-million-jobs-will-be-lost-or-degraded-by-artificial-intelligence.

32 Bethan McKernan and Harry Davies, "'The machine did it coldly': Israel used AI to identify 37,000 Hamas targets," The Guardian, 3 April 2024, at https://www.theguardian.com/world/2024/apr/03/israel-gaza-ai-database-hamas-airstrikes. Estimates are provided by the parties involved, so bear in mind the possibility of bias in either direction.

33 "Five challenges in designing a fully autonomous system for driverless cars," IIoT World, 21 August 2017, at https://www.iiot-world.com/artificial-intelligence-ml/artificial-intelligence/five-challenges-in-designing-a-fully-autonomous-system-for-driverless-cars.

34 Joe McKendrick and Andy Thurai, "AI Isn't Ready to Make Unsupervised Decisions," Harvard Business Review, 15 September 2022, at https://hbr.org/2022/09/ai-isnt-ready-to-make-unsupervised-decisions.

35 Iain Borner, "The Implications of AI Governance: Challenges and Opportunities for Businesses," Data Privacy Group, 28 October 2023, at https://thedataprivacygroup.com/blog/the-implications-of-ai-governance.

36 Rachel Lim, "AI fuelling more sophisticated phishing attempts, cyberattacks," Channel NewsAsia, 30 July 2024, at https://www.channelnewsasia.com/singapore/ai-phishing-attempts-cyber-attacks-technology-scams-deepfakes-ransomware-4506631.